Flying with Cuckoos

Michael Patrick Clark

Published by MDB Publishing

ISBN: 978 0 9572489-1-5

Dedication

For the mother I lost all those years ago

and

the loving wife who found her for me.

Contents

Author's Note

Few of those mentioned are truly innocent; fewer still would bother to read this, or any other book, for that matter.

I have, nonetheless, decided to change their names, but while the majority of names are indeed fictitious, the characters, places and events portrayed within these pages are as true as memory permits.

Prologue

Now, there are those who would entice a young man into the military by using all manner of seductive promises and half-truths. They will talk of patriotism, or seeing the world and learning a trade. They will undoubtedly highlight the comradeship and sense of belonging, and possibly even hint at the chance to actually live out some 'Call of Duty' fantasy for wholesale slaughter. Should any obstinate young Lochinvar remain unconvinced, they'll add the clincher:

'Women go crazy for men in military uniforms . . . you'll have to fight them off.'

Well, that's what they told me, and I can remember being pretty convinced.

Sadly, the truth is seldom so fanciful. The truth is, for all of the glossy brochures and whispered inducements, for all of the camaraderie of a life in the service of monarch and country, for all of the undoubted fringe benefits, the vast majority join up for one reason and one reason only. . .

They have nowhere else to go.

They may have been friendless at school, unpopular with their peers, disliked by teachers, or unloved at home. They may have been following in the footprints of overly-demanding fathers; footprints that were always half-a-pace too wide and half-a-size too large. They may have lacked basic academic ability, or raw athletic prowess, physical appeal, or intellectual maturity. They may have had no one to care for, or no one who cared for them; or simply found themselves lost in the middle of a world that didn't give a damn.

Or they may, like me, have been all of those things.

On killers and killing

"God preserve us. What are you . . . dense as well as stupid?"

I sat quietly looking back at him, seeing only disappointment and contempt, hearing only hostility and anger; suddenly remembering all of those reasons I so rarely visited.

"We always knew you never had much of a brain, but now you've lost your bloody common sense as well."

It had been over two years since my last visit, and four since the one before that, and yet he was still finding the showing of any affection for me to be as difficult as I had always found any discussion with him. I stood listening to yet another lecture in a familiar line of the same, and made myself an unspoken promise . . . The next interval would be longer still.

"Now listen to me and listen carefully, Michael, because I want you to think long and hard about this. This isn't a game, and these people aren't like regular armed forces. These people are killers, born killers."

I had only broached the possibility of my transferring to the regiment to fill one of our many embarrassing pauses in conversation, but the intensity of his reaction surprised me. I smiled inwardly at the description, knowing how exaggerated it was; knowing that no human being is a born killer. Whatever we become is a product of teaching or environment, and more often both.

"I met some of them in Cairo, during the war," he went on. "They had a different name in those days; called themselves the Long-Range Desert Group, or some such nonsense, but they were just the same bunch of cold-blooded cut-throats they are today. Even in those days they considered themselves an elite force, but in my book there is nothing elite about wanting to kill your fellow man. . . And they wanted to kill, believe you me. You could see it in their eyes."

I couldn't agree with that, but knew exactly what he meant, because I too had met some of them, and I too had seen those eyes. There was a special look to those eyes. It was a strangely disconcerting look: a vacant and yet penetrating stare that went through your own gaze and then focused on a point at the back of your head. That look had nothing to do with being a born killer, though, or a cold-blooded cut-throat. That look was just like everything else to do with the regiment: tutored, and practised, and intentional.

"Well, I've been on exercises with them all over the world, and I believe they're the best of all the Special Forces, but they're not all killers. That's just media hype and nonsense. They may have been in your day, but not today. Oh, and they never worked as LRDG. They sometimes worked with the long-range guys, but mostly they worked ahead of them."

From infancy, and on through the various stages of childhood, moving my lips to silently rehearse whatever I had intended saying was something I'd always done, often when I felt unsure or intimidated in some way, and always when I spoke to him. In those days it had been one of the many faults he so often criticised me for, further undermining my self-confidence and further compounding the problem. But that had been then, and this was now.

"Mind you, that doesn't mean they don't kill. You know as well as I do that they do, when they have to, when it's necessary, but forget all that born killers stuff. They're simply doing the job they're paid to do; a job they happen to be good at. Anyway, what on earth's the point of belonging to any branch of the armed forces, if you have no expectation of fighting and possibly killing? I mean, let's face it, apart from anything else, it's sheer hypocrisy."

For the first time in living memory I was arguing with him; stating my case and contradicting him, without rehearsal or hesitation, on a subject I knew better than he. I watched his amazement, at the uniqueness of such an event, and then noted the confusion that followed as he considered the argument's merit and my authority to make it.

"Anyway, I didn't say I was going to join them. I just said I was thinking of applying. They probably wouldn't take me. They're incredibly selective, and even if I did manage to get through the weeding-out period, the training programme after that is long and tough . . . and I mean tough."

I couldn't tell you why I had felt the need, but I had lied about my misgivings to somehow comfort his; childhood conditioning perhaps. It looked to have worked, though, because the tone of voice responding to my carefully-worded olive-branch was one I'd not heard before. It was softer, less aggressive, and almost conciliatory: well, perhaps not that, but definitely less aggressive.

"But there is a chance you will apply, and there is a chance they will take you?"

I shrugged my shoulders in feigned nonchalance and answered in the same manner.

"It's a possibility. I've got some skills they could use . . . well, as a basis for further training."

"What skills have you got that could possibly interest people like that?"

The scorn had returned to his tone and was plain. He seemed mildly annoyed that anyone would ever confess to such ability, let alone boast about it. Then again, maybe he was still smarting from my earlier contradiction. It seemed the greater the proverbial absence, the colder our hearts had grown; colder even than they had been those five or so years earlier, when I had walked away from this place to begin a new life and find a new home.

"Well, there's mobile and fixed comms, I seem to have an aptitude for that, and I've got some good field experience from all over the world. Then of course there's small arms and basic survival stuff. And I've done some boxing; oh yes, and some unarmed combat training." I watched the eyebrows rise and the brow furrow before hurriedly adding, "It was something I mostly did in my spare time. Just some basic throws, with a bit of karate and savate thrown in. Nothing compared to their level, but it could be something to work on."

Once again I had stood my ground and given my answer, without rehearsal or waver. Once again he appeared surprised by the show of self-confidence.

"Well, I just don't understand you, Michael. I never did, and I doubt I ever will. Isn't the outfit you're already serving with demanding enough for you?" I watched the eyes narrow, as doubt returned to the features and a possibility occurred. "You did go back into it, didn't you, after you came back from Libya? I mean, we just assumed that . . ."

Five short years ago the thought that he didn't know or care, or hadn't even bothered to find out where I was or what I was doing would have deeply wounded. But, as I said, that had been then and this was now.

"Yeah I went back into it, but it was never all that demanding. Anyway, it's changed; it's not the same. The old spirit's not there any more, and the edge is gone. They're talking about transferring the wing up to Benson; moving us in alongside the Queen's Flight. If that happens, it won't be five seconds before there'll be more interest paid to polishing cap badges and painting pavements than understanding whether we can do our job. I was thinking, maybe it's time for me to move on; thought I'd see if the regiment can use me . . . assuming I do decide to move on."

"But haven't you considered the alternatives? Surely there must be something, and just about anything would be better than that? What about trying the RAF Regiment? They do some interesting work, I'm told. What about transferring to them?"

"Become a Rockape, you mean? Automatically present arms, or shoulder arms, or do an about-turn every time I hear a click? No thanks. I'm looking to move forward, not take ten steps back."

"But surely there must be something else you can do; some alternative to that?"

"Yeah, I could always buy myself out; go work in a factory."

"Don't be flippant."

"I'm not; it's a serious possibility."

The only father I had ever known was clearly seeing less of the boy he had once tried to mould into his own image, while I was finding less of the authority I so vividly remembered in him. Perhaps he saw no further need to preserve the pretence of caring, especially for an adopted son with so little gratitude in his manner and so little warmth in his heart.

"Frank, what on earth are you doing? We're due at Angela's in an hour."

My mother had made her entrance, seemingly unaware of my presence. She suddenly noticed me as I rose from the corner armchair, and made no effort to disguise her disappointment.

"Oh, it's you, Michael. What an honour. So what do you want?"

I looked across, firstly to my mother and then on to my father, as if seeing each of them for the first time. I saw her aggression and disenchantment, and wondered what unhappy combination of misery and circumstance had conspired to make her that way. Then I turned back to him, and felt a peculiar sorrow as I saw his previous interest and intensity fade to nothing.

I watched his head drop and his shoulders slump as he shuffled away from centre stage and into the wings of his favourite armchair. I saw the life visibly drain from him in just a few short seconds, and suddenly understood why.

"Hello, Mother . . . just dropped in for a quick chat, and to see how you were both keeping."

I crossed the room to plant the obligatory peck on a proffered cheek. She eyed me suspiciously, and then snorted disapproval as she looked me up and down.

"Well, we haven't got time for any of that now. We're on our way over to Henley. And before you ask, the answer's no. We can't take you with us, because you're not invited. Anyway, you look like a yob with that haircut and those filthy-looking jeans."

She knew I had no wish to join them, and no intention of asking. Her comments had all been to do with an imaginary world, which she held in her mind like a delicate long-stemmed rose. Everything at the top of the stem belonged to her and to hers, and was fragile and perfumed and tinted pink. Everything below that belonged to me and to mine, and was dark and hostile and barbed.

"I wouldn't want to take you over to Angela's new house looking like that. They've just elected Alasdair captain of the rowing club."

"Good for him."

Another suspicious look surveyed my thinly-disguised sarcasm, before she puffed the feathers and began again.

"Angela's been promoted, you know. She's the new staff nurse on the ICU, over at Battle Hospital. That's the Intensive Care Unit."

"Good for her."

This time the sarcasm had been a little too overt.

"It is good for her. She didn't waste every opportunity she got, unlike some I could mention. She's made something of her life. Her new house is beautiful, and in a very well-to-do area."

"Yes, I know the area. They're thinking of transferring the wing up to Benson, and that's just outside Henley. We'll probably bump into each other down at the Leander Club bar."

I watched her falter, take in the interruption's annoyance, consider the irrelevance, ignore the flippancy, and carry on regardless. I should have saved my breath.

"She's got it looking an absolute picture. Of course, Alasdair's in overall charge at the brewery now. He's doing ever so well. Such a charming young man. There'll be a new edition along soon, if I'm not mistaken. You know, Michael, with our Angela making such a success of her life, I do sometimes wonder where we went wrong with you."

"It's all in the genes, Mother . . . it's all in the genes."

My mother had obviously forgotten the comment, made all those years before, because her expression didn't alter by as much as a flicker.

"Well, if you're expecting to stay the night, I'm afraid . . ."

"I'm not, Mother, you don't have to worry. I only stopped in to say hello."

"Well, I've got nothing in for supper and we've got to rush. If you're hungry, you'll have to get fish and chips. Come along, Frank, we don't want to be late. Michael, if you're not staying the night you'll have to go now. I've got to lock up, and I'm not giving you another key to lose."

She had never given me a key in the past, but the assertion that she had and I'd lost it seemed to please her. I said nothing to contradict, and smiled politely. She ended the audience with the toss of a regal head and the sweep of a dismissive hand, before ushering me out of the front door.

I stood watching as she glided down the pathway, slipped through the dutifully opened door of the family saloon, and assumed pride of place on the front passenger seat. There she perched, looking neither left nor right, presumably intending to block out my unwelcome presence to all but the most peripheral of vision.

My father nodded a cursory goodbye, and had been about to drive away when a further curt instruction caused a long-suffering husband and father to draw the car alongside the kerb. He sat quietly, while a domineering wife and mother lowered the passenger window and called out.

"I do hope you're not leaving that monstrosity there."

This time the look of disgust only briefly surveyed me, before turning to deride my aged motorcycle. It was a classic, a Beezer C15, and my only serviceable transport.

"I'm only leaving it there while I wander up to the fish shop. Don't worry, Mother, we'll both be long gone before you get back."

"I should hope so, too. We have a position to keep up in this community. Having a scruffy-looking object like that cluttering up the drive isn't part of it. Oh, and incidentally, Michael . . . I do hope that monstrosity isn't leaking oil all over my drive."

"It wouldn't dare, Mother . . . It simply wouldn't dare."

In truth, I'd only said that after they'd driven away. Although I had only visited my parents on three brief and less than memorable occasions during the previous five years, the lessons that we learn in childhood last a lifetime.

I watched the back of the latest Wolseley in a long line of similarly-styled cars disappear around the corner, then thrust my hands deep into my pockets, and set off to the other side of the village and the fish and chip shop. With the weather turning chilly, I walked briskly out of the close, and on up to the High Street, where I slowed the pace and began idly reminiscing as I wandered past familiar places and took in the tranquillity of a deserted village centre.

I can't tell you why, but as I wandered along in front of my old junior school I suddenly stopped and peered through the metal railings, hazily recalling the painful memories that still echoed around the emptiness. I looked for the gap by the steps where I used to hide myself away at break times, and remembered just how confused and disoriented and lonely I had been during my schooldays there. From there, my thoughts moved on to recall so many other days of loneliness and isolation, in different schools and in later years.

A frosty morning in late January of 1965 came to mind, and all of those other unhappy memories that had constituted my life until then came similarly flooding back.

They were memories from the years of childhood naiveté; the trusting years, the unknowing years. Memories of a time of ignorance. Memories formed before I came to understand that any available love for me had been conditional. Memories formed before I came to realise the true legacy of an orphanage, and the true value of an unwanted child.

To a truly square peg, every hole is round

"Well, come on then; say something to help me out here, for goodness sake. Surely you can give me some sort of clue, some sort of idea as to what you think I should do with him. Well, at least during the few meagre hours he condescends to spend here."

That freezing winter's day, back in late January of nineteen sixty-five, had been my day of destiny; a day that I would forever recall; a day that others would do their utmost to forget.

On this occasion, however, the head teacher's despair, and my adoptive parents' larger than usual dose of pessimism, wasn't due to the freezing January weather, or even the death of Churchill. It was to do with my somehow achieving the most appalling set of year-end examination results in the long and uninspiring history of the school's incongruous GCE stream.

They had scrubbed me down and dressed me up, treated me to my mother's individual interpretation of The Riot Act, and escorted me to the headmaster's study. There, they pointed to a bench at the back of the room and ordered me to sit down, and sit up, with chin up, chest out, stomach in, shoulders back, feet together, hands in plain sight, ears tuned, and eyes front.

It was all too much to take in. I sat down and pursed my lips, hoping that would suffice. To my amazement, it did.

In truth, the meeting hadn't started well, because Illingworth Duxbury arrived late. He rushed into the room, slammed the door, and then sat himself down behind his desk; well, not so much a desk, more a stained-oak barricade and corporal punishment rack.

On our side of that barricade, my parents, the locally renowned and evidently uncomfortable Grace and Frank Clark, appeared embarrassed, defensive, and unified only by a similarly unflattering opinion of 'yours truly'. My mother answered the headmaster's appeal, and subsequently monopolised the conversation, as was invariably the case.

"We're so sorry you've had to call us in here, Mr Duxbury; we are, aren't we, Frank? I mean, we'd love to be able to suggest something, honestly we would, but he can be such an awkward little cuss when he wants to be, even at the best of times, and God knows, there are precious few of those. I mean, he just doesn't want to do anything that normal children do, not around the house or in the garden and that, not at school, not even down at the church.

"I've talked to him until I'm blue in the face, but he just shrugs his shoulders and goes off fishing on that bike of his. I'm absolutely serious. We don't see him from dawn till dusk. He just sits there, all by himself, down at that scruffy-looking Johnson's Pond, watching a float bobbing up and down. I sometimes wonder what goes on in that head of his. Most of the time I shudder to think. It's no wonder the other kids can't stand him. He's the proverbial square peg."

Sitting there, in my less-than-splendid isolation, I had to admit there was something in that. But as to the fishing? Well, that was my way of escaping it all; my way of finding some peace.

It had all started some years earlier, when I saw an elderly fisherman catch a tiny silver roach. The old man had been about to return the fish to the water, when he caught sight of the look of wonder in a young boy's eyes, and kindly showed me his impetuous catch. Little did that elderly fisherman know that while snaring one nuisance small fry he had similarly snared another, but this time far more securely and far more permanently than any hook ever could.

I will always remember staring in fascinated awe at the miniature perfection of those fragile red-tinted fins and shimmering silver scales, and then watching in open-mouthed excitement as the elderly fisherman carefully returned that tiny silver roach to the water.

And, as one reckless small fry sped away to the safety of the nearest reed-bed, another ran all the way home and pleaded with his father to give him a fishing rod for his birthday.

My father said no, of course, but after seeing me heading off to the ponds on the snobbish Wentworth Estate with a cotton reel, a sliver of kindling, and the proverbial bent pin, he reassessed the potential for public humiliation and bought one of those all-in-one fishing outfits from Woolworth's in Windsor's Peascod Street.

My mother gave a visible shudder as she told the headmaster of my love of fishing, and then turned to look at me, presumably to deflect her embarrassment to where it rightly belonged.

Then again, maybe it was true. Maybe my mother really did have eyes in the back of her head.

"Michael. Stop picking your nose. It's a filthy and disgusting habit. Use your handkerchief, and for goodness sake, sit up straight."

I would never have done anything so disgraceful, of course, but I did have this maddening itch in my right nostril. I gazed to the heavens with a suitably angelic expression on my face, while my mother relaxed the posture of revolted indignation to resume a damning monologue.

"I'm sorry about that, Mister Duxbury. Now, where was I? Oh yes. Well, I mean, half the time, well that is, whenever he deigns to honour us with his presence, he comes home covered in fish slime and God knows what else, and he smells like a rotting haddock. He doesn't try to make himself look presentable, doesn't try to be pleasant, not to anyone; doesn't try to conform or fit in. I mean, he just doesn't seem to want to make any effort; not in any way, shape, or form."

For his part, Illingworth Duxbury sat quietly listening, while my mother gulped in another lungful of air before venting an over-emotional spleen with a further crushing tirade.

"And, apart from that, he can be such a cantankerous little sod when he wants to be. Not that he ever says much, but he'll argue black's white and white's no colour at all if it suits him.

"It's the same with anything and everything he does. I mean, while every other kid in Christendom is listening to the new pop groups, like those Liverpool mop-heads and those filthy-looking rolling whatnots and what have you, he locks himself away in his room. Sits up there listening to music: blue and rhyming music, he calls it . . . a blooming dirge, that's what I call it.

"It's not so bad now we've got our new bungalow, we can shut the doors and block him out, but when we were at the old house in Sunningdale . . . It used to come down through that kitchen ceiling, thump, thump, thump, like a formation of bloody German bombers. I could hardly hear myself think. Frankly, I was amazed we had any plaster left over the stove when we moved out. Anyway, I ask you: what's he want to listen to African music for? It's not healthy. I mean, after all, and when all's said and done, he is white, isn't he?"

Explaining the subtle differences between the basic twelve-bar chorus of commercially adapted rhythms exported from the United States and the more elemental rhythms hailing directly from southern and central Africa would have served little purpose.

"I honestly believe he only says and does it to be different, just to be awkward, and that's not all . . . I mean, while all the other kids are doing what normal kids do, when they're growing up, what does he do? I'll tell you what he does. He goes off up to London, all by himself, bold as brass; goes up on the train and then wanders around the West End all day. Don't ask me what he does when he's up there, and don't ask me why he does it.

"I've given up on him, I have honestly. He earns all that money, caddying up at the golf club, but we never see a penny piece of it. I was tidying his room the other day and twenty-five pounds fell out of his pocket: twenty-five pounds. You could have knocked me down with a feather. God alone knows what he does with it all. He really is the most peculiar child."

She paused, and glanced across the desk at a nonplussed Illingworth Duxbury, who gathered his shattered wits and volunteered a suitable endorsement.

"Yes, I have noticed; he is something of a loner."

As a breathless wife and mother paused to rack her brains for further negative inspiration, the brief respite allowed a usually reticent husband and father to express an opinion.

"Ungrateful little bastard. He's just bloody-minded, that's his trouble. For two pins he'd get the toe of my boot up his backside."

Illingworth Duxbury made a belated attempt to get the meeting back on track.

"Well, yes, I suppose there could be some truth in that, but let's get back to the issue, shall we. Now then, short of drowning him in the bath, what are we to do with him?"

There had been no mirth in the question. As the headmaster watched parental anger subside into mild embarrassment and vacant indifference, the deathly silence that gawped back at him somehow encapsulated both the utter futility of his damning summary and the sheer time-consuming nonsense of such ineffectual proceedings as these.

He picked up the report from where my mother had thrown it, and then sat and scanned the detail, obviously seeking some previously overlooked glimmer of light or hope among the many entries of doom and gloom. The resulting summary was painfully predictable.

"Well, I'm afraid we have to face the unpalatable fact that he has no faculty for any form of academic study, and no especial talent for any mainstream sport. He has no friends to speak of, and no aptitude for languages, even though he specifically asked, and we agreed to put him on extra periods of French. He's unable to read music, or play any form of musical instrument, despite the best efforts of our music teacher, Mr Wingate. To cap it all, from the little I've been unfortunate enough to witness during morning assembly, he appears to be completely tone-deaf."

My mother couldn't possibly allow the indictment to pass without some form of embellishment.

"And on top of that he's, bloody well bone idle."

Strangely, my father suddenly decided to make a token defence of the ungrateful little bastard. Sitting at the back of the room, it was unclear to me whether this was a result of paternal obligation, an innate sense of fair play, or simply a need to prevent my mother from completely monopolising the conversation.

"He plays basketball. They say he's good at that."

Illingworth Duxbury shrugged.

"Yes, I suppose that is true, but even if he were good enough to play professionally, which he isn't, I somehow doubt he'd interest the Harlem Globetrotters." He smiled briefly at my father, noted the blank reaction, and explained further. "As your dear lady so rightly pointed out a few moments ago, he is undoubtedly lacking the necessary pigmentation."

Some sort of sixth sense must have allowed him to realise the utter dejection and demoralisation that had washed over me, because he continued scanning and hastily added, "He is, however, an exceptional mile and cross-country runner, and he also exceeds at swimming; represents the school in both . . . Well, that's what it says here."

My mother seemed impressed.

"Ooh, is he good at swimming? We didn't even know he could swim, but then, no surprise there; getting him to tell us anything at all is like getting blood out of a stone."

Illingworth Duxbury was insistent.

"Oh yes, it says here: backstroke at fifty and a hundred yards. They think he could be a genuine talent, given the right training and equipment. We only have a twenty-five-yard pool."

As I soaked up Illingworth Duxbury's words of praise, while selfishly basking in the glorious sunshine of a rare achievement, it was hard to keep my chest from expanding or a smile from my face. However, as my father dragged me back into the cold reality of failure's shadow, I realised that his earlier defence of me had obviously been for the last of those three possibilities.

"Typical. Little bastard excels at the only sport in Christendom, where looking to see where you're going is a positive bloody disadvantage."

With flagging impetus rejuvenated, my mother resumed her customary command of the baton.

"Michael. For the last time, will you please use your handkerchief. Now, stop slumping and sit up straight. Slouching like that; you look like a common navvy. I've told you a thousand times not to slump. You can laugh, but I'm warning you, Michael, you'll finish up with a curvature of the spine one day. There are times when I wonder why we bother to waste our breath.

"Now then, what was I saying? Oh yes, surely there must be something you can come up with, something that you can suggest?"

The head teacher shook his head from side to side in a façade of sad contemplation.

"If there is, then offhand I can't think what. I'm at my wits' end. How old is he now?"

"He'll be fifteen on July the fourth."

"You do know that's American Independence Day?"

"Yes, we do."

"Well good, good. Not long to go now then, and he'll be someone else's problem. . . can't say I'm not looking forward to that."

The winsome chuckle that followed went down like the proverbial lead balloon, met by two indignant stares, three open mouths, and a young man's sinking heart.

Illingworth Duxbury saw and quickly blustered both apology and qualification.

"I'm sorry. I didn't mean to be dismissive, but given the abomination of these results, I can see little point in any extended education. Although, now that's strange. It says here that he passed his eleven-plus. Mmm, I must have a word with Mrs Jewel. I'm seeing far too many of these typos."

As Illingworth Duxbury began clinically scoring out the offending entry with the rubberised end of a 2B, my father interrupted.

"Oh, but he did."

The enquiring look demanded more.

"Pass, I mean."

The headmaster viewed the errant amendment and snapped a question.

"Well, for goodness sake, why didn't you say so?"

"I just did."

The worm had finally turned, occasioning an uncomfortable clearing of my mother's throat, and causing Illingworth Duxbury to bluster yet another apology.

"I'm sorry, forgive me, of course you did. So, what happened? I mean to say, if that's the case, what the hell is he doing here?"

Having apparently gained some peculiar form of conversational second wind, my mother glared at my father before resuming her previous monopoly.

"Yes, that's right, Mr Duxbury. He went to Windsor Grammar School. Nothing but the best would do for him, of course. He couldn't have made do with going somewhere ordinary, like Bracknell. Oh no, it had to be Windsor Grammar. We bought the uniform and everything; new leather satchel, all the books. What with one thing and another it cost a blooming fortune."

"What happened?"

"They kicked him out after the first year. They said they couldn't do a thing with him; said it would have been easier to educate a chimpanzee, and the eleven-plus result must have been a fluke. But then, we knew that. I mean, we should have expected it."

"Oh, I see, yes, um, most unfortunate, but it happens; an exception to prove the rule, perhaps?"

"Mmm, yes, possibly, but then we had to go out and buy another set of uniform for this place. Not that he could give a damn about it. . . water off a duck's back."

"Oh, yes, that reminds me. Come to think of it, there was something else."

Illingworth Duxbury had remembered a more delicate issue. My mother gave a groan.

"Oh God. Not more embarrassment?"

"It is, I'm afraid. You see, one of our young graduate trainees, Miss Bridges, caught him trying to look up her skirt in French language class the other day. He claimed he was trying to pick up a ruler from under the desk, but she was certain he'd dropped it on purpose."

"We didn't think he had any interest in girls. We were starting to worry about it."

"Well, Miss Bridges assured me there was no doubt about it whatsoever."

Two hugely relieved parents could find little to warrant censure. A smiling mother explained.

"Oh come on. It isn't that serious, is it? More of a blessing in disguise than a problem. At least he might start washing himself properly from now on. God knows, we might even get him to change his vest and underpants without having to be constantly told. After all, it does mean he's not a pansy, or one of those flouncing nancy boys who are always on the telly these days.

"Anyway, I thought all young boys did that? They do, don't they? I mean, let's face it, that little strumpet does insist on wearing skirts with hemlines that hardly cover her knicker elastic. Half the time they're not even close to being decent. Mrs Flood was only saying that, just the other day."

My mother always used to slip dear old Mrs Flood into the conversation whenever she was unsure of her argument, or needed independent validation or third-party support for a controversial statement. Gallantry, professional loyalty, and a well-known fondness for voyeurism caused Illingworth Duxbury to spring to the defence of the voluptuous Miss Bridges and her celebrated miniskirts. It was an ill-conceived crusade that he would equally swiftly have cause to regret.

"My dear lady, I do understand your concerns, but such outfits are of the fashion these days."

He smiled, fully expecting boyish charm to win the day, but a belligerent stare told him that he had underestimated the depth of feeling involved. The dear lady was having none of it.

"Fashion, you say? Oh, come off it. In the few short months she's been here that little madam must have had more men clinging on for dear life on the back of that red and white Vespa than I've had hot dinners. Looking up her skirt? Huh. Show me a man who hasn't had a bloody good eyeful of that little trollop's wares. From what I hear, most of them have had guided bloody tours."

A beleaguered Illingworth Duxbury had been about to signal the retreat and change the subject, when it became clear the dear lady wasn't finished. The dear lady was far from finished.

"I've got nothing against fashion. I like fashion. Well, Norman Hartnell and that; you know, proper, decent, fashion design. Not all this latest disgusting Mary Quant, show men everything you've got rubbish. All fashion means to little tarts like that is an excuse to show off a pair of skimpy little knickers and what have you to any man who wants an eyeful. I mean to say, remember the exhibition she put on at the Christmas Bazaar? I know I bloody do."

Illingworth Duxbury opened his mouth, presumably hoping to placate, but missed his cue by a good country mile.

"It wasn't enough for her that she'd spent the entire morning batting her eyelashes at anything in trousers; common little tramp had to take it to extremes. And when she bent over at the lucky dip, she had to go right for the bottom of the barrel, didn't she; had to make sure every man in the place got a bloody good eyeful of next week's washing. Not that there was all that much of it to see. I've got lace hankies in the drawer at home with more cotton in them than that.

"Filthy little slut, left nothing to the imagination. Disgusting display, and in front of all those children. No, I'm sorry, but if the boy went back for another look, she's only got herself to blame."

The head teacher's mouth was still hanging open, but any short-lived opportunity for comment had once again come and gone before he'd formed the first syllable.

"I said to Mrs Flood, when she was doing it, I said, she's scraping the bottom of the barrel in more ways than one. I don't know about lucky dip. She'll be bloody lucky if she doesn't catch pneumonia. . . and God knows what else, if you follow my drift."

She finally paused, presumably for breath, and everybody in the room took the welcome opportunity to gulp in a lungful of blessed air. Then she was off again.

"Anyway, I think that we've all wasted more than enough time talking about your little miss Lucy-lastic. So, as I said before, isn't that normal? Don't all young boys do that, at some time or other? Isn't it all supposed to be a healthy part of growing up?"

Clearly taken aback by the degree of hostility that his passing mention of the debatably offended Miss Bridges had induced, Illingworth Duxbury stuttered an answer.

"Well, uh, yes, uh, some of them do, yes; yes, of course they do, uh, I suppose most of them do, but with your Michael . . . Well, I'm afraid the problem is rather more complex."

Career guidance by default

Aah, Anthea Bridges. I can still hear the echoes of that sexy French accent she always affected during French language classes; still see the mesmeric perfection of that unbelievable wiggle as she sashayed her way out of one schoolboy's fantasy and pouted her way into the next.

I remember that just about every other boy in the fifth form claimed to have some exclusive inside knowledge on the many and varied and sadly all-too-often-imagined indiscretions of Anthea Bridges. Three or four even claimed to have known her, in the biblical sense, that is. Not that I understood the term at the time, but that was what they had claimed.

My father knew her, of course, in just about every sense of the word, and in some that decent society has yet to define. I know that to be true, because I'd heard my mother complaining about it to Mrs Flood. At the time I found it impossible to understand just what it was about the voluptuous Mademoiselle Bridges, more than any of his many other female friends, which so incensed my mother and so often confused, embarrassed, and excited me. There was no doubt about it, though; the wiggling and giggling Anthea *femme fatale* Bridges did have something about her.

Thankfully, in those days there were so many other more interesting distractions available to me: fishing for one, earning easy money caddying at the golf club for another, and wandering the streets of the West End of London for a third.

All solitary pursuits, you may notice, because my mother had been absolutely right. The other kids couldn't stand the sight of me.

I don't know if it was the short-back-and-sides hairstyle. It could have been the plain white starched collar, or the beetle-crusher lace-up black shoes, or the Sloane Street accent, or my seeming refusal to mix with the other kids after school. It could have been or all those defamatory rumours, mostly started by my elder sister, or my failure to make the grade at Windsor Grammar School and resulting dismissal to the depths of academic mediocrity in the wilds of Sunningdale. Maybe it was because I came from one of the more socially acceptable areas, or that I always went to church on Sunday, and always raised my cap to ladies.

It could even have been the simple fact that I was an all-round pain-in-the-arse weakling. Whatever the reasons, the other kids definitely didn't like me. Neither did the three discontented adults meeting in the headmaster's study that day.

I could feel the colour rise in my cheeks as the head teacher shuffled uncomfortably in his chair and valiantly strove to cushion the words.

"You see, looking up a young woman's skirt is understandable; not something to encourage, of course, but nonetheless forgivable for a lad of that age. However, with your Michael, I'm afraid the problem is more complex, because, well you see, I don't know how to put this, but . . ."

"Oh, for God's sake, spit it out, man."

"Well, it's just that . . . I don't believe he had the faintest idea of why he was doing it."

"What do you mean? He's nearly fifteen, for God's sake."

"I know, and I'm sorry, Mr Clark. I questioned him about it at some length, but I still couldn't get a sensible answer. He said all the other boys did it, so he thought he ought to do it, too. But I do believe the 'why' remains as something of a mystery to him."

Visibly staggered by yet another glaring educational defect, my father looked at me in open-mouthed disbelief. The news didn't surprise my mother, though. I was, after all, a member of a lesser species.

"Look, you can't blame a dim-witted boy for the sins of half the planet. I mean, I ask you, does any man ever know what he's doing it for when he does that sort of thing? Looking up your skirt, gawping down your cleavage, grabbing and mauling and pushing up against you. They're all the same. I doubt any man could tell you why they do it, and having suffered from it for the last twenty years I'm bloody certain I can't either. No, that's men for you; just the way God made them. His little jest at the expense of we poor helpless females."

Three normally divergent male opinions were suddenly in accord. There was very little that might be, even charitably, described as helpless about this particular female. She went on.

"I've told you before, Michael. If you want to know about that sort of thing, ask your father."

She switched her glare to my father, who pretended not to hear.

"He's the expert on that . . . or he is in this family."

Illingworth Duxbury glanced uncertainly from one to the other. There was clearly nine-tenths of this particular iceberg hidden below the waterline. Incredibly, instead of changing the subject or glossing over the incident, the foolish man heaped folly on to folly by completing the tale.

"Uh, yes, well, anyway, I let him off with a stern warning. In all conscience, I didn't have the heart to cane him . . . Well, I mean, given the lad's obvious naiveté."

It seemed to my mind, and I do believe my patently incredulous father's, the school's principal was behaving like some sort of retarded mongrel with a dry bone. There clearly wasn't an ounce of nourishment to be had from the damn thing, but he was refusing to let it go.

"Have either of you ever talked to him? I mean about sex and all that?"

My mother turned to stare blankly at my father. He stared blankly back at her. She shrugged her shoulders matter-of-factly, and then turned her palms outward, like a second-hand car dealer caught red-handed clocking a Ford Popular. My father followed suit, using the self-same mannerisms, and that self-same expression of ignorance mitigating inactivity. My mother finally accepted the stalemate and added words to clarify the charade.

"No, we never did. We didn't know we had to. I mean, we never did with our Angela, did we, Frank? And she found out well enough for herself."

I watched my father frown as he assessed the alarming implications of his beloved daughter's apparently more than comprehensive education. Then, sensing a charge of parental failing, he defensively added, "Nobody told us we had to. The subject never came up. Anyway, shouldn't you lot handle subjects like that?"

"No, I'm afraid not. We're only trained to deal with the basics of human biology. I'm sorry."

I had no idea why Illingworth Duxbury kept apologising. I suppose he found it easier than confrontation. Mind you, given that my mother could verbally strip a man to the bone without pausing to draw breath, he was probably showing more sense than I gave him credit for.

"Well, I suppose Frank had better choose the right moment. Did you hear that, Frank? It should be easy enough for you to explain to a fifteen-year-old boy why it is that men who should be old enough to know better find such fatal fascination in gawping up some little strumpet's miniskirt."

It was now clear, even to an embarrassingly obtuse headmaster, that his mentioning of the voluptuous Miss Bridges had stirred something of a hornets' nest reaction.

"Oh, and you can also give him all the graphic detail on what's expected of him when that same little strumpet slips her knickers off and entertains rather more than just a glance. Perhaps when she's sprawled across the back seat of a bottle-green Wolseley on Lock's Ride playing-field on a wet Wednesday evening. Or, maybe you could tell him what happens at Christmas bazaar time, when the key to the stationery cupboard disappears, along with a half-naked strumpet and some poor woman's sod of a husband. You should be able to manage that without troubling the old grey matter, shouldn't you, Frank?"

A spluttered cough allowed a dumbstruck Illingworth Duxbury to focus his mind, cover his embarrassment and clear his throat before pressing the point.

"I rather think it would be prudent, to talk to Michael, that is, before it becomes an issue. Nip it in the bud, as it were. I'm sure your husband will find the right words."

It wasn't often anybody saw my mother cornered like this. She glared, first at my father and then at me, before blustering an answer.

"Oh, very well, I suppose he'd better do that then. We'd better get him a copy of *Health and Efficiency* or something. Now then, what about manual subjects like woodwork or metalwork? He said something to Mrs Flood about liking art. She mentioned it to me."

Unified once more in shared misfortune, two unhappy parents nodded an enthusiasm they were far from convinced of. The headmaster's response was cruelly predictable.

"He may like art, but art doesn't like him, and, as for woodwork? Well, I couldn't say with any certainty, because Mr Casey told me that he sawed off his half-lap dovetails in the middle of the last exam before walking out."

"Metalwork?"

She was grabbing at straws, and everybody knew it.

"Uh, sorry, no. Mr Johnson in the metal-shop told me he couldn't get the lad to file a straight edge to a piece of ten gauge; not if he stood over him for a month of Sundays."

"Well, there must be something you can recommend. After all, you are officially responsible for his career guidance."

Illingworth Duxbury suddenly spied a gap in the fence, one that he'd long been searching for.

"Well, now you come to mention it, I'm not, well not officially. You see, that responsibility belongs to our Mrs Henderson. Have you met her? No? Oh you should, she's probably far better qualified to involve herself in this. After all, she is his form teacher. I'll set up an appointment for you. No, better still, I'll get her in here to discuss it with you now. She should be free."

If Illingworth Duxbury thought he'd slip the noose that easily he didn't know my mother. With a quick flick of her verbal lasso the hapless man was back under control and trotting to order.

"And who, might I ask, does she report to?"

"Uh, yes, I see what you mean, but, strictly speaking. . ."

One of my mother's famous 'don't bandy words with me, if you know what's good for you' snorts had interrupted the headmaster's feeble effort to evade responsibility, before she added, "Right then, that's settled. We'll leave you to talk to her, should you feel the need."

With miscreant colt suitably gelded, and gap in the fence repaired, she glared triumphantly.

"Now, where were we? Ah yes, what about college; further education or something?"

"Before we could consider further education, a fundamental appreciation of the basic academic curriculum is prerequisite. I'm sorry to be so blunt about all of this, Mrs Clark, but I believe honesty is crucial in these matters."

My mother's offer of conciliation was instant and unreserved.

"There's no need to apologise, Mr Duxbury. We understand perfectly. So, the future for this gormless flippin' article doesn't look particularly encouraging then?"

The headmaster made a weak attempt to cushion the blow with levity.

"Well, I'm certain the acne will go in time, but the rest of his future is less easy to predict."

"What about getting him into the Army? Isn't that what people do in cases like this?"

"Yes, that is a possibility, I suppose, but according to this report from our Mr Jennings down at the gymnasium, even that might prove difficult. You see, he's got two left feet and they're both a trifle on the flat side. Not sufficient to cause any great concerns, but it did get me to thinking that maybe we should consider . . . The Navy?"

The response was in perfect unison.

"Seasickness."

"Badly?"

A reluctant agreement overshadowed the collective look of distaste. My mother explained.

"We could try, I suppose, but he threw up all over the Weymouth to Jersey ferry a couple of years ago. I've never been so embarrassed."

She was right, of course. All those partly-digested carrots and tomato skins, sprayed all over the till at the buffet checkout. I can still remember the look of horror on the young checkout girl's face in that ghastly suspended moment before the tidal wave of mustard- and maroon-coloured vomit arrived.

The restaurant manager called me 'a disgusting little shit' and opened another till on the opposite side of the cafeteria. I was frogmarched out to the main deck and left hanging over the railings at the back of the ferry for the rest of the voyage into St. Helier. I still have vivid memories of it, and have hated anything to do with boats from that day to this.

"What about trying the police?"

"Already did; assessed him against the criteria for cadetship and everything."

"And?"

"Well, he was tall enough, and given their less-than-exacting educational standards, he was also bright enough, surprisingly."

"But?"

"Well, height and intellect seemed all right, but . . . Look, I'm sorry to have to tell you this. We hadn't even given it a thought, well, not until the school health visitor told us, but it seems he's got a cast in his left eye. They say he'd fail to meet the minimum eyesight standard on that basis."

"Yes, a specialist at Reading General did tell us he's got a lazy eye. Had it since birth."

Clearly disgruntled by his lack of involvement, my father muttered, "Little bugger's got a lazy bloody everything."

Yet another period of shared discomfiture followed, before a comedy of nods and winks from an insistent husband and father persuaded a reluctant wife and mother to apportion the blame.

"You see, he's not really ours."

I have no idea why she suddenly blurted that out; hoping for absolution, I suppose. Then she saw the resulting look of horror and tried to repair the damage. It only made matters worse.

"Well, I don't mean he's not ours. Well, I do, but I don't. I mean, he is ours, but, then again, he isn't. It's all a question of interpretation, if you see what I mean."

Illingworth Duxbury clearly didn't, and I wasn't sure I did. Finally, and to the blessed relief of all assembled, my mother qualified the explanation.

"Well, by that I mean, well, we adopted him, you see, when he was two-and-a-half."

The general relief felt all around the room at that moment had been tangible. My mother saw, relaxed, and immediately resumed her more usual ground-swallowing conversational stride.

"He already had the problem when we got him, honestly he did. It was nothing to do with our genes. Frank didn't notice, of course; well, not until it was too late to do anything. I mean, it's not something you look for, is it? We didn't. Most people wouldn't, and that bloody orphanage never said a word. Well, not until we'd signed the papers. Not so much as . . ."

Not wishing to appear callous, my father bravely interrupted.

"Not that we wouldn't have taken him anyway."

He flashed a comforting smile in my general direction, while my mother returned her attention to a bemused headmaster. She leaned closer as she confided, obviously in a token effort to save me from the unwholesome truth.

"His real mother was a shop-girl in London – useless strumpet, by all accounts, but aren't they all these days? The father was some wandering Irishman. Rumour was that . . ." She leaned even closer and spoke out of the corner of her mouth. "Well, there were so many rumours about that one nobody knew what to believe, but we all know what those randy bloody paddies are like, don't we? Populate half the damn planet before they're finished."

Not for the first time that morning, Illingworth Duxbury looked lost for words. She went on.

"Well, anyway, to cut a long story . . ."

If there was anything in this world that my mother had never tried to do, it was to reduce a story by as much as a raised eyebrow.

"That was the last anybody ever heard or saw of him. He didn't even leave his name, or if he did, they never told us. All the SOB left behind, apart from a million unsavoury rumours, was a pronounced cast in the boy's left eye."

Illingworth Duxbury summoned what little remained of his senses.

"So that's why the lad goes a bit boss-eyed now and then? Irish background, huh?"

As I sat quietly at the back of the room, trying to study my left eye with my right in cross-eyed confusion, my mother returned to a pet subject.

"Blooming Irishmen, they're everywhere these days; swamping the whole damn country."

She was off again, and not a man in the room was possessed of the courage to stop her.

"There's a gang of them digging holes in the road up in Sunninghill High Street, outside Mathew's hairdressers; long-haired bunch of yobbos. All didicois of course; and all about as foul-mouthed as a truckload of bargees . . . whistling at all the women; making disgusting suggestions.

"I said to Frank, when he got home. I said, surely we have enough English yobbos hanging around the labour exchanges to be able to dig a few holes in the road, without having to send out for gangs of Irish yobbos to do the job for them. I said that to you, didn't I, Frank?"

"Yes."

It was that precise moment when Illingworth Duxbury entertained the spark of inspiration that would be destined to change my life.

"Wait a minute, hold on just a moment. You know, I've just had a thought."

"What's that, then?"

"Let's think about this for a moment. What have we got? A loner, two left feet, ham-fisted, short-sighted, prone to seasickness, unpopular with his peers, and everybody else; stranger to the arts, awkward as the day is long, naïve, bone idle, and not so much as a brain in his head."

I had been sitting quietly at the back of the room, half-listening and half-daydreaming. It was only when my mother turned and glared her concurrence that I realised he'd been describing me. The glare remained fixed as she confirmed the sorry truth of it all.

"Yes, we already know all of that, but what's the alternative?"

"Maybe we should get him into the Air Force. Can't imagine why I didn't think of it before. You know, I think they might take him. I hear tell they'll take just about anybody these days."

My mother bristled.

"Well, you do surprise me. My Frank was an officer in the Royal Air Force. Sir Denis Spotswood always sends us a Christmas card. He and Frank were squadron leaders together."

A proud nod of my father's head confirmed the boast's legitimacy before an equally proud wife extended her boastfulness beyond that which might be excused as a passing reference.

"You did know that Frank's Treasurer of the Council?"

"Yes, I think you mentioned it. " Illingworth Duxbury skilfully guided the conversation back. "However, I rather think we may be aiming a trifle lower with your young Michael."

"So just how low are we talking?"

"Maybe even as low as aircraftman, but at least that's a step in the right direction. Then again, with your husband's connections, we might even get him an apprenticeship. After all, it'll get him off your hands that much sooner; you won't have to wait until he's seventeen."

Mutual and genuine interest was immediately apparent.

"How much sooner?"

"They'll take him at fifteen or so. Well, they will if we play our cards right."

Despite the façade of nonchalance, there was no disguising the sudden flurry of excitement.

"But that's less than six months away. We could start planning now."

Positions to keep up

With the cantankerous little bastard's future secured and previous humiliations forgotten, my parents' disposition visibly improved. The wily Illingworth Duxbury pressed on with more productive matters.

"Now, if I remember rightly, you've got a daughter, haven't you? I think I heard you mention her. So, tell me, how's everything with her?"

For once the response was both genuine and encouraging as my father drew himself up in his chair and proudly announced, "Yes, you must remember our Angela, beautiful girl. She's training to be a nurse, over at St. Peter's. Going to be an SRN."

An equally proud wife and mother swiftly added, "Of course, she never had Michael's advantages. She had to work for everything she got. We couldn't believe it, could we, Frank, couldn't believe it when she didn't pass her eleven-plus. I still say they made a mistake with the results from her year; maybe the tests were on the wrong subject or something. Either way, they must have been a lot harder than they were when that lazy little bugger took his. Well, I mean, what happened afterwards proved that, didn't it?

"We couldn't believe it when we found out he'd passed, especially when Angela had been so unlucky with her result. Poor darling, she was ever so upset; had every right to be, as far as I'm concerned. She was always much brighter than him. Talk about bloody injustice."

A dutiful nod confirmed the idiosyncratic and prejudicial nature of the much and justifiably maligned eleven-plus examination scheme.

"Such a lovely girl, our Angela, but what am I saying? Nowadays, she's a fully-grown young woman; well, she's not a little girl any more. She has to fight the men off these days, I can tell you."

What utter nonsense my mother did sometimes talk. My sister hadn't known what it was like to fight any man off since her acne had miraculously disappeared after that rendezvous in the garden shed with Tony Jarvis's older brother on the night of her fourteenth birthday. She may have declined one or two offers from the decrepit and ugly, but never from anybody under the age of fifty, at least not to my knowledge or recollection.

"She's going to make some lucky man a fine young wife before long, I shouldn't wonder."

Good God. Talk about a day of destiny. Pack me off to some previously unmanned radar station on the Outer Hebrides, and marry my wayward sister off to the local headmaster. Not a bad result for one morning's efforts. Clearly not realising the danger, or the depths that a doting mother's strategy might plumb, Illingworth Duxbury smiled in reminiscence of the precocious Angela.

"Yes, I remember: lovely girl, and one of our more advanced pupils. Well-proportioned for her age, I always thought. Long, athletic limbs, used to run like the wind, and very popular with the staff. A very willing girl; used to help out with half-time refreshments for the soccer team."

By this time a doting mother was positively bursting with pride.

"Oh yes, our Angela was always a keen supporter of both the soccer and rugby teams, especially the rugby team. She knew all the rules, and she used to keep score and everything. She even used to travel with them to the away matches, in the team bus and that. There was never any shortage of volunteers to run the line when our Angela handed round the oranges, I can tell you."

That was true. She did keep score. Although, whenever my sister travelled to away matches, the reserves, the coach driver, and even occasional spectators, scored more freely than the team. While the team sweated to trouble the scorer on the pitch, the number of tries successfully converted between an eager pair of horizontal thighs spread-eagled across the back seat of that rickety team coach was mind-numbing. I don't know what her end of season tally was, but it undoubtedly exceeded that touched down or booted high between battered uprights on some worm-infested swamp of a rugby field.

Illingworth Duxbury smiled lasciviously.

"Yes, I remember her. So she's a nurse, eh? Your own little Florence Nightingale. I can just see her now, all decked out with her hair pinned up under a bonnet, wearing black stockings and a freshly-starched uniform. All that rustling and bustling around the wards. You must be so proud."

"Oh, we are."

"Yes, and rightly so. You must ask her to pop in and see me when she's got a minute, maybe show me her new uniform. I'd like that, and I always like to keep in touch with former pupils."

"Yes, of course, Mister Duxbury. She'll be over to see us later in the week. It's her birthday, she's eighteen. Doesn't time fly? I suppose she'll be ready to settle down with some lucky man soon, and I'm sure she'd like to see you again. She always used to speak very highly of you."

I could see the chest expanding and drops of saliva forming at the corners of the mouth as Illingworth Duxbury beamed an enthusiastic agreement.

"Good, good. I'll look forward to that. Well, if there's nothing else, perhaps I'd better let you get on. I'll send you the forms and brochures, then."

"What?"

"The forms and brochures. For Michael. For the armed forces."

A wife and mother was already intent on marshalling her troops.

"Well, say thank you to Mr Duxbury for all the trouble he's gone to, and for the umpteenth time will you please stop picking your nose. How many times have I got to tell you to use a handkerchief? Now get the door, and for goodness sake be quick about it."

The itch had mysteriously returned and she had caught me attending to it yet again. There was no doubt about it, I decided: my mother definitely had eyes in the back of her head.

"Well goodbye, Mr Duxbury. Oh, and thank you for all your help. For goodness sake, Frank, do come along. Michael, put your shoulders back and stand up straight; and put that filthy-looking handkerchief away. For heaven's sake, there must be a dozen in the drawer and you have to bring that disgusting-looking object with you. I'm sure you only do it to embarrass me. Oh, and I'll ask Angela to pop round; get her to call you in the week and make an appointment or something."

Illingworth Duxbury looked bewildered by the sudden flurry of activity.

"Yes, yes, do that. Please do ask her to, uh, bye now, Mrs um . . ."

A shell-shocked headmaster returned to more rewarding deliberations, while two demoralised parents walked to the car in silence. I clambered on to the celebrated back seat of our bottle-green Wolseley and slammed the door. They climbed on to theirs. My father broke the angry silence.

"Why did you have to push Angela at him so blatantly? You know what a reputation he's got."

"Don't be ridiculous. Talk about people in glass houses. Anyway, our Angela's a grown woman, and he seems a pleasant man."

"She's still an eighteen-year-old child as far as I'm concerned, and he can keep his hands to himself. He's got to be almost forty. In my book that's all but bloody illegal."

"Yes, but he's got lovely hands. I always say you can tell a man by his hands; beautifully manicured fingernails, and he always keeps them that way. I've noticed before. Anyway, Angela likes her men that little bit older."

I hadn't notice my sister being all that fussy in the past. Neither had my father, but then he'd been blissfully unaware of a lot more than that. Nor did he share my mother's admiration for the headmaster's well-manicured fingernails and dubious motivations.

"Bloody Bluebeard. Black stockings and starched uniforms. He can keep his beautifully manicured fingernails out of her bloody knickers, or I'll bloody well cut 'em off."

"Oh, for goodness sake, Frank, stop being so silly. Angela can look after herself. Anyway we need Illingworth Duxbury to help sort out this useless article behind us."

"I suppose there is that."

For once there was grudging concurrence.

"Anyway, he won't be the first, and I doubt he'll be the last. Our Angela's far too sensible to get herself into trouble. She is a nurse, after all."

"What was that? He won't be the first to what?"

"For goodness sake, keep your eyes on the road. This is a bad junction. Mrs Flood told me there was a nasty accident here only the other day."

"The first to what? Grace, are you listening to me? I said, he won't be the first to what?"

"To slip his fingers inside her knickers, of course. Oh come on, Frank, for God's sake, she's not a baby any more. She's a fully-developed young woman, and mothers and daughters do discuss such things. Anyway, if she is a bit too free-and-easy, we both know which side of the family she gets that particular trait from."

For a while they each sat in a cocoon of silence, until my father said, "I can't believe you waited until now to tell me. Why the hell didn't you tell me before?"

"It was none of your business. Angela's a sensible enough young woman, and that was a private conversation. Anyway, you've no room to talk. Don't think I didn't see you with that Susan Stringer the other day. What is it about you and common little tarts like that?"

"Oh, give it a rest."

"Give it a rest? How about you giving it a rest for a change? I've still not forgiven you for that time in the kitchen, or spoken to Vera bloody Kenilworth."

"That was a long time ago."

"Well, I can still remember every vivid bloody detail. Pinned up against the fridge, blouse undone, skirt up around her waist, legs at ten-to-two, stockings at half-mast, and a pair of white Marks and Spencer's hundred per cent cotton knickers dangling from one ankle.

"She looked like she'd just surrendered to the bloody enemy. And when the little bitch shot out of the back door, I swear I could see Hotpoint Iced Diamond stamped across her backside. Oh, and while we're on that subject, if you catch so much as a cold from that Anthea boomerang-knickers bloody Bridges, I'll be doing some cutting-off of my own."

As we neared the High Street, my mother brought matters to an abrupt conclusion.

"Look, we're coming into the village, so just let it drop. I don't want anybody to see us arguing like this. You know how these small-minded people love to gossip."

Angela arrived home later that week. My father was working in the garden shed. My mother greeted her in the usual fashion.

"Darling, you look so tired. I'm sure they're working you too hard over at that hospital."

I watched my sister grimace as she offered her cheek for a doting mother to kiss.

"No, it's just that we had a hectic time last night. We were up for most of the night on men's surgical. She giggled. "So were they."

"I didn't think they allowed you to do night duties, darling, not as a trainee? Oh, I'm sorry, I almost forgot. . . Happy Birthday, darling. Your cards and presents are on your bed. Frank. Come and wish our darling baby a Happy Birthday."

A doting mother rattled out question, greeting, and instruction in mechanical fashion, but then noticed a blonde-haired woman standing behind Angela. The woman was attractive, aged in her mid-twenties, with sparkling eyes and a ready smile. However, it wasn't the smile but the outfit that captured the attention.

It was a bright red dress with a low-cut top, and the shortest skirt I'd ever seen. It was even shorter than Anthea Bridges wore, and that wasn't an easy fashion statement for any young woman to make, not within the bounds of the decency laws.

I wondered whether my father would approve, and somehow guessed the answer.

"This is Diana Clifton, Mummy. She's my best's friend in the world. I said she could stay with us for a couple of days." Then, in that maddening high-pitched whine she always affected whenever she wanted something, "That is all right, isn't it, Mummy?"

"Of course it is, darling. I'm afraid your father has taken over the spare bedroom for an office, but Diana can have Michael's room. He can sleep on the settee."

I watched in silence as two dainty noses turned skyward.

"Oh no, Mummy, you can't do that. His room is such a pigsty, and if I know anything about this little toad here it'll probably still stink of fish, like last time." She eyed me disparagingly and then turned to her friend. "At least, I think it was fish. I brought Julia Simpson home. We had to block up the bathroom keyhole with loo paper. We never do know what to expect with this obnoxious little pervert, do we, obnoxious little pervert?"

My sister had a history of thinking up ever more disparaging descriptions of me. This was obviously the latest.

"Been peeping through any more keyholes, have we? You sad obnoxious little pervert."

I hadn't been peeping through any keyholes. I merely wanted to see if the bathroom was free. I flushed red with embarrassment and studied my shoes, while my sister and her friend broke out into fits of giggles and a doting mother glanced uncertainly from one to the other.

After an uncomfortable silence, my sister smiled coyly across at her newest and best's friend in the world, and then announced, "Diana will share with me, Mummy. We've shared before. It's a double bed; there'll be heaps of room. You don't mind sharing with me again, do you, Di? It's just like riding a bike, they do say, or do they say riding a dyke, I can't remember."

Not understanding, but sensing it to be improper, I looked at my mother, while my sister and her friend dissolved into more fits of giggles. My mother smiled politely and changed the subject.

"Oh, you're not still in training then, Diana, not like our Angela?"

As spoilt and precocious as ever, my sister sulked her disappointment at the lack of reaction, then loudly scoffed, "Well, of course she's not. Don't be so silly, Mummy. Di's a qualified staff-nurse over on men's surgical. She'll be twenty-five in May. She's got her DN Cert and midwifery, but she's just split from her husband. He was a bastard, wasn't he, Di? Real shit of a man. Never you mind, you poor darling, you'll be in my bed tonight, I'll help you forget about all those rough nasty men."

Diana Clifton stifled a giggle and looked down at the floor, while my sister waited expectantly for a reaction that never came. Presumably reasoning that my mother was either senseless or naïve, she shrugged and continued prattling about nothing and everything.

"Poor Di, she just got divorced. The bastard went back to Glasgow, that's where he came from, and she needed to get away from all of that messy nonsense. You know what divorces can be like, especially when there's other people involved. She still hasn't got a penny piece from the lousy bastard. You know how tight these bloody Scotsman can be."

Diana Clifton sniffed her contempt.

"Tight isn't the word that instantly springs to mind."

Yet again, the two of them dissolved into fits of giggles, while my mother stared vacantly back at them with that same polite smile playing across her lips. The giggles finally subsided. My sister finished her introduction.

"But anyway, that's why she came back to regular nursing, and that's how I met her, and that's how she came to be my best's friend in the world. Isn't that lovely, Mummy?"

"Yes, it is." My father had returned, taken one look at my sister's best's friend in the world, and begun openly salivating. "Hello, darling. Happy Birthday. Well now, who is this gorgeous creature? Will she be staying for long?"

"We're just staying for a couple of nights. Oh, I'm sorry. This is Diana Clifton, Daddy. She's my best's friend in the world, so you have to be nice to her."

"Oh I will, darling. I promise. Well, hello there, Diana Clifton, and how do you do?"

Diana Clifton's self-assurance and sensuality were even more powerful than her perfume.

"I do everything very well, thank you, and whenever I please, Mr Clark."

My father deftly sidestepped my mother's blocking manoeuvre and closed in for the kill.

"Well of course you do. You're an intelligent, beautiful and sexy young woman, and so why shouldn't you? But you must call me Frank, and I shall call you. . . let me see now: the gorgeous Diana, I think."

And that was how I always thought of her. . . the gorgeous Diana. However, it didn't appear my mother shared our masculine opinions.

I looked on as my father clasped the outstretched fingers of Diana Clifton. I watched my mother glare her anger and contempt as she studied his foolishness and considered his weakness. I watched my sister smiling mischievously as her eyes flickered between those of my father and those of my mother. I watched 'the gorgeous Diana' playfully hold his admiring gaze with a similarly candid one. I watched my mother turn the glare on my sister's best's friend in the world. I watched a mischievous smile broaden as my sister's eyes flickered back and forth between them. I watched it all, and considered it all, and decided that this was not a good place or time for an ungrateful little bastard like me to be around.

The following morning I was in my room, listening to the risqué conversation in my sister's room.

"I always fancied him, at school and that. I think he fancied me, too, but he never came on to me, not like that randy old bugger Jennings. He'd always find an excuse to brush up against me, or accidentally on purpose grope my arse. Illingworth Duxbury wasn't like that, though. He used to look, they all used to look, but he never touched."

The gorgeous Diana scoffed at that.

"Well, darling, I can't say I ever felt that way about my old headmaster, but what the hell. I'm the last person to start lecturing you or anybody else on a girl keeping her knees together. I will tell you something, though. If he sees you in that outfit, you're going to get the old sod's blood pumping somewhere and you'd better be ready to deal with it. . . Just a minute. Have you taken that hemline up? If matron sees that, she'll go berserk."

My mother had always been one of the world's worst eavesdroppers, but that didn't stop her being self-righteous, because she would see me listening and say, "Michael. You do know that people who listen to other people's conversations never hear anything good about themselves?"

On that particular morning those words were to prove sadly prophetic, but this conversation was far too risqué and intimate for an inquisitive teenage boy to ignore. I crept to the doorway and peeped through the gap between frame and door.

My sister's bedroom door was ajar. I could see her cavorting back and forth in an obviously customized version of her nurse's uniform. However, the precocious Angela wasn't the object of my teenage voyeurism, and never had been. Neither was she the reason that my eyes bulged in their sockets and my heart started thumping against my ribcage. Oh no. It was the gorgeous Diana, leaning against the wardrobe, dressed only in the briefest underwear.

My only previous experience of a semi-naked female was an elderly lady on the pebbles at Bracklesham Bay. She'd been exchanging her knee-length knickers and liberty bodice for a heavy-duty woollen bathing costume. Although protected by a huge beach towel, the wind suddenly whipped across the pebbles and snatched away the towel, leaving the poor woman displayed in all her glory and balanced precariously on a single shapeless leg. It left a scar that remains to this day, but this was the first time I had seen an attractive woman so much as even partially undressed, and the gorgeous Diana was every inch the stuff of a young man's dreams.

I can remember standing motionless and mesmerized, like a rabbit frozen in a shaft of light. Holding my breath, with my eyes boring through the liquid translucence and my teenage naiveté racing, I was only vaguely aware of my sister sashaying back and forth as she answered, "No, she won't. She won't say anything, because I haven't taken up the hem. I've just folded the waistline over. See, the belt's wide enough to hide it nicely, and when I sit down and cross my legs, he'll just be able to see the stocking tops without having to grovel on the floor."

She was obviously giving a demonstration, but I hadn't the slightest interest in her, or any intention of tearing my eyes away from the gorgeous Diana. As she moved away from the wardrobe and stopped to study the adjustment, she lolled her head and shifted her weight from one long smooth leg to the other. I was spellbound.

I remember an incident involving one of the more boastful boys in my class at school. He was standing by the tennis courts, watching the girls through the wire, and holding court with some of the boys from 4G.

Everyone admired Gerry Hitchcock, because he was one of the few boys in 5G who claimed first-hand sexual experience with a real, flesh-and-blood female. He was boasting of his latest conquest. We gullibly clung to every word.

"She had incredible tits," he loudly and crudely declared, "huge bloody knockers that stood out like this." He used his hands to provide graphic assistance, and we stretched our limited imaginations in an effort to imagine the poor overladen creature.

"I'm a tit man from now on," he confided. "You've got to be one or the other, you see, 'cos everybody is." To confirm his extensive knowledge and improve our feeble understandings, he explained further. "Some men are arse men; some are leg men, and if that's what they want, well I guess that's O.K., but I'm a tit man . . . As long as they're huge, bloody great big ones."

I hadn't the faintest idea why it should be necessary to choose, and I don't believe anybody else had any more idea than me. However, some of the more vocal, boastful, vulgar and undoubtedly untruthful had instantly made up their minds. They loudly announced individual preferences, amid much schoolboy sniggering and nudging of elbows.

Fearing someone might demand I make a similarly chauvinistic choice, and more importantly justify my decision, I said nothing and slipped unobtrusively away.

Six months on from that I still wasn't any closer to an opinion, but that morning it was if a cloud had lifted. I gawped at the gorgeous Diana's satin-clad rump, and instantly decided.

"Oh yes," she said, "that works, but are you sure the old sod will be able to stand up to the strain of it all? I mean, have you done any cardiology yet?"

"Of course, but he's not that old; less than forty I think, and reasonably good-looking for a teacher. Mummy always says she likes his hands, but I always liked his feet."

"Why's that?"

"They're enormous."

For the umpteenth time, they collapsed into fits of giggles, before the gorgeous Diana said, "Well, darling, if they're that big, perhaps I'd better come with you . . . help massage his toes."

"I'm sure I'll manage. Anyway, you'll be too busy flirting with my father. Now you be careful there, Di. He's a real bastard with women. He always has been, and he always will be. And don't go thinking that just because you're my best friend, he won't shove you up against the fridge and do you if you give him half a chance."

"You can't be serious? Sweetie, that's positively Neanderthal! Up against the fridge?"

"Oh, yes. Height's good for a knee-trembler. Mummy caught him and our next-door neighbour doing it there. He had her shoved up against the fridge. Mummy never got over it. Now she won't even sleep in the same bed. Horny old bugger never could keep it zipped up. He must have screwed half the women in the village over the years."

"Oh that's priceless! I don't believe it. What a scream! Did she actually catch him, seriously, *in flagrante delicto*?" My sister must have nodded. "So she doesn't sleep with him?"

"No. She never was all that keen, but now she flatly refuses to let him anywhere near her, silly bitch. That's the real reason you can't use his office for a bedroom, because he has to."

"Well then, you can't blame him. It's no wonder he wants to screw women wholesale. Poor man must be walking around with a permanent hard-on. So what does he do, to relieve all those pent-up masculine tensions and that?"

"Shags anything and everything. Mummy says he's hardly ever home. I reckon he's only hanging around today in the hope that you might be up for it."

If my sister had intended to dissuade, she clearly failed.

"Well then, maybe I'll pop into the kitchen later; check out his lettuce crisper."

"You bloody well wouldn't?"

"I bloody well would. Between you, me, and the fridge door, if you're at your old school this afternoon, and your mother's still up in town . . . I more than likely bloody well will."

"Diana Clifton, I sometimes think you're too disgraceful for words."

"Me disgraceful? I'm not the one who'll be bent over some leery old schoolmaster's desk this afternoon, getting shagged senseless."

"Neither am I."

"Oh, yes you bloody well are."

"I'm not, honestly." She paused before adding, "Well, maybe, but only if I get six of the best."

The same annoying and predictable fits of giggles followed, then the gorgeous Diana asked, "So what's wrong with your brother, then? Why don't you like him?"

"He's not my brother; never was, and never will be. Anyway, I hate the little bastard."

"Well, he seemed all right to me; a bit shy, in fact a lot shy, but he's still young."

"Oh come off it, Di, he's almost fifteen, for Christ's sake. I'd screwed half of Bracknell track and field when I was his age. He still thinks it's for pissing out of. Anyway, as far as I'm concerned, he doesn't belong here. We were a happy little family before he arrived."

"What do you mean?"

"He's adopted. Mummy didn't want more children, but Daddy wanted me to have a brother. We got him from an orphanage, but I never wanted a brother. I never wanted anybody else in our family. I was happy with everything as it was, and he never fitted in . . . . just shoved his way in, like some sort of bloody cuckoo. We always had trouble with him, and I never liked him."

"Oh come on, Angie, don't be so hard on him. It was hardly his fault, poor little sod."

"I don't care whose fault it was, I just wish he wasn't here. Mummy thinks so, too. She can't wait to get rid of him. Even Daddy admits he made the biggest mistake of his life in taking him. We keep hoping and praying that one day the little shit will finally take the hint and fuck off."

"You don't suppose he's listening, do you?"

The gorgeous Diana had suddenly become aware of the open door. I stepped back as she pushed it closed, but not before I had heard my sister say, "I don't care if he is."

It's strange, but until I heard my sister utter the words, I hadn't actually realised that my family had never loved or wanted me. It was only then that all of those experiences I had suffered and endured for so many years were suddenly and alarmingly focused. All the bias, all the negative and disparaging comments, the absence of any warmth or affection for me, and the resulting emotional emptiness: they were all the result of one simple, unpalatable fact.

I remember sitting on the edge of my bed with all thoughts of the gorgeous Diana forgotten, and only those terrible words echoing inside my head. At last, I finally knew the truth.

I don't believe I have ever suffered from emptiness and loneliness and unhappiness as acutely as I did at that particular and most dreadful moment in my life.

Everyone is good at something

The following Sunday my parents took me to see my grandmother. As we walked from the car to the nursing-home entrance my father was his usual happy-go-lucky self.

"Well, I can't see what we need to do this for. Just kick him up the backside and tell him to do as he's bloody well told. Why go to the bother of all this palaver? Just send off the application forms and boot him into whichever one is desperate enough to take him."

My mother provided her usual arbitration.

"I've told you a thousand times. If we're serious about getting him into the forces this year we have to get him an apprenticeship, and if the little bugger decides he doesn't want to go . . . Well, you know how bloody-minded he can be. He'll dig his heels in, and heaven and earth won't budge him. Michael, for goodness sake, stop dawdling; we're only doing this for you."

The matron greeted us at the entrance.

"Mrs Clark, how do you do? Oh, and Mr Clark, too. It's nice to meet you at last, and you've brought young Michael with you, I see. The whole family."

"Good morning, Matron. Yes, the whole family, apart from our Angela, of course."

"Yes of course, apart from Angela. How is she? Training over at St. Peters, I understand."

"She's doing very well, very well indeed, Matron, we couldn't be prouder. She's simply flying through her examinations. They're so pleased with her over there, I just can't tell you."

"Well, that must be lovely for you, and of course there's your young Michael here as well. Now, how's he doing these days?"

"My mother . . . She's in her room, is she?"

The matron paused for a moment, unsure if she should repeat the question.

"Um, uh . . ." She wisely chose not to. "Yes, oh yes, she's up and waiting for you in her room."

"Good, good. Well we won't keep you then, Matron, good to see you again. Michael, do take your hands out of your pockets. I don't know, you look more like a yob every day."

The matron retreated along the corridor. My mother muttered out of the corner of her mouth.

"I didn't want to say too much in front of her. You know what a gossip she is. They say when she's not gossiping here, she spends all her time over at the Cannon; propping up the bar with a gin-and-tonic in one hand and someone else's husband in the other."

My father hadn't been listening. He'd been watching the nurses hurrying to and fro, and one in particular. She returned his stare with a provocative smile, then flashed a confirmation of interest as she squeezed past. We watched her sashay along the corridor. My mother was not amused.

"Don't you ever stop? For God's sake. Is no woman safe where you're concerned?"

"What?"

"I should have known better than bring you to a place like this. Like letting a fox loose in the hen-house. Now don't go upsetting my mother. We need her support on this."

She tapped lightly on the door and walked on in. My grandmother was sitting in her chair by the window. The old lady spoke, but she didn't get up.

"Good God, what have I done to deserve this? So what do you want this time?"

"We've just come to see you, Mother. Why on earth should we want anything?"

"Because you only ever come to see me when you want something."

"Good morning, Agatha."

"Well, good morning, Frank. What do you want this time . . . more money?"

"Of course not, Mother. What a shocking thing to say."

"It wasn't so shocking the last time you came around here cap-in-hand."

For once in her life my mother allowed the subject to drop. She kissed my grandmother on the cheek, then sat down on the only other chair. My father stood shuffling uncomfortably with a pained expression on his face.

"Where am I supposed to sit?"

"Sit on the bed, Frank, and stop being so childish. Michael, give your grandmother a kiss."

My father gingerly tested the counterpane with one fingertip.

"It's not wet, is it?"

My grandmother glared at him.

"If I have to pee on anything, Frank, you'll be the first to know."

"Frank, don't be so silly. Now sit down and be quiet. Michael, did you hear what I said?"

I walked over to my grandmother and gave her a kiss on the cheek. She gave me a hug.

"You two seem friendly enough."

"He's a good boy, is Michael. He comes to see me every week, don't you, darling?"

I nodded, feeling slightly embarrassed, and then backed away to sit alongside my father.

"Is that true, Michael?" Why she thought my grandmother would want to lie about it escaped me. "Is that true? Do you see your grandmother every week?"

"When I can."

"What an honour. Getting him to say two words to us is a minor miracle."

"Perhaps he speaks, Grace. Perhaps you don't listen. So, what is it?"

"We saw Michael's headmaster. He said Michael's been a disaster at school, and his only choice is to join the armed forces."

"Well, that doesn't unduly surprise me. That school was about as much use to him as nipples on a boar, or his parents for that matter."

"What do you mean by that?"

My grandmother shook her head and wagged a finger.

"When Michael passed his eleven-plus did either of you even bother to say well done? No, of course you didn't. Your only interest was telling the world how unfair it was that he somehow managed to scrape a pass, and that little madam of a daughter of yours didn't."

"What do you mean, little madam? She's a lovely girl. I wish I had two like her."

"And did either of you ever help him with his homework, or take any interest whatsoever? No, of course you didn't, because you were too busy putting him down and puffing her up."

"What do you mean: little madam?"

"Because she takes after you, Frank, that's always been her trouble; brains in her knickers. And don't you sit there with that sour look on your face, my girl. You were no better at her age."

"You know that's not true. Anyway, I thought we were talking about Michael."

Unusually, my mother was trying to get the conversation back on track. I could see where her verbal aggression came from, because sweet harmless Granny was in battering-ram mode.

"Oh, you want to talk about him, do you? So, are you aware that he's the subject of continual victimisation at that damned school? Did you know he's regularly beaten up by the other kids, punched and kicked around at break time and lunchtime, and on his way to and from school?"

"Well, you notice things now and then, of course you do, but he's a boy, he's going to get himself into scrapes. He has to learn to defend himself. That's what becoming a man is all about. It would be a fine state of affairs if Frank had to fight his battles for him, wouldn't it now?"

"For goodness sake, Grace, you know I wasn't suggesting anything of the sort, but haven't you ever considered the reason behind it all; the reason they always pick on him?"

My mother eyed me up and down.

"What's wrong with him?"

"For God's sake, just look at him, and listen to him."

"He's smartly dressed and he speaks well. What's wrong with that?"

"He doesn't speak well, Grace. He speaks like he's got a plum in his mouth, and the other kids hate him for it. Your Angela never spoke like that."

"Well, it's more important for boys, and how do you know what the other kids think?"

"Because I've got two eyes, two ears, and a brain in my head, and I happen to use them. You should try it some time. I mean to say, look at the way you dress him and send him to school."

"Well, there's a surprise. So that's wrong too, I suppose?"

"Yes it is, Grace. He goes to school looking like a throwback from the nineteen-twenties."

My father took up the challenge.

"I'm sorry, Agatha, but I'm not having a son of mine going out dressed like a yob. I don't care what passing fad or modern social claptrap you spout at me. I have a position to keep up in this community, and I'm not having it undermined by that little sod."

At that moment a tapping at the door caused everybody to stop in mid-argument. My mother opened the door to find an embarrassed-looking matron.

"I'm sorry, Mrs Clark, but this is a nursing home, you know, and these walls are thin."

My mother flushed to the roots and mumbled an apology.

"I'm sorry too, Matron. Families; you know what they're like, but we'll do our best."

The matron muttered her thanks. My mother pushed the door shut and glared at me.

"Now see what you've done. I don't know . . . the trouble you cause."

With the culprit identified and admonished my mother continued.

"There's a shop at the bottom of Peascod Street. Frank gets all his clothes there."

"And I always look smart enough."

"Yes, you do, Frank, but you're not a teenage boy with a dozen millstones around your neck, desperately hoping the other kids will accept you so you can somehow find yourself."

"Find himself? What is he, lost?"

"In a way, Frank, yes, he is."

"Well I'm sorry, Agatha, but I've never heard such bloody rubbish in my life. If he's bullied at school, then it's high time he stood up for himself. If he wants to be a long-haired layabout, he can bloody well leave my house first. If he doesn't like the clothes I buy for him, he can bloody well go without, or get a job and buy his own. And if you don't like the way I send him to school and discipline him, you can bloody well lump it, because it's none of your bloody business."

"None of my business? In that case, what the hell are you doing here? Now, I've had just about enough of this. So, out. Go on, get out of here, the pair of you. I want to talk to Michael."

"So, what's the problem with you today?"

We could hear my parents bickering as they walked down the corridor, but now I was alone with my grandmother, and that was how we preferred it. She was a lovely lady, my grandmother, with a gentle manner and a kind heart. She was both friend and mentor to me during those unhappy years. I will always remember her with the greatest affection, but for some reason my parents always brought out the worst in her.

"They're trying to get me to join the Air Force, become an apprentice. I don't want to go."

"Why on earth not? You can't hang around the golf club for the rest of your life."

"Why not? It's not bad money, and other people do it?"

"Because people who hang around places like that aren't living their lives, Michael, they're wasting their lives. You're far too bright to settle for anything as mundane as that."

"I don't see why; everybody else tells me I'm thick."

"And who might everybody else be?"

"The teachers, everyone at school, my mother and father: just about everybody."

"Well, I can't agree with them. I happen to know you're not thick. You may be a little confused, even a trifle awkward at times, but you're not thick. I've seen enough thick people in my time to know the difference, and you're not one of them.

"You just haven't found out what it is that you're good at yet, but you've plenty of time, and you'll discover it one day. You may not know this, Michael, but everyone is good at something, and I mean everyone. You just wait and see if I'm not right.

"All those smug academics at that snobby grammar school, and down the road at that other dump, aren't worth tuppence in my book. A major part of their job is to find out what youngsters like you are good at, and they didn't even bother to try. All people ever want these days is an easy life, and getting the best out of youngsters never was easy. You'd think teachers, of all people, would understand that."

"But Windsor's got one of the highest Oxbridge entry rates. That's why I went there."

"Oh, I'm sure it has a sparkling record in that department, but that's not what it's all about, or it shouldn't be. Kids like you are the real measure of a teacher's worth, kids who take some effort and skill to bring along, not the naturally gifted children. They're no challenge at all.

"Don't you ever let those fur-trimmed capes and tasselled mortarboards fool you into believing that these people have some God-given right to mark you down as a failure. In my experience, people who look down their noses as they push kids like you aside haven't got a worthwhile success or useful qualification between them.

"No, you keep on looking, and don't ever let anybody call you thick. You'll find out what it is that you're good at; you see if I'm not right."

"And so you reckon I'll find it in the Air Force?"

"Who can tell? It's a possibility, I suppose, but there's something I do know. You'll have more chance of finding it out there than you will by hanging around this backwater."

There was a pause after that as we drank our tea. She could see I was upset, but didn't press me. She knew me better than anyone, and she knew I would tell her.

"Why don't my parents love me, or want me, Gran? Is it because I keep messing up?"

I had finally blurted it out, half afraid that any form of answer would somehow validate the question. She looked surprised, but then looked hard at me.

"Who says they don't want you?" she asked.

"Angela was telling her friend. She said Mother and Father told her that they wish they hadn't taken me . . . you know, from the orphanage. She said I was just like a cuckoo."

"Well, that tells me a lot more about Angela than it is does about them, or you for that matter. Why would you want to believe her, anyway?"

"It's not just that, Gran, you know it isn't. It's just that I'd never thought about it before, but it's true, I know it is. I hadn't realised it, not before she said, but it's true."

"And I know it's not true, but you must understand something, Michael. You must understand that even though they cut the umbilical cord, they still leave all the other ties in place. That is a basic fact of life, and you're just going to have to learn to deal with it."

I obviously hadn't understood a word. She tried to explain.

"You know, Michael, it took me half a lifetime to realise that my daughter can be a spoilt and selfish child, but I still love her. I made her, you see, I gave her life. She is a part of me that will never change, and I would never want it to. We're none of us perfect, Michael, not me, not you, and certainly not your mother and father. They'll come to understand that one day, when they look at Angela and themselves through the same microscope they use when they look at you."

"You're saying they'll change their minds some day?"

"One day they will, but Angela will always be their natural daughter, and you will always be their adopted son. You can't change that, Michael. You just have to accept it, and get on with living your life."

She patted my arm as she spoke, and I felt a profundity of warmth for her.

"Go and join the Air Force, or the Army, or something; anything that will take you away from here. Get out there and see the world, leave all of this behind you. You know something, Michael: problems always look smaller and less overwhelming when you look back at them. You jolly well get out there and start enjoying your life. You'll find out what it is that you're good at. It's out there somewhere. . . all you have to do is find it.

"Right then, that's that. Now, shall we have another cuppa?"

Three days after that most significant chat with my grandmother, the various pamphlets arrived. My mother handed them to me, allowing me the illusion that it was still my decision. I remember saying I would 'think about it' as I carried them up to my room.

I discarded the Navy pamphlets. Leaving embarrassing seasickness problems aside, I had been watching old films and newsreel footage of life on the ocean wave since the age of seven, everything from *Mutiny on the Bounty* to *Battle of the River Plate*. Had I shown any inclination to enjoy months of cramped deprivation and boredom, throwing up rancid food, while at the mercy of some despotic ship's captain, I would probably have failed the medical on grounds of insanity.

I moved on to the Army brochure, a glossy document suggesting I enrol in the 'British Army Junior Leaders Regiment'. Both glossy document and glossy idea initially impressed, but, thankfully, common sense prevailed. I say thankfully, because I later discovered that it was little more than a government-sponsored oxymoron.

How anyone could claim that shaving a child's head, shoving him into uniform, and screaming obscenities at him until he moves his limbs in concert with other similarly-brainwashed children somehow constitutes leadership development escapes me.

That aside, it did occur to me that in the regular Army there's altogether too much shouting and hollering. Too much yes sir and no sir and three bags full sir, and marching up and down for no obvious reason, and a whole raft of other unnecessary and menial tasks. Worst of all, there was the distinct possibility of my getting killed. While it was good to know that desertion only demanded negotiating the traffic along Aldershot High Street and not breast-stroking through man-eating sharks to a barren south seas island, it couldn't possibly compensate for that.

That was it then: a no-brainer. I didn't fancy dysentery, scurvy, or being eaten by sharks. I didn't fancy becoming a robot, or getting blown-up, bombed, or shot at. There was nothing else for it. I would have to join the Air Force.

I picked up the brochure and scanned the preconditions for fighter pilot training, desperately searching for some loophole that might allow me to apply. It seemed simple enough: minimum of five 'O' levels and three 'A' levels GCE passes, preferably a good degree, supremely fit, perfect eyesight, demonstrable maturity and mental agility. The result of all that was not an opportunity to take over from Charlton Heston in some Cecil B. DeMille blockbuster, but possible acceptance into the academy at Cranwell.

Undeterred, I continued scanning the brochure, reasoning that if fighter pilot training was beyond reach, then maybe I should become the brains behind the brawn. Perhaps a navigator, or airframe or propulsion technician; maybe a radar boffin or weapons-guidance supremo, maybe even an air-traffic controller. I could just see myself studying complex battle plans and plotting bomber formations across a war-torn continental chessboard. The possibilities were endless.

I hastily chose three or four of the more exciting looking possibilities, haphazardly scribbled a few details across the application form, and then nipped out to catch the five o'clock post.

I spent the next two weeks hovering by the front door with my heart in my mouth while I waited for an answer. It finally arrived, second post, on a wet Wednesday, a large and important-looking envelope full of more brochures and a two-page typewritten letter.

The first paragraph thanked me for writing, and went on to say how much my application had impressed them. The second paragraph was even better than the first. It said young men of my calibre were always of interest to the Royal Air Force and invited me to Royal Air Force Stafford to take a physical and some aptitude tests.

My mind was racing. This was better than I could have possibly hoped. I began daydreaming about my career, imagining myself in full Air Force blue regalia, looking dapper and deadly and handsome. I began to consider the vast range of technical skills that I would undoubtedly develop; in addition, of course, to a comprehensive assortment of more lethal skills.

It wasn't until I picked up the next page and read through, then re-read the letter in its entirety, that reality dawned. It seemed the Royal Air Force had carefully appraised my skills profile and come up with some 'exciting opportunities' that would undoubtedly appeal to an ambitious young man of my unquestionable talent and potential.

Fireman, Cook, and Clerk Secretarial were the cream. However, should I be willing to undergo a frontal lobotomy, wait a further two years, and then take an intensive course in human robotics, there was the possibility of adult entry into the RAF Regiment.

I shuffled into the lounge and broke the sorry news to my parents. My father looked to the heavens and then walked away, mumbling something under his breath, but my mother was furious. How could she possibly tell her friends that I was training to be a fireman or a cook? The shame of it all would be too much to bear. Admittedly the term 'clerk' covered a multitude of sins, but the secretarial attachment would tell people all they needed to know.

In a despairing gesture and keen not to be seen as in any way unsupportive, she telephoned the RAF careers office. I shuffled closer, and tried to hear what was being said.

"A cook. A lousy cook. A bloody spud basher." Were they bloody well mad? Her husband had been a squadron leader in the war. He was one of those people who had saved this country for people like you. He was a friend of Sir Denis Spotswood, and now you want his son to peel bloody potatoes in some greasy godforsaken kitchen?

"Who's he? What do you mean, who's he? He's the Chief of the bloody Air Staff, that's who he is. I'll tell him you said that." She frantically screamed her displeasure into the mouthpiece and the poor man at other end of the line went strangely silent. "The Army may well march on its stomach," she added, "but did you really fly aircraft on the same basis?" By this time she was warming to the task. "A clerk. A lousy, pen-pushing, Uriah bloody Heep of a clerk, with ink-stained fingers and national health glasses, typing inconsequential memos and poring over columns of meaningless figures . . . you have to be bloody well mad."

A further pause for oxygen and inspiration allowed the beleaguered sergeant to calm her with a further well-intentioned suggestion. Then she started again.

"What was that?" she barked. "A fireman, is that what you said? Is that really what you said?" She caustically begged his pardon, but . . . "Wasn't that always supposed to be a part-time job?"

The Sergeant begged to differ, insisting that fireman was indeed a most important job, but then wisely changed tack.

"What about a telegraphist, then?"

"What about it? A telegraphist, a bloody telegraphist. Are you serious?" She paused, then looked across at me with one of those 'hold on a minute that sounds interesting' looks on her face. "I'm sorry,

Sergeant." She hadn't meant to interrupt. "Please go on. What exactly was that again?" We both listened, hopefully and carefully, as the Sergeant explained. Morse code, radio, teleprinters, telecommunications, high technology. He even threw sophisticated code machines and the latest computers into the equation.

Well now, finally she was getting through to them. "That's more like it, young man." She could happily boast to Mrs Flood about how she had managed to use the family influence to get me that. She finally released the poor man from his torment and replaced the receiver. Well, it was better than sweating over a hot stove and peeling potatoes, or filling in boring forms, or shinning up ladders and rescuing overfed tabby cats.

I nonchalantly announced my decision to the world.

"I might as well do that then, I suppose."

For a fleeting moment of uncharacteristic caution, I did wonder why there had been no specific educational or physical preconditions mentioned.

God, I was young.

Royal Air Force Stafford proved a friendly little camp, with happy smiling faces and flowers growing in the guardhouse window box. According to the smiling warrant officer who greeted me so warmly at the camp gates before taking me through the various tests, they'd received over eleven-hundred applications for one-hundred-and-fifty vacancies . . . talk about a sought-after cross-section of professions.

As you might imagine, they hooked me with little difficulty. By that first lunchtime I was begging and pleading for them to accept my application. At one point on that first evening, I was even willing to consider spud-bashing or pen-pushing. No, they had me all right; snared with a quick flick of their 35 millimetre projector and landed in style by teatime. I was going to be a highly-trained, impeccably-suited lethal weapon: a Royal Air Force technical specialist. Not just anybody could do that, you know.

The following day's aptitude tests had been a breeze. The only tricky bit came when they needed to know if I could distinguish between short and long blips, heard through a set of World War Two headphones.

'Don't try to read it,' they said, as I sat there with strings of Morse code going in one ear and out the other, and my eyes flickering between bossed and crossed. Don't try to read it? They had to be joking. I'd had enough trouble with semaphore in the Wolf Cubs. As for understanding this fellow, Samuel Morse, and his half-duplex, variable length, electronic pulse code, I didn't see a snowball in Hell's chance of that ever happening. Happily and inexplicably, they decided that I could just about spot enough of the essential differences between the two pulse lengths and that was that. I was through. For once in my miserable life I had succeeded, and I couldn't have been prouder.

When that smiling warrant officer called me into his office and told me that I was one of the privileged few who had passed, I can remember beaming with pleasure and puffing out my chest. Maybe it wasn't my finest hour. That dubious honour still belonged to a two-pound-eight-and-three-quarter-ounce stripy perch, caught along the tree-lined banks of Johnson's Pond. However, it was right up there among the best of them.

Royal Air Force Cosford would be my training arena, they loudly announced. The exciting metropolis of Wolverhampton my carnal stomping ground, I silently deduced. All those sexually aggressive females, with their loose elastic and Birmingham accents, must have been waiting with bated breath. I was on my way, courtesy of a Royal Air Force travel warrant, and a liberal measure of homespun ambition.

You see, she had warned about them, my mother, and the sexually aggressive females, I mean. One day, in a bizarre fit of maternal obligation, she told me of beautiful and sensuous women who were in reality nothing more than voluptuous sirens, intent on ravishing the virginity and plundering the flesh of a young and handsome warrior such as myself.

Now, thanks largely to an unexpected moment of glory at RAF Stafford, and a cautionary tale or two from an unexpected quarter, I was more than ready and willing to do my bit. All I had to do in the meantime was survive until the beginning of the apprentice year.

And survive I did, hiding myself away, playing truant for most of that year, and giving a wider berth than usual to the other kids.

It wasn't so much the well-adjusted majority of the school that I was avoiding. I had long ago learned to live with the comments and the sniggers and the sneers. . . it was the gangs.

There were three distinct local gangs, for whom my short back and sides and Sloane Street accent acted as a proverbial red rag. Two of them arrived by coach from North Ascot, and left by the same means, which meant I only had to avoid them at school. However, the third gang was cobbled together from local council estates and more difficult to avoid.

A local celebrity called Bobby Day ran the gang. He insisted people call him Bad Bobby Day and did all he could to live up to the nickname. As you might imagine, Bobby Day boasted a limited intellect. In truth, he was a junior car mechanic from the local garage, but he had a liking for cruelty and viciousness that knew few bounds. At first he would simply catch me on the way home from school, or down at the lake, and knock me about for the benefit of his juvenile entourage. However, after a year or so of this ritualistic bullying, he tired of such simple victories and allowed his entourage to do the honours instead.

Now, I was a weakling at school, but I never considered myself a coward, or I tried not to be. I knew that if I fought back against these boys, many of them from my own age group and some even younger, then Bobby Day would undoubtedly step in and finish the job. The choice was a simple one. I could fight back, with a guarantee that Bad Bobby would step in and finish the job, or stand there and take a minor beating from the younger kids, with pride the only casualty.

To my eternal shame, I elected to suffer the latter, and so, for, the last two years at school, I had to suffer pint-sized bullies as well as the more mature variety.

In Bobby Day's absence a boy named George took charge. George was six months younger than me. I called him 'Punchy George', because he rarely lashed out with his feet, well, no more than the odd kick of two after I had hit the deck, but would happily rain a flurry of unanswered blows with his fists.

Punchy George took great pride in combining a sequence of four or five punches at a time for the benefit of watching gang members. Those who had both spoken to him and seen him fight said he could string punches together better than words. I hated him, because he was a bully and a coward, who used the wrath of Bobby Day as a shield to further his own aggressive reputation. I hated myself more, though, because he made me ashamed of myself and my unwillingness to fight back.

For most of that last six months at school I managed to avoid the gangs. I would take lengthy detours home from school, and started fishing up at the Obelisk Pond rather than down at Johnson's. I spent my remaining free time and truant time up at the golf course, or hidden among London's West End streets. With one or two exceptions my new avoidance strategy worked well.

I remember that blessed last day of school as if it were yesterday. It was a day when everybody forgave everybody else for just about everything they had ever done during those five years of misery. Perhaps I should say, everybody who mattered forgave everybody else who mattered.

True to form, Gerry Hitchcock, who had by that time added the f-word to his already extensive vocabulary, generously shared his latest words of wisdom with the rest of 5G. I found him ensconced in a corner, advising the most suitable time in any given foreplay scenario for a young stud to don the essential prophylactic, explaining how it was best to be subtle for fear of alarming the fortunately selected, and presumably heavily overladen female of the moment.

"You've gotta be a bit shrewd about it all," he said. "I once banged this gorgeous-looking bird in those woods over by Fireball Hill." He glanced around the room, as if searching for eavesdroppers, before continuing. "She was something else; talk about a seriously fuckable piece of arse." He paused again, waiting expectantly for knowledgeable nodding and wide-eyed stares of hero-worship. "But d'yer know something, I nearly didn't get there at all. You see I was whacking the old rubber on, and I let her have an eyeful of what she was gonna get a bit too early on in the proceedings, if you know what I mean? Well, I'll tell yer, her eyes came out on stalks, her jaw dropped to the floor, and her thighs snapped together like they was on fucking elastic. I'll tell yer, I didn't manage to get 'em apart again for about an hour after that."

One of the green and the gullible at the front of the auditorium concernedly enquired, "But she went all right, once she'd calmed down, didn't she? That wasn't the end of it? She did come across and that?"

"Oh yeah," the maestro hastily confirmed, as if there had ever been any doubt. "She went like a fucking rocket, once I'd pushed the right buttons. They all do, if you know what you're doing."

By this time, even I was beginning to doubt the authenticity of the worldly-wise Gerry Hitchcock's many and fascinating carnal chronicles. I wandered away and left him and his admiring audience to their individual fantasies.

Unaware of my father's regime, Doc White spoke of his grudging admiration for me. How, despite all of those beatings and the constant verbal abuse, I had always stoically refused to allow my hair to grow, or wear modern dress, or look normal, or speak sensibly, or mix with the other boys after school. I hadn't enlightened him as to my lack of influence or control in such matters, because I had been far too busy bathing in the shallow waters of an unearned compliment.

Few of the others bothered to speak to me, apart from Pauline Bell. I had always thought Pauline one of the prettiest and most sophisticated of the girls at school. She asked how many 'O' level passes I had mustered. When I blurted out the unhappy truth of my miserable performance, she seemed genuinely concerned. She told me that she had always liked me, before leaning forward to kiss me on the cheek and wish me luck.

I blushed like crazy at the time, and doubted that her sentiments were due to anything more than pity and the emotion of the moment, but I will always remember her kindness and the gentleness of that kiss. It was just about the only enduring memory of school that I ever treasured, or can these days recall with any fondness whatsoever.

Nine weeks later I stood in front of my parents for final inspection, pretending not to notice the look of relief on their faces, while they pretended not to notice the same look on mine.

I remember shaking my father by the hand and kissing my mother on the proffered cheek before picking up my suitcase and walking away from them. I believe I skipped the first few yards down the driveway, passing the post office at a trot, and then heading down the road towards Sunningdale at a canter. I passed the doctor's bungalow and then climbed the hill, before stopping all too briefly to say a genuinely fond farewell to my grandmother. Then I was off again, down The Rise and past the bicycle and fishing tackle shop, before turning towards the footpath leading around the back of the playing fields to the station.

I loved that walk to freedom and that train journey to my new life. I was timid, uncertain and insecure, but happier than I could ever remember being.

Five hours and three train changes later I was there . . . a clean slate and a new life; a fresh beginning and a new opportunity.

A Brave New World

My first impression of Royal Air Force Cosford was of a tiny railway station with a simple wooden platform that could well have been described by Enid Blyton. Not that I had read the dear lady for some ten years or so, but some characters and places leave a lasting impression, and Cosford railway station bore a remarkable likeness to her description of Toytown.

Dear Enid Blyton. I loved those books, and I never did have any time for the politically correct. They always struck me as interfering busybodies, left-wing loonies, and inverted snobs; people with nothing better to do than pollute innocent childhood memories with ridiculous accusations.

But then I met Corporal Campbell and suddenly understood why the world needs left-wing loonies. It preserves the balance by adding a similarly weighted psychosis to either end of the sanity scales. It is so most of us are better able to plot a meandering course between the two.

Corporal Campbell was a fearsome, five-feet, eight-inch, right-wing loony with a shaved head and a daunting expression. He gleamed from head to toe, and had the strangest habit of ostentatiously stamping his feet every time he mentioned something dear to his heart, or whenever he needed to adjust position or change location.

He met me at the camp gates, and formally introduced himself as my new discipline and drill instructor. He snapped to attention, presumably to demonstrate competence, but then relaxed both posture and formality to advise me that I should simply refer to him as Corporal.

I was to discover that he was a Wee Beastie from the dark side of the Black Isle. There was nothing even faintly timorous about him. Rumour was that he'd suddenly appeared at an Inverness mobile recruitment centre one morning, claiming direct lineage to a Highland Regiment Fusilier who'd fought alongside the vicious and victorious Duke of Cumberland on Culloden Moor.

Whatever the truth of that particular claim, there was no doubting Corporal Campbell's credentials. He was a twenty-two-years-service proudly completed, dyed-in-the-wool, gleaming from head to toe, RAF Regiment man, and a total sociopath. My first experience of him was unnerving, to say the least, because he was one of those utter morons who 'slash their peaks'.

Allow me to explain. 'Slashing one's peak' is nothing to do with incontinence, or an unsteady aim in the ablutions. It is a trick of those armed forces personnel whose purpose in life was, and I presume still is, to intimidate little lads like me into mechanical and emotionless conformity.

The trick they employ is simple. The number one dress hat for non-commissioned ranks has a shiny peak that juts out to the front at roughly ninety-degrees. Smart and practical uniform, for most normal well-adjusted human beings, most would concede, but not for drill instructors, station warrant officers, and overbearing guardians of military law.

For such peculiarly regimented psychopaths and all-round charmers as these, the standard government-issue uniform is incapable of providing a sufficiently frightening appearance. When issued with a new service-dress hat, they apply a razor blade to the supporting stitching beneath the shiny peak which results in a dropped peak that rests on the bridge of the nose.

So what? I hear you ask. What possible advantage could be gained from such an adjustment? What benefit could such flagrant abuse of government property achieve? The answer, dear reader, is thus . . .

By covering the eyes it provides a bland, almost robotic, quality to the individual's character. It shields the windows to the soul, and thus ensures the beholder can detect no emotion in the wearer. It also demands the wearer looks down his nose at you and everything and everyone he meets, which places him in a position of authority, or so he fondly believes. However, that assumes the wearer is around six-foot-something inches tall, and the beholder some inches shorter.

Corporal Campbell was five-feet, eight-inches tall in his shiny boots. I was of similar stature at the grand old age of fifteen-and-a-bit years, or maybe even slightly taller. You can probably imagine the problem. For most of that absurd first conversation I found myself talking to a hat with a mouth underneath, frantically manoeuvring my eyes up and down in the hope of detecting some form life above the national health dentures and shaving rash.

That was until the Wee Beastie decided to assess my youthful complexion, and tilted his head back at such an acute angle that I found myself addressing the bottom of his chin. Immediately above the chin, and dominating what little I could see of his face, two oversized nostrils bristled with thick black wiry hair. Completing the abomination, from deep within the blackness and beneath the drooping peak two beady black eyes glinted angrily back.

"Well, laddie, this is it. Welcome to the Number Two School of Technical Training. Welcome to Royal Air Force Cosford."

He aggressively stamped his feet, as if in some mechanised reverence to the hallowed ground upon which we were fortunate enough to be standing. I jumped at the suddenness of movement before collecting my wits and nervously answering.

"Uh, thank you, sir."

"Thank you, Corporal."

He had screamed the contradiction. I jumped again.

"I'm sorry, I meant thank you, Corporal."

I'd stammered my response. He seemed pleased at that.

"That's better. Now then, you can wait in here. The bus will be along."

"Yes, sir."

"Are you deaf, as well as stupid? It is not sir, it is Corporal. You understand? It is Corporal. I am the backbone of this man's Air Force, not some chinless flaming zobbit. I am a Corporal; a Corporal. Can you get that through your thick skull? When you address me you say, yes Corporal."

I had no idea what the decibel rating on that little speech might have been, but it would undoubtedly have registered on some scale or other.

"Yes, Corporal."

"That's better, laddie, and don't you forget it."

"No, Corporal."

"You don't say no to me, laddie: not ever. You say, yes, Corporal. Do you understand?"

"Yes, Corporal."

Those simple pleasantries, which had been awkwardly but politely exchanged only a few moments earlier, were suddenly forgotten and I was in childlike awe of the man. He had screamed every syllable of those instructions as if trying to rouse me from a coma, and I knew that I had never before met anybody like him. I shuffled, nervously and obediently, into the waiting-room, and then peered cautiously at the other boys, who were similarly waiting for the bus.

There were three of them, all clutching their suitcases as if their lives depended on it, and all looking similarly terrified. One of them visibly shrank into his seat as the psychotic Corporal Campbell suddenly appeared framed in the doorway. I understood the boy's nervousness, because this spectre of military precision had similarly unnerved me, but that was as far as it went.

You see, so many people had religiously punched and kicked me around for so many years that I found the verbal version of bullying something of a welcome relief. Someone shouting instructions at me, even someone as menacing as the psychotic corporal, might have intimidated, it might have made me jump, but it held few, if any, real fears.

"Wotcha."

I nodded as I spoke, in a gesture of juvenile bravado, hoping to display my great courage to the three timid-looking boys who were still hiding behind their suitcases. Since listening to my grandmother scolding my parents for teaching me to speak with such an affected accent, I had been secretly practicing my slovenly speech. I would practise words and phrases like 'wotcha' and 'streuth' and 'cor blimey' and 'leave it out, mate' whenever I was on my own. I heard myself saying the word and felt pleased, reasoning that it had sounded suitably slovenly and convincing.

One of them said 'wotcha' and similarly nodded a greeting, but the other two simply stared blankly back from behind their suitcases and said nothing.

Another dozen or so boys joined us during the next twenty minutes. The psychotic corporal loudly announced each new arrival with the same staccato stamping of those shiny boots and the same series of basic instructions, bellowed at the same unholy decibel rating. The result was the same in each case: a wild-eyed fifteen-year-old boy, who had arrived full of hope and was now in an emotional state that ranged between acute nervousness and terror. A soon-to-be automaton, who already understood the appropriateness of the words 'yes' and 'corporal' and the sheer folly of using the words 'no' and 'sir'.

"Right then, you lot, the coach is here."

He'd delivered the announcement matter-of-factly. Everybody looked from one to another.

"Didn't you hear me? I said the coach is here. Get up off your lazy backsides and pick up those bags. Come on. Come on. Move it. Move it."

The corporal's screams died away, replaced by a glare of hostility, a second of intimidating silence, and then instant panic. As one, we rushed to collect belongings and pour through the narrow gap of the open doorway.

"Stand still, you lot. Did you hear what I just said? I said, don't shove. What are you; a rabble? Single file. I said one at a time. Don't you understand 'single file'? Come on then, move it. Move it. Hurry it up. Wait for it. Wait for it. Did you hear me, laddie? I said get a move on. So do it. I said move it. You. That's right, laddie. I mean you. Stand still. Who told you to move? Well come on then, don't just stand there. Jump to it. Jump to it. I haven't got all day to waste on you lot."

It was the same performance five minutes later when the coach drew to a halt outside the barrack block.

"Right then, lads, we're here."

Once again the comment seemed innocuous. Once again everybody looked uncertainly around. And once again the screaming began.

"I said we're here. So get out, and get out now. Come on, I haven't got all day. I said out. Come on. Come on. Out. You there, stop pushing. You there, what are you dawdling for? You there, get off this bus now, and I mean right now."

Most of us fell out of the coach. Some went sprawling across the road in their haste to escape the corporal's wrath, with bags and baggage sent similarly flying in all directions. We collected our strewn belongings and nervously assembled in the road. There, he bellowed some more well-chosen phrases of abuse, and then unceremoniously frogmarched us into the block. He then herded us up four flights of stairs, along a corridor and into a dormitory. Once inside the dormitory he bellowed an instruction to 'fall out', which was a term that meant nothing to me at the time, and still perplexes me to this day. After that he assigned each boy a bed space, with one metal bedstead supporting a lumpy-looking mattress, a plain wooden wardrobe, and a plain wooden locker.

Even in the barrack block the fearsome Corporal Campbell continued to bellow a never-ending series of conflicting instructions. First do it, then don't do it, then do it quicker, then stop, then start, hurry up, slow down, turn round, face the front, on your feet, stand still, sit there, no not there, move it, move it. He continued with that same routine for the next hour or so, screaming each conflicting instruction into our shattered consciousness until we were more nervous and confused than many of us had previously thought possible.

However, it wasn't until six months or so had passed that I came to understand the tactic, which was a relatively simple one. First calm, then fear, then panic, then control, then calm, then fear, then panic, then control, and finally back to calm again. It was his quick-fire method of achieving emotionless conformity from a quietly spoken command, because, after an hour of this verbal St. Vitus dance, he had us frantically complying with the mildest of spoken orders while subconsciously awaiting the next.

I am sure that dear old Ivan Pavlov would have been proud of him. Irrespective of any inherent logic, rationality, or sense, he had tutored us to instantaneous reaction, instantaneous obedience, and full and mindless compliance, while subconsciously primed to obey any subsequently murmured whim or conflicting order. One screaming, glistening, foot-stamping Scottish Corporal had managed to achieve all of this within less than two hours of our stepping from the train. It was like a psychopath's guide to behavioural science.

There was, however, a secondary objective. By stampeding us like cattle that same psychotic Scottish Corporal had ensured that he was the unchallenged leader of that herd, and that no other hierarchy would be necessary, or tolerated. Nobody had any opportunity to dominate, or impose an aggressive personality, because each boy had been as frightened and pathetically obedient as the next. Clichéd maybe, but in his own psychotic fashion Corporal Campbell had created 'comrades in adversity' from a wildly-diverse group of frightened boys.

Fulton Block was the name of the grim-looking barrack block. It was typical, if oversized, and much as you might imagine. Built in an oblong, it boasted three floors, varying wings with barrack rooms leading off, and a quadrangle in the centre. They said the formidable, but sadly late Lady Fulton had gifted the building to the apprentice wing during the thirties. Rumour had it that she still haunted a closed-off portion of the block. They claimed the area was unsafe, but we visited it one night and found it to be in no worse condition than our wing, and so rumours of ghostly goings-on in Fulton Block's infamous west wing became rife.

To say that Fulton Block was spartan would have been fair, but there was nothing dingy or Dickensian about it, or at least not the occupied sections. Every floor shone, every window was spotless, every brass door handle gleamed, and every porcelain sink sparkled and reflected every similarly sparkling tap. In fact, every surface, every item, every crevice and corner in the place glittered and gleamed like new.

Each floor of each wing comprised a long polished corridor with four extended U-shaped dormitories. Each dormitory contained the same basic inventory: Twenty-two beds, twenty-two lockers, twenty-two wardrobes, twenty-two bedside mats, and twenty-two apprentices, with each reflecting from the polished wood flooring. The apprentices on each floor shared two or three sets of spotlessly clean ablutions, and each floor also boasted storage cupboards and meeting rooms.

Roughly three hundred apprentices lived their lives within Fulton Block, but when we arrived they were mostly over in the training hangars on the other side of camp. I was in awe of the place and wondered how the cleaners managed to keep everything in such perfect condition. It was not a mystery that would trouble the old grey matter for more than the next few minutes.

The base itself was a sprawling metropolis, mainly housing the many apprenticeship courses, but it was also the RAF centre for anything physical training. Cosford had suffered from this dual identity crisis since some well-meaning fool had naively converted a disused aircraft hangar into an indoor athletics stadium. I imagine the cream of the United States and Warsaw Pact athletes must have been sick with envy.

However, this in turn meant that the place was teeming with international athletes and muscle-bound Olympians, a comparison that could only aggravate the already rife inferiority complexes of three hundred emaciated teenagers.

As well as an endless supply of athletes and physical training instructors, inexplicably drawn to this Mecca of indoor athleticism, there was a socially cosmopolitan assortment of other less focused individuals. There were cooks and clerks, drivers and mechanics, technicians and aircrew, fireman and policemen, educational support staff, and drill instructors by the truckload.

Finally there was nirvana, or in Cosford's case the Women's Royal Air Force or WAAF block, stuffed to the rafters with a misshapen assortment of clucking females, all with varying sexual proclivities, and all in high demand. Incidentally, if you find the acronym confusing, it stems from the original Women's Auxiliary Air Force, a title given long before uniform hemlines hurtled skywards and the seductive charm offered by a young lady's trim and dainty ankle became passé.

Cosford boasted a many and varied assortment of technical and craft apprentice training courses, each conducted within the wire fenced surround, and each married to its own hierarchical assemblage of apprentices. Allotted to each course was a flight lieutenant, and allotted to each entry within that course was a sergeant, a corporal, and a unique entrance number.

At the top of the tree were the technician apprentices, chinless wonders with phony Oxford accents and emotional or allergic conditions to replace the working-class blight of teenage acne. They were training to be aircraft technicians and obviously destined for greatness via the hugely costly apparatus of a three-year apprenticeship. They rightly considered themselves above the rest of us, but not above reminding us of it.

Next, came the craft apprentice ones, only worthy of a two-year apprenticeship. The technician apprentices looked down their noses at them, and had some justification in doing so. To a man, they were less than intelligent, and almost all of them had psychological problems brought on by years of under-achievement and academic failure. Poor buggers, they didn't fit into any of society's categories and they knew it, but to their eternal credit they never stopped trying, never paused in their individual struggles for social status, technical expertise and academic recognition.

Me? I was a craft apprentice two, on a one-year apprenticeship; known, less than fondly, throughout the Royal Air Force technical community as a 'crap app'. You could get lower than that, but not without the frontal lobotomy mentioned earlier.

Not that I cared. A lifetime of raised eyebrows and sadly shaking heads had prepared me well for my lowly allotment in Royal Air Force society.

Sergeant Dickie James was theoretically in charge of both the aggressive Corporal Campbell and us. Less intimidating than the Wee Beastie, Dickie James was also more comfortably dressed, more comfortably spoken, and more comfortably mannered. However, I believe he was just as secretly frightened of the pint-sized Scotsman as we, and so he rarely appeared, unless the corporal was away. On our arrival the comfortable Dickie James introduced himself, sat us down, and explained some of the basic rules of life in military service.

"Good afternoon, everybody," he began. "My name is James, Sergeant James. Can everybody hear me all right? If you can't, you had better move closer, because this is important."

By this time there were almost fifty of us crammed into that barrack room, but nobody moved closer, presumably because they could all hear, or maybe because they couldn't. Either way, the comfortable Dickie James seemed happy enough.

"Right then, a few dos and don'ts for you."

The next fifteen minutes involved a seemingly unending string of don'ts, with two exceptions: do as you're told, and do as I say. For all of that Dickie James was a cheerful and comfortable enough man, more at home raking around in the blackened bowl of an old briar pipe than screaming orders across a parade ground. The terrifying and undersized Corporal Campbell appeared toward the end of the lecture. He leaned his head around the door, and screamed, "And the next man who says to me, 'Would you like a sweetie, Corporal,' will be on jankers quicker than you can say bulled boots. I'm not here to play favourites, I'm here to give you lot some discipline."

The mildly mannered Dickie James didn't complain about the interruption. Instead of any show of indignation or annoyance, he took the opportunity to refill his pipe, seemingly engrossed in packing the tangled strands as he benevolently allowed the corporal his moment of celebrity.

We sat and looked on in astonishment, having no idea what jankers or bulled boots might be, and flabbergasted that anybody had found the time, the inclination, and especially the courage, to speak civilly to Corporal Campbell, let alone offer him a sweetie.

We were to learn a lot about ourselves during the next twelve months. We were also to learn about the gleaming Corporal Campbell and the comfortable Sergeant James; about the unwritten protocol existing between them, and the character traits, strengths and weaknesses that each man possessed. Corporal Campbell and his phantom offer of a sweetie was a case in point. Whenever he felt left out, or somehow inferior, Corporal Campbell would interrupt proceedings by claiming to have recently received or overheard something of note. It could be comments of admiration for him, or tokens of esteem and various gestures of friendship. It might be sycophantic observations, similarly levied by doting apprentices, or spiteful and disparaging remarks, which always seemed to be about someone other than the hugely popular Corporal Campbell.

Dear old Dickie James was the usual target of the Corporal's malicious fantasy, but sometimes he'd mention the Flight Lieutenant, or the Warrant Officer, or one of the other officers. All the claims were untrue, of course, not because we didn't make remarks of that sort, but because we would never have allowed Corporal Campbell to overhear us making them. However, each interruption, and each successive and ever-more-fraudulent claim, taught us ever more about Corporal Campbell, and ever more about his many and varied psychoses.

The only excursion of that first day was a trip to the bedding store. We each collected two plain white sheets, one under-blanket, three top blankets, a striped counterpane, two pillows and two pillowcases, all under the watchful but not especially vigilant gaze of Dickie James. As we wandered along I chatted to a boy called Stephen Walters. He came from Dorset, and seemed a pleasant enough lad. In truth, I think he chose me because I was the only other boy out of the fifty or so in the entry who had arrived with the same short back and sides hairstyle. I can't remember all that much about him now, but I do remember he talked non-stop about his dog, a border collie named Bonnie. He even showed me a picture of it.

When we returned from our pleasant afternoon stroll the Wee Beastie was waiting.

"I suppose you lot think that you're now going to make up your beds, and then Corporal Campbell's going to tuck you in for the night?"

At four-thirty in the afternoon the only logical answer to that was of course the dreaded 'No, Corporal'. However, we now understood the folly of any apprentice using those words and wisely kept our own counsel, or most of us did.

"Well, do you?"

"No, sir."

We looked around in astonishment, wondering who held the nerve, the effrontery, the sheer mindless stupidity to even consider uttering such words. It turned out to be a tall boy, with red hair hanging down to his shoulders in lank and matted strands. He was a newcomer, allotted a bed at the end of the dormitory, and had obviously arrived too late for any formal introduction to the Wee Beastie and his decibel-loaded conditioning routine.

For his part, The Wee Beastie was clearly beyond rage. What made it even worse for the highland warrior's overstressed blood pressure, was that a boy sporting a girl's hairstyle had volunteered the answer in a broad Glaswegian accent.

"Do I know you, laddie? Or should I say lassie?"

"No, sir."

This was getting worse; it was like a lowland version of the highland charge, not at any thin red line, although by this time Corporal Campbell was looking decidedly pink around the gills. This was a one-man suicide charge, straight over a cliff into a bottomless ravine.

"No, sir?"

"No, sir."

He'd said it again. Corporal Campbell stuck out his chin and double-dog-dared him.

"Say 'no sir' to me, just one more time, laddie, just one more time."

Thankfully, the red-headed Glaswegian declined the dare.

"I'm sorry, Corporal."

Instead of replying, the furious-looking Corporal Campbell glared long and hard, and then effected a thunderous about-turn before stamping his way to the door. For a second we thought he was about to leave in a huff, and that our redheaded Glaswegian had unintentionally discovered the Wee Beastie's Achilles heel. However, at the end of the dormitory he stamped to a halt and then turned to the first bed.

Now, standard-issue metal bedsteads came in three main sections. The rectangular base was a heavy iron frame enclosing the springs and supporting the mattress. It had four studs welded to it, two at the foot and two at the head. The independent head and foot sections were simple heavy tubular frames, with U-shaped slots above each foot to house the welded studs and support the frame. A simple enough arrangement, which, when new and in good condition, fitted tightly and solidly together and provided a stable support for both lumpy mattress and slumbering apprentice. Over time, however, the studs became worn, as did the U-shaped slots, leaving a poorly-fitting connection and an unstable bed that would rock back and forth like a baby's cradle.

Corporal Campbell wandered casually down the line of beds, pushing and pulling at each, and testing the fit. The first few were relatively new, well-fitted and unmoving, but then he found what he was looking for, a bed with a good eight inches of movement. He rocked it back and forth with a finger and thumb, and for the first time since arriving at Cosford I saw him smile. It wasn't the warm and comforting smile of that cheery Warrant Officer who had greeted and interviewed me at RAF Stafford, but the cold and malicious smile of a psychotic drill corporal.

"Do you know what this is, laddie?"

By this time even the foolhardy red-headed Glaswegian had learnt his lesson, and so the answering silence was deafening.

"I'm talking to you. . . Bonnie Princess Charlene."

Somebody sniggered, more from nervousness than humour, I'm sure, but the beastie's glare was plain. The interruption halted in mid-snigger.

"I said, Bonnie Princess Charlene, do you know what this is?"

"It's a bed, Corporal."

There was no mirth in the mimicry.

"It's a bed, Corporal." The pause was punctured only by the nervous breathing of the red-headed Glaswegian, before the decibel rating suddenly increased "It is a wanker's bed, Princess Charlene, that is what it is, a wanker's bed. And do you know what else it is?"

"Corporal?"

It was as if a cloud of confusion had suddenly lifted. The hapless Glaswegian had discovered a method of negatively answering the Corporal without saying no. The Wee Beastie roared back.

"It is your bed, laddie, that is what it is; it is your bed. So bring your suitcase here. From now on, whenever anybody wants to know who the biggest wanker in the block is, he only has to wander down the line and test the beds. He's going to be able to find the biggest wanker in the block without having to speak to him, or even look at him. You see how it works?"

"Yes, Corporal."

"Then get over here, now."

As the hapless Glaswegian hurried to his new bed I gingerly tested my own, having no idea what a wanker might be, but certain in my own mind that I didn't want people to think I was one. Thankfully the fixings remained firm and the bed didn't rock, but the eagle-eyed Beastie had spotted my testing of the assembly and equally swiftly recognised my concern for what it was.

"Oh don't you worry, laddie; if you're a wanker, we'll know about it soon enough."

He then showed us how to make a bed military-style, and to unmake the same bed and assemble a bed pack, which was a method of folding all the sheets and blankets into a squared-off pack. The counterpane provided the only colour, placed precisely and tautly across the mattress, with the corners folded at precisely forty-five degrees, and the completed bed pack centred at the head of the bed. All pillows confined to wardrobes during the day.

More instruction followed, including how to clean windows with newspaper, and polish the wooden floors with a partially liquidised yellow polish, and heavy bumpers on six-foot-long wooden handles, and followed that with details on how to polish the brass and clean the ablutions.

He then left us to polish what I had previously thought to be an already spotless dormitory floor, make up our beds and bed packs, and be ready for our first inspection in one hour's time. As he marched out of the dormitory we could hear him clicking down the corridor and into the next dormitory. There, he performed precisely the same routine and similarly identified that particular 'dormitory wanker'. The red-headed Glaswegian with the tell-tale bed frame glared after him.

"Tongs, yer fucking baz."

The red-headed Glaswegian's name, we later discovered, was Archie. He had lived in one of the infamous Glasgow tenements, and claimed loyalty to one of the city's notorious street gangs. According to Archie, there were two main gangs in Glasgow, the Tongs and the Fleet, and he claimed allegiance to the Tongs. 'Tongs, yer baz' was seemingly a challenge, issued by a member of the Tongs to anybody not similarly allied, and especially to members of the rival Fleet.

We listened to his tales of belligerence and destruction, and instantly christened him 'Tongs yer baz'. However, when he rolled up his trouser leg to show us an old axe wound across his knee, I had to admit to scepticism. He claimed to have received the wound during a street fight with the Fleet, but to me it looked like a scar I once got when I fell down in the school playground.

Although not fully understanding the term 'wanker', I have to admit that I privately sided with the Wee Beastie when it came to the red-headed 'Tongs yer baz'. I decided to place him in the same category as the boastful Gerry Hitchcock and his carnal chronicles, not having the necessary experience to question either, but considering the pair of them as dubious raconteurs, whose tales of skirmishes past demanded salt in very large pinches.

We spent the rest of that week and most of the next two in one-size-fits-all dungarees, and this was for two reasons. The first was solely economic, because for fourteen days from the date of our arrival, the Air Force generously offered any of us who wished to leave the opportunity to do so. All we had to do was state that this was not the life as advertised or anticipated, and was therefore unacceptable. Anyone so deciding could pack their bags and head for home, with no hard feelings on either side.

Now, while this might seem to be a noble and generous gesture by the Air Ministry, in truth it was little more than a public-relations exercise. There was always the possibility that someone might make a dash for the gates, but the reality of why each of us had signed up in the first place meant that nobody did. In short, none of us had anywhere else to go, and they bloody well knew it.

However, this meaningless gesture of Air Force compassion caused a problem for the administration. It prevented the camp tailor from beginning adjustments to precious stock items of uniform until everybody was certain there would be an apprentice left to wear it.

And so they kitted us out in one-size-fits-all dungarees, partly for logistics and partly for what I can only describe as a dehumanising process.

Started on our first day by the psychotic Corporal Campbell and his behavioural science technique, it now graduated to personal grooming and a visit to the dreaded camp barber.

Now, I always found the camp barber to be a pleasant enough fellow. He was a Greek Cypriot, with gold teeth and a pock-marked face, who would always smile cheerily at you and wish you 'good day' as he passed on his way to and from the shop. He boasted a plump and attractive Greek Cypriot wife and two slightly plain little girls with ribbon-festooned pigtails and braces welded to their teeth. I know this, because the entire family sat beaming out from a black-and-white photograph on a shelf alongside the razor strop.

There were, however, a good many of the apprentices, in fact the vast majority, who didn't share my opinion of our little dark-skinned Cypriot, and for a very good reason.

Now, if there is ever a wholesale wailing and gnashing of teeth it will undoubtedly be a mournful and terrible event. I know, because when I was seven years old the otherwise-benign Reverend Forecast indoctrinated me in the teachings of the Sunningdale Congregationalist Church and I became an instant believer. However, I also believe it will prove no more harrowing and terrible than that first-ever visit by fifty-or-so fashionably diverse and collectively trepidant young men to the camp barbers.

For me it was no problem; the tidying-up of a few unruly hairs along the back of the neck and I was done. However, for those with hairstyles ranging between loudly fashionable and quietly sensible, which included everybody but me and the boy with the border collie, it was an event that either left them traumatised into incoherence or sobbing in anguish.

The act itself was as rapid as it was clinical, and, with the exceptions of me and the boy with the collie dog, there was no variation in technique. A half-dozen rapid and seemingly careless hacks, using the largest pair of scissors I'd ever seen, preceded eight upward slashes with the razor. This left a single tuft of hair protruding from the top of the skull and wafting in the breeze, which he then trimmed to all but nothing, presumably for reasons of aesthetics and aerodynamics. All this took place within the bat of an astonished eyelid, while the shell-shocked apprentice gazed at his own reflection with eyes bulging and jaw dropping ever lower.

Irrespective of the length or style of the original hairstyle, the entire procedure took less than sixty seconds from gun to tape. Sixty of the briefest seconds between the arrival of strutting young Lochinvar, with flowing tresses and carefree smile, and departure of timid automaton, with glistening cranium and shattered ego.

Each shell-shocked apprentice left a scene of such clinically coiffured devastation in his wake that to enable our little brown barber to manoeuvre without hazard or hindrance around each successive shrunken head, the shop employed a full-time sweeper-up, who then gathered the debris into oversized plastic sacks.

Where it went to from there nobody was ever to discover, or not with any certainty. The barber would never discuss it, and the sweeper-up was sworn to secrecy. For me, however, there was no escaping the coincidental arrival of a newly-refurbished consignment of mattresses, three weeks to the day after the similar arrival of each newly-sworn apprentice entry.

Nowadays the impact of having one's image transformed from long-haired trendy into scrotum-headed village idiot is, for most young people, less than disturbing. Many of today's pop stars, film stars and football icons do it almost routinely. However, in the sixties, when every able-bodied man under forty wore his hair long, and those who didn't were either accountants or bankers, or people hoping to be accountants or bankers, the effect on the individuals concerned was devastating. So devastating, in fact, that it was often days before many of the former young Lochinvars could string together any form of coherent speech.

For me, though, it was heaven. Thanks to that one innocuous little Cypriot, a set of one-size-fits-all dungarees, and my slovenly speech exercises, I now looked and dressed and sounded just like everyone else.

This heralded an astonishing period of emotional growth for me. Suddenly people didn't sneer when they addressed me, or glance knowingly at one another as they stifled a snigger. Suddenly people no longer threatened me with physical violence. Suddenly I was an equal, and whatever I had to say was just as important as whatever anyone else had to say.

I must admit I made the most of it.

I got to know everybody, and they got to know me. I got to know their opinions, and they got to know mine. I got to understand their prejudices, fears, strengths and weaknesses, and they got to understand mine. I got to decide which of them I liked, which of them I agreed with, which of them I could share a discussion, an opinion, or a joke with, and I avoided the rest.

For the first time in my life, it was me who got to choose, me who got to say what he wanted to say, me who got to stand tall and equal, me who got to be a real person. It was also me who looked for the person inside, and discovered he was no less important than anyone else in the overall scheme of things.

There were all sorts, and shapes, and colours and sizes gathered in that humble barrack room. We ranged from the tall and thin to the round and bulbous, from the violently aggressive to the cowardly effeminate, from the pseudo-intellectual to the overtly thick, from the sexually experienced to the embarrassingly naïve. We had arrived from twenty-two different areas of the United Kingdom, and twenty-two different walks of life; from belligerent of Belfast to nervous of Knightsbridge, from fast-talking Cockney wide boy to slow-moving west-country farm-hand, from the great unwashed to the quietly fastidious, and from the palest pink to the deepest ebony.

Each of us had own reasons for being there, our own private skeletons to hide, our own inner demons to deal with, and our own emotional baggage to carry. Now we each held a degree of commonality, which would serve to mould individuals into comrades and overshadow any previous superficial differences.

The clothing and presentation were the same for each. We each had the same spartan bed-space, and the same basic equipment, and enjoyed the same lowly position in life. We each held roughly the same fears and concerns, and the same ambitions. We each felt the same previously unfamiliar sense of belonging, and shared a similar dislike for the same psychotic little Scotsman.

In the weeks following that first haircut the Air Force gave me a rank, craft apprentice, and an individual number, which I often repeated in my sleep but won't bore you with. They gave me my first uniform, supposedly tailored, which only fitted where it touched, and a selection of other equipment to keep me looking both spick and span, and lice, nits, and scabies-free.

That first uniform issue included a battledress, which was a roughly hewn two-piece working dress with a monkey-jacket tunic, and two pairs of ill-fitting trousers. The trousers were only estimations of the stated size and needed a set of adjustable braces to keep them in place. There was also a beret, with a detachable badge and a coloured disc, two pairs of ankle-length boots, three pairs of knee-length underpants, and a similar quantity of cotton vests.

Further additions included three blue shirts, with four detachable collars, two sets of collar studs, four pairs of black socks, two pairs of blue shorts, a pair of blue plimsolls, and a pair of lace-up beetle-crusher shoes.

There was a blue webbing belt, with matching shoulder bag for holding cleaning items, a large blue canvas holdall for high-days and holidays, and two plain white towels. There was also a spare cap badge and pin, a thick webbing belt with a large brass buckle, and a thin trouser belt with a small brass buckle. Finally there was a complicated brass button stick, to use when cleaning all those buttons, badges and buckles.

My weekly salary was ten shillings, or fifty pence in real money, with a further twenty shillings a week held back for annual leave, scheduled at the completion of basic training.

For some, those first few months of training were a living hell, but for me they were some of the happiest times of my life. I had finally found a place where I belonged, and I learnt so much in such a short time. On the upside, the Air Force trained me in telecommunications and transmission technology, teleprinters and tape relay equipment, radio receivers and transmitters, communications techniques and various transmission codes. They taught me to reduce any sentence to phonetic parts, and to use a thousand different acronyms, mnemonics, and procedures for military and civil telecommunications.

I learnt to assemble, disassemble, clean and fire the bolt-action three-o-three rifle, to feed myself, and survive in the great outdoors, to contribute to the success of others, and understand that any individual success needed the whole to be greater than the sum of the parts.

I also learnt to march in step and complete two-dozen different drill manoeuvres. I played the snare drum in the apprentice band, and wielded the drum-major's mace on each weekday morning march to the apprentice hangars. I learnt to obey orders, and to clean everything to the point of obsession. I learnt to bull boots and shine webbing belts, press creases and polish floors and windows and doorknobs and toilets and sinks and baths and taps and walls and ceilings. I learnt to be precise in everything I did, and take a curious form of pleasure from cleanliness and hygiene.

And that was the strangest thing. A few weeks earlier, if someone had asked me if I enjoyed cleaning and polishing and personal grooming, and all those tasks that teenage boys naturally detest, I would have laughed, but the truth is I did.

However, three of the lessons were not on any curriculum, but were of importance beyond measure. They were more important than teleprinting, or Morse, or any other code, for that matter. They were more useful than any technique for encryption, more essential than servicing telecommunications equipment, and more memorable than the million different procedures and codes for transmission, kept in parrot-fashion style between youthful ears.

The first occurred after lunch, one Saturday, around four months or so into my training.

Lessons in life

That Saturday I decided to take a stroll into Albrighton, the local village. By then I had moved on from basic working dress to wearing the number-one dress, or best blue, with the peaked SD hat.

None of the others wanted to go. They had spent the morning marching back and forth across the parade ground, and said I needed my head examined. I'm not sure why I had wanted to go either. I guess I must have needed to get away from everything Air Force for a couple of hours.

It was around three, and I was passing one of the pubs as a group of revellers were leaving. There were four of them, aged in their late teens to early twenties. One of them sneered when he saw me. When he said something, the rest laughed and then spread out to block the pavement.

It was then that I made the first of two mistakes. Instead of walking straight through them, I crossed to the other side of the road. They watched me and one of them said something else.

I couldn't hear what he said, but it drew another round of sycophantic laughter, which I didn't much mind, but then they followed me across the road, and I knew there would be trouble. It was then that I made the second and most foolish mistake. I turned and started walking back to camp.

Now, I was always a weakling, but never a coward, or I hadn't previously thought so, and so I walked quickly but refused to run. They started after me and caught up within a few yards. Three stood blocking my way. The fourth stood behind me.

One of them asked where I thought I was going. I mumbled something about going for a walk. He asked why nobody had told me that Albrighton was off-limits to Cosford apprentices. When I didn't answer, he stopped laughing and shoved me in the chest. A slap across the back of my head made me turn. Someone punched me, and I went straight to the pavement.

All those memories of Bad Bobby Day and Punchy George came flooding back as they started kicking. I closed my eyes and covered up, but then everything stopped.

I lay there for a few seconds before I realised. There was scuffling and shouts, some in anger, some in pain, and a voice cursing above all the kerfuffle in a clear and clipped Highland accent.

I looked up to see Corporal Campbell, wearing an Air Force blazer and grey-flannel slacks, and obviously in genuine beastie mood. One of the gang was on the tarmac. Another was about to join him. A third was leaning against the wall and holding his groin. The fourth was running away. A few moments later, three battered and bruised companions hobbled off in his wake.

Corporal Campbell glared after them and called out some sort of Highland insult as he brushed imaginary dust from his spotless blazer and straightened the flawless knot of his Royal Air Force Regiment tie. I got to my feet and mumbled my thanks.

"Thank you, Corporal."

I expected him to nod, or say something derogatory, but when he turned to look at me his face was blacker than it had been when despatching the thugs.

"What the hell were you doing, just lying there on the ground?"

I mumbled something about them hitting me when I wasn't looking. He nodded.

"I can understand that, it happens, but why the hell didn't you get up again?"

I didn't want to tell him the truth, which was that I had learned from bitter experience if you stayed down and covered the essential parts you got less badly hurt. Instead, I mumbled something about there being four of them and that they were obviously so much older and bigger. He didn't buy that. He moved closer, until his nose was only inches away from mine, and snarled his anger.

They were words I would never forget.

"Let me tell you something, you snivelling little wanker. You may have no self-respect, and I couldn't give a shit about that, but you're wearing a Royal Air Force uniform and that I do give a shit about. And let me tell you something else, you spineless little bastard. If I ever see you disgracing this uniform again, you won't have to worry about scum like that. Next time it'll be me standing alongside them, and I'll be giving you the biggest kicking of your miserable bloody life. Do you understand me? You pathetic little worm."

I nodded meekly and mumbled the compulsory "Yes, Corporal", but the words had been superfluous. My shamefaced look confirmed my disgrace without any need for comment.

With a disparaging snarl, he marched back across the road, to where a woman stood waiting, and they continued their stroll through the village; without a backward glance.

I remember walking dejectedly back to the camp, feeling more miserable than I could possibly have felt if the four thugs had finished the job. I knew the worst part of it all was that he had been right. To the uninitiated, the fact there had been four of them might have made my surrender more acceptable, but I knew that even if there had only been a single belligerent idiot, it would have made no difference. I would have behaved in exactly the self-same cowardly fashion.

Neither was there any solace to be had in my usual litany of excuses: I didn't fit in. I spoke with a plum in my mouth. I wore old-fashioned clothing. My father didn't allow me to join in with the other kids and behave normally, or make friends. Suddenly I knew why I hadn't had any friends to support me at school. Suddenly I understood the real reason people didn't like me.

Suddenly I didn't much like myself.

There was no one here to point the finger of responsibility at, and no more excuses to be had, or none that didn't sound hollow and implausible. Somehow this pint-sized, gleaming, foot-stamping, psychotic Wee Beastie had forced me to face a simple and unpalatable fact of my young and useless life. Somewhere along the line, as well as being unloved, as well as being a failure, as well as being a disappointment, as well as being universally disliked, I had become a coward.

I believe there are defining moments in everyone's life, and that was mine. On that walk back to camp I was more ashamed than I had ever been before, or since, and that moment changed my life. Or, should I say, that moment, and support from an unexpected quarter, changed my life.

I barely spoke to anyone over the next week. During free time I sat around, pretending to read and listening to the radio. I was thinking about those unhappy and lonely schooldays; about Bobby Day and Punchy George and the gangs that had terrorised me. I thought about my adopted family, and how I had always blamed them for every weakness and problem. I thought about my birth parents, and how much I hated them for abandoning me to the orphanage. I thought about my loneliness, and why God had chosen to make this world such an unfair place.

Mostly, though, I was thinking about how ashamed of myself I was, and how all those disparaging comments about me had been absolutely true.

It was Tuesday evening, on the following week, when the Wee Beastie marched into the barrack room. All the other apprentices were in the television room, or playing snooker, or in the cafeteria. I was alone, and still feeling sorry for myself.

"What are you doing, laddie?"

I put down the book I had been pretending to read, climbed off the bed and stood to attention.

"Reading, Corporal."

It seemed he had been keeping more than just a casual eye on me during the last week or so.

"Wallowing in self-pity, more likely."

"Yes, Corporal."

My expression told him I believed no such thing.

"Tomorrow afternoon, two o'clock, my office."

"Yes, Corporal."

He marched out of the room, leaving me to ponder something more immediate than self-pity. I could hear him clicking his way down the corridor and snapping orders at anyone foolish enough not to have fled at the sound of his approach. What he wanted I wasn't sure, but I was certain it would involve some form of punishment meted out to you-know-who somewhere along the line.

The following afternoon, at precisely 1.59, I knocked on his office door and heard him call for me to enter. I stood smartly to attention, hoping there wasn't anything he could find fault with; knowing that if he wanted to find something, he would.

"What are you doing?"

"You asked to see me, Corporal."

"Isn't it sports afternoon?"

"Yes, Corporal."

"The go and change, and hurry up about it."

"Corporal?"

"We're going to the physical training hangar. I want you back here in three minutes."

"Yes, Corporal."

As I hurried off to change into my gym kit, none of the thoughts that came and went during those frantic three minutes was comforting. I considered a dozen reasons for him taking me to the gym, and a dozen scenarios that might occur when we got there. I finally decided on one unpleasant thought, and one unpleasant scenario. He was taking me to the boxing ring, to beat me senseless for disgracing the uniform.

Just as I feared, we headed straight to the boxing area. The physical training instructor, or PTI, in charge of boxing was a sergeant. He was a tall barrel-chested man, with muscles in places that most people didn't have places. When he saw us he studied me for a while, and then said, "Afternoon, Jock. . . this the one?"

"Ay, that's him, Terry. See what you can do with him. I'll be back in a couple of hours, to see how he's getting on."

The Sergeant was in the middle of a training session. He pointed to a group of a dozen or so young men who were hard at work training. It seemed I was to watch and learn, and so I tried to do just that. A couple of them were in the middle of a sparring session in the centre of the main boxing ring, but most were exercising and practising on the equipment around the gymnasium. Without exception, they were faultlessly turned out, with lace-up boots and expensive-looking boxing gear, well-toned muscles, sturdy-looking thighs, and well-developed biceps. What most captured my attention, though, was the degree of intensity and concentration on each of their faces.

None of them took any notice of me. Some were skipping and shadow-boxing, while others pummelled heavy bags and worked on routines of combination punches. I stood in silence, meekly watching, in my knee-length Air Force-issue blue shorts, with blue plimsolls and an open-necked white cotton sports shirt; with my spindly legs and woefully-thin arms looking for all the world like pale pink pipe-cleaners sticking out of the bowl of one of Dickie James's cavernous pipes.

They boasted well-muscled torsos, powerful athleticism, focused aggression and consummate expertise. I was spindly-limbed, nervous and emaciated. The contrast didn't bear comparison.

I remember standing there in dread of them as I awaited my fate, wondering which of them would be the chosen executioner: The Marquess of Queensbury's grim reaper, specially selected to prove his overwhelming power by snapping my limbs, or knocking me out with a single punch.

A few minutes later the Sergeant blew a whistle and everyone stopped. It seemed the moment had arrived. My eyes flickered nervously from one to the other as I considered their respective physiques and abilities, before deciding that it didn't make much difference who he chose. Any one of them could have slaughtered me with one arm behind his back.

"OK, lads, shower and change, and get back here at five-thirty for circuit training."

Well, that settled that; the big slab-sided sergeant wanted to keep the fun for himself. He would be the over-muscled and under-educated instrument of my doom. I stood warily considering him as he approached.

"Right then, boy. Alec Campbell tells me you're such a pathetic little weakling, a girl's netball team could bully you."

It seemed, for some inexplicable reason, he believed such a comment to be an indictment and insult, designed to raise the hackles and summon the blood. I remember thinking, if he'd seen the size of some of the girls in our school's netball team, he might not have been so derisory.

"Well, we're going to change all that, and we're going to start right now. Come here."

He pointed to the heavy bag and told me to hit it. I looked uncertainly back at him, and he bellowed the instruction again. I stepped nervously up to the bag, then let fly with a straight right that failed to crease the outer casing and almost dislocated my index finger.

"What the hell was that?"

"A punch, Sergeant."

"A punch? You big tart's blouse. I've seen gnats piss harder than that. Hit it again."

I performed the same straight right, and almost dislocated my thumb and the remaining fingers. The bag remained singularly unimpressed.

"Jesus Christ! What are you trying to do; hit it or dance with it? Get out of the way."

He stepped forward and hit the bag with such force that his right fist almost disappeared into the stuffing. Suspended from a hook on the ceiling by a heavy rope, the bag gave a jolt and then started swinging slowly back and forth. He hit it again, and then again, and again, giving a little snort from his nostrils at each moment of impact, and with each dull thwack echoing inside my head. I remember thinking that if he didn't stop soon his knuckles would be red raw. Given all that snorting, I also wondered what would have happened if he'd had a cold. Finally he stopped punching, held the bag to stop it swaying, and then looked at me with a strange gleam in his eyes.

"Your turn." He noticed my lack of enthusiasm. "What's the matter? Don't think you can do it?" I didn't answer. "Think you're too puny and weak, do you? Think because I'm twice your size it makes it easier?" I still didn't answer, but that was precisely what I'd been thinking. He sniffed contemptuously and called to one of the junior instructors. "Get young Spencer out here, would you? He's in the changing rooms."

The junior PTI went to collect whoever young Spencer was, and I stood nervously anticipating being on the receiving end of a delayed beating. However, when young Spencer finally emerged from the changing area, dressed only in a towelling robe, I breathed a sigh of relief.

Young Spencer was two or three years older than me, I guessed. He was eighteen or nineteen, maybe a few months more, but at least an inch shorter than me and, if his ankles were anything to go by, his torso was even thinner than mine. He sauntered over and asked the PTI what he wanted. The sergeant grunted and pointed to the heavy bag. Young Spencer grinned back at him.

"Sure."

He moved over to the bag and hit it just once, with a thwack the equal of anything the sergeant had managed. Then he stood back and shed the towelling robe.

I thought. He's naked. That's disgusting. He could at least have put something on. It was bad enough having to give up my afternoon's tennis practice just to punch a lump of leather. Having to do it naked and in front of everyone was taking the punishment too far.

Then I looked a little closer, and saw that Spencer was wearing a flesh-coloured jockstrap. With some relief, I began more objectively studying the diminutive torso. He was thin, there was no question of that, and he was short, but that was the end of any similarity between us, because wherever there could possibly have been muscle there was. This wasn't the puny pint-sized weakling I had assumed to be cowering beneath the towelling robe. This was a pocket Hercules. But what was even more impressive than the powerfully-muscled torso and awesome punching power was the speed; the sheer, phenomenal, crazy speed of the man.

He began punching the bag with a quick succession of loud heavy thwacks that had the bag swaying back and forth in a few seconds. Then he increased the speed, dancing left and right and punching faster and faster until his fists were almost a blur. Thwack, thwack, thwack, thwack, thwack. A few more skips left and right and then thwack, thwack, thwack, thwack, thwack.

By this time the bag had begun swaying alarmingly, with the all but naked Spencer dancing around it like some demented savage around a campfire. His eyes were wild, and yet strangely focused, his face red and angry, the nostrils flared and snorting in time to the punches. As he grunted and snarled and weaved and skipped, he continued to rain those punches into the heavy skin faster than the eye could possibly have followed.

I didn't know anything about conditioning or stamina at the time, but I do know that I felt tired just watching him. The PTI halted proceedings with a word, and the pocket Hercules grudgingly ended his decimation of the bag. He stood back, allowing his breathing to soften and the composure to return, and then began shaking his arms and kicking his legs, presumably to loosen the tension. Finally, he undertook a series of uncomfortable-looking neck-stretching exercises, rolling and lolling his head, presumably with the same intention.

A few further moments of stretching and kicking and shaking passed before he turned his attention to me, but, instead of the expected homicidal glare, he simply grinned at my open-mouthed astonishment and nodded. The grin faded as he casually considered and nonchalantly dismissed my insignificance, before slipping the robe back on and sauntering off to his interrupted shower.

"Still think you can't do it, boy?" The PTI looked hard at me, but my jaw was still hanging somewhere around ankle-high. He went on.

"That's Ronnie Spencer. He's one of my boys; tri-services champion, gonna be ABA champion this year, if there's any justice." He nodded towards the changing rooms. "They're all champions, service champions, inter-services champions; come here to train, from bases all over the world. They've all got speed and skill and the strength of lions, they have. Each one's got raw, natural, God-given talent, and each one's got two fists of steel. But, do you know what they've got most of all, boy? Do you know what makes them champions?"

It was clear I still hadn't a hope of finding my voice, and so he didn't wait for an answer.

"Guts, boy. That's what. More than anything else, they've got guts." He thumped his stomach with the flat of his clenched fist and the sound of the contact echoed around the hangar. "You see, that's the real difference between them and you, boy. When it comes down to that final stretch, it doesn't matter who you are, or what your reputation is. It's got nothing to do with bulk, or power, or speed, or skill, or training, or even raw ability. When it comes down to the wire, boy, they're champions for one reason and one reason only. . . they've got the most guts."

Again he smacked himself in the stomach, and again the sound of the contact echoed around the emptiness. I must have still appeared bemused, because he stared earnestly at me and said, "I can give you most of it, boy. I can give you the power and the muscles, the stamina and the conditioning, the boxing skills, even the speed, but I can't give you the guts; nobody can. You're the only one who can do that. You're the only one who knows if you've got any guts to find. Do you understand me, boy?"

"Yes, Sergeant."

He glared at me again.

"Don't you 'Yes, Sergeant' me, you little shit. I'm not your drill instructor. I'm not looking for some fawning little sniveller to agree with everything I say. If you agree with me, you say 'Yes, Sergeant' but if you disagree with me, you bloody well say so. Is that clear?"

For once the answer was genuine.

"Yes, Sergeant; yes it is."

He seemed satisfied.

"Good. Well, let's get on with it then."

For the next hour and a half he showed me some of the basics. I remember thinking that apart from those two days of potato picking when I was ten years old, he was making me work harder than I had ever worked. I did circuit training and shadow-boxing, tried and failed at combination punching, skipped until I couldn't lift my legs, and jabbed and weaved around the light bag until I couldn't hold my arms up.

But no matter how hard I tried, I still couldn't get that heavy bag to move.

I was still trying to crease the bag's outer casing when the Wee Beastie returned.

"How's it going?"

"I reckon he'll do. He's got a good strong pair of legs."

That was true about the legs. Although nobody had seen fit to make an issue of it on that day in the headmaster's study, I ran the mile for the school and for my age was among the best cross-country runners in the county. The Wee Beastie clearly hadn't forgotten the original reason for my attendance at boxing class.

"Yeah, well, with all the running away he's done, he probably needed a strong pair of legs."

The sergeant grinned.

"Maybe so. He's got basic co-ordination, and he's not slow, but he needs to build some bulk in a hurry. I can't build strength without muscle, and I can't build muscle on bare bones."

"Drop of the Liffey, you think?"

"I'd have to say so, Jock. A pint in the evening, just to start, and then we'll see how we go."

I knew that 'a drop of the Liffey' was Guinness, but I couldn't believe they were conspiring to encourage my under-age drinking. Not that I was unaware of the demon drink, because when I had finished my morning round caddying up at the Golf Club, I'd sometimes nip down the hill and into the Chequers. There I'd enjoy a ham sandwich and a half of lager and lime before returning to the club for a further round in the afternoon. I remember the elderly landlady always smiled quietly, pretending not to notice my youthful countenance, while directing me and my illicit half-pint to a quiet corner of the lounge. However, Guinness, the genuine Liffey water, was a different matter. I'd tried a sip at a wedding, and could distinctly remember not enjoying the bitterness.

They ushered me into a side room, where the sergeant produced three pint bottles of Guinness from a stack of cases, and three tankards from a cupboard. We both looked on, me apprehensively, the corporal in reverence, as he poured each pint. They each took a hefty swig, while I pulled a face and swallowed hard as I anticipated the bitterness.

"Slowly now, boy. Don't want you necking it."

I sipped at the froth, took a tentative mouthful, and then grimaced as the bitterness offended the senses. It was exactly as I remembered: harsh and black, and, to my untutored palate, thoroughly obnoxious. The two of them swigged happily and laughed as they studied my disgust.

"You'll get used to it, boy. Six o'clock each evening: one full hour of training and a full one of these afterwards, understand?"

I nodded, and took another bitter mouthful, finding it hard to swallow, but accepting the medicine as part of my penance for being such a coward. I saw they had finished, while my glass was still three-quarters full, or one-quarter empty, depending on one's perspective. The Wee Beastie wiped his mouth with the back of his hand, and then nodded at me.

"Get the rest of that down you and then back to the block. You're to say nothing about any of this, not to anyone, clear?"

Six days, six hours of training, and six pints of Guinness later, the taste was slightly less offensive, but the heavy bag still hadn't moved. I was back for my Wednesday afternoon penance and spent the first twenty minutes training, but stopped when he called me over to the boxing ring. He took the gloves from me, gave me another pair and a protective helmet, and then climbed up and into the ring. When he signalled me to follow, I knew it could only mean one thing.

I looked up at the ring, and realised my worst nightmare. Ronnie Spencer was in town and he was there, looking down at me with that same disarming grin on his face. He slipped a gumshield into his mouth and the grin disappeared, replaced by a look that I can only describe as homicidal. I looked on with my heart thumping and my legs feeling strangely weak.

I climbed uncertainly up and into the ring, not sure whether I should crawl under the bottom rope or step over the second, before deciding on the latter and clambering ungainly through. I stood in the centre, in a confused no-man's land that lay somewhere between nervous confusion and mesmerised fear, cautiously studying my opponent, while feeling self-conscious at my sudden celebrity status and desperately embarrassed by my inadequate physique. The sergeant tightened the strap on my headgear and babbled some brief instructions into an incognizant ear.

"Now then, boy, remember what I said. Chin tight in, hands high, elbows in, small target, small target, keep working, keep working and keep moving the feet. Remember what we worked on. Keep behind the left and keep moving. Whatever else you do, keep everything tight and keep moving. Now go to your corner, and then come out punching."

The barrage of instructions, so clearly designed to inspire, served only to further clutter an already frantic mind. Nervous tension gripped at the stomach walls and tightened my facial muscles into a mask of dread. The PTI nodded encouragingly and directed me towards a corner. I stumbled across to it, not certain that my legs would get me there. Through my fog of panic and cowardice, I vaguely heard him issuing instructions to Ronnie Spencer.

"And you remember, Ronnie, he's just a youngster, so take it easy. I don't want you killing him. Just show him a few moves."

I wanted to ask him to repeat those instructions, in case 'Ronnie The Reaper' hadn't understood, but I'd forgotten how to move my lips. By the time I remembered, it was too late.

"Ding." He rang an imaginary bell and waved me forward. I staggered to the centre of the ring.

Ronnie Spencer touched his gloves against mine, and then began dancing from side to side, with his head bobbing and weaving and his gloves making little feints. I peered up at him from underneath the headguard, thinking he looked so much taller than I remembered before realising I was on the floor. How I'd got there I hadn't the faintest idea, but there was no doubt I was there, and no doubt who'd put me there.

The sergeant ordered me to my feet, then took my gloved fists and began to brush them down my front, as though brushing the dust from me. I looked vacantly back at him and then on to Ronnie Spencer, who was still dancing from side to side in the other corner. The sergeant stepped away, and I was down again, but this time I'd half seen the first punch. It was a straight left, which speared its way through the gap between my two gloves and caught me squarely on the chin. The second had landed from out of thin air, and caught me like a hammer across the left temple.

Once again the Sergeant ordered me to my feet, and once again he performed the same brushing action with the gloves. Again he stepped aside, and again I went down like a deck of cards. I didn't bother to wait for the order. I clambered to my feet and mechanically brushed my gloves down my front, swaying in the breeze like a punch-drunk robot and preparing to go down for a fourth time. Then, in a blessed moment of mercy, the sergeant halted the slaughter.

I stopped following the mesmerising motion of Ronnie Spencer's dance routine and looked gratefully at the sergeant, seeing him not as a referee but as a saviour. He looked bemused.

"What's the matter, boy? You do know that you're allowed to punch him back, don't you?"

"Yes, Sergeant."

"Then well why the hell weren't you doing that?"

I remembered that first meeting, and his demand for my total honesty.

"I didn't want to piss him off."

We both looked across to Ronnie Spencer, who was leaning against the ropes kicking the tension from his legs and looking thoroughly uninterested. The PTI looked back at me.

"Piss him off? There's not much chance of that happening, but I'll tell you something, boy. You are in danger of boring him to death." He looked hard at me, and I knew he was about to ask one of those searching questions. "Now tell me something, boy, and I want you to be honest with me. Did any of those punches actually hurt you? I mean, did any of them genuinely hurt you?"

I wiped my glove across my mouth and studied the resulting smear of blood, then stood looking back at him with glazed eyes and a vacant expression written across my battered features. He carefully and deliberately repeated the question. I blinked, to clear the haze and began seriously considering my answer. I thought back to those two minutes of mayhem, trying to remember my feelings, and trying to revitalise whatever limited senses remained.

I came to an astonishing conclusion. Despite the battering and the blood, the punches hadn't actually hurt. Their arrival had shocked me and knocked me off my feet; three times in quick succession, to be precise. They'd temporarily winded me and wounded what little remained of my pride, but the punches themselves hadn't physically hurt, or not at the time. He watched the light of recognition appear in my eyes and grinned back at me.

"You see? It's not so bad after all, is it now?"

"No, Sergeant, no, it's not."

For once I was being truthful. He grinned again.

"So what's to stop you having a go, too?"

I thought hard about that, but couldn't think of anything.

"Nothing, Sergeant."

"Right then, so get out there and get into him."

I'd love to be able to tell you the boxer was born at that moment. I'd love to be able to tell you that I came out of my corner dancing and punching, floating like a butterfly and stinging like a bee. I'd love to be able to report a looming disaster converted into a memorable victory at the final hour, with an Ali shuffle and a triple combination.

But sadly in life truth is rarely stranger than fiction, and the unhappy truth was that I was still a long way from being a born-again pugilist, or even a workmanlike sparring partner.

Despite pulling punches, moving at half speed, in low gear, and under orders not to hurt me, the magnificent Ronnie Spencer still ensured that I spent most of those two rounds looking up at him from a depressingly familiar position on the canvas. The difference now was that each time that I clambered back to my feet and came staggering out of the corner, I was swinging punches of my own, or what I fondly imagined to be punches.

Others afterwards remarked that I had looked like a frantic spider, stuck in his own web. However, I can also happily report that on one memorable occasion I caught my opponent with a roundhouse blow, which may have only glanced harmlessly off his head, but did cause the sergeant to caution him for a momentary lack of concentration. It also brought a fleeting smile to my lips, before he dumped me back on to the canvas for the umpteenth time, with my eyes glazed and my head spinning. But at least I had laid a glove on him, as they say.

When that final simulated bell blessedly sounded, I had lost each of those frenzied two-minute rounds by an embarrassingly hefty margin. Battered and bruised and thoroughly dazed, I had blood seeping from my nose and mouth, a badly swollen eye, and a fat lip that was getting fatter by the second. I was so close to exhaustion that I could hardly lift my arms. I had spent more time sitting on the canvas than standing on my feet. I had only managed to connect with one non-scoring punch, and a significantly better athlete than I could ever hope to be had publicly destroyed me.

But I had tried to fight back, and I was as proud of myself as any boxing champion ever was.

For his part, in the slaughter's aftermath, Ronnie Spencer shed the gloves and then skipped over to me. He tapped me on the shoulder and grunted something that I assumed to be complimentary, but may well have been an ultimatum to get out of town. He then leapt out of the ring and moved toward the heavy bag, presumably needing to practice on something that could withstand more than two lightweight punches in quick succession.

The sergeant PTI grinned affably down at me.

"Well done, lad," he said.

That was it. My triumph was complete. He'd instantly promoted me from boy to lad, and my world was suddenly sweeter than it had been for some time.

I floated back to the apprentice block, looking for all the world as though I'd walked into a revolving door, but with my chest out and my head held high, determined that I would become the consummate fighter I had secretly always wanted to be. Determined too that I would never again allow anyone to push me around with impunity.

It was four months after that, and more pints of Guinness than I care to recall, when the inter-flight boxing championships came around. The inter-flight championships were a series of local competitions between apprentices in the various apprentice wings. They automatically selected the winners in each class to represent the Cosford apprentices in an annual tournament against the other apprentice camps. Considering my efforts of the previous months, I was a clear favourite, not only to represent the Cosford apprentices, but also to win my class outright.

By then I had put on a fair amount of bulk and muscle, and could dance and string together some impressive combinations of punches. Most importantly, I could get that heavy bag swinging alarmingly within seconds. The sergeant PTI now called me by my Christian name, and most considered me a fair boxer and budding athlete, one who might go on to represent the service, and maybe even compete in the ABA championships.

I spent almost all of my spare time down at the gymnasium, and, whenever moving around the block, would skip and shadow-box my way from room to room. Most of the entry rather wisely steered clear of me, and almost everyone treated me with varying degrees of healthy respect. The inter-flight tournament was, I reasonably assumed, a formality.

The tournament's first hurdle was to decide who would represent our apprentice entry, and so they pressed-ganged another apprentice into providing some basic opposition. I knew him, vaguely. His name was John, but everyone called him Jack. He was a friendly enough sort, but had a reputation for being able to handle himself, and so they chose him on that basis. Once drafted into the competition, he took matters seriously enough, setting about the task by practising and sparring and working-out down at the gymnasium. For all his efforts, we both knew that he was no boxer, and we also knew he would provide little or no competition for me when the moment came.

And so it proved. He stepped into the ring, looking as nervous as I had been when I first stepped into the ring with Ronnie Spencer, and I felt an overwhelming sense of superiority. Most of our entry was watching. I was the star attraction. I decided to make the most of it.

I remember that I knocked him down twice in quick succession, and could see any willingness to make a fight of it go out of him, but then I made the most arrogant and unnecessary mistake. I decided not to knock him down for a third time and finish the bout, but instead began proving my superior ability at his expense, humiliating him by dancing around and tapping at him with lightweight combinations, then skipping away as he lumbered after me, before dropping my arms and shuffling and playing at being Cassius Clay. To give him his due, he didn't give up, but kept on swinging and missing, and so I kept on tapping him on the chin with an impressive succession of unanswered punches, and then dancing away.

At the end of the round he had hardly laid a glove on me. He stumbled back to his corner and I danced back to mine, feeling secure in the mastery of my art and gloatingly proud of myself. I was leaning against the ropes, arrogantly basking in the premature glory of what would inevitably be my one-sided victory, when the Wee Beastie came over to my corner.

"What are you doing?"

I grinned arrogantly back at him.

"Sorry about that, Corporal. Did you want me to finish it off?"

"No, I want you to go and get changed."

"What?"

"You're disqualified., Now get out of my sight."

With that said, he walked over to Jack and raised his arm into the air. I looked on in numb disbelief, not understanding what had happened, only knowing that my chance to succeed as an athlete and boxer had gone, cruelly stolen in a shattering moment of patent unfairness.

I climbed from the ring and staggered back to the changing rooms in a daze, not understanding what had happened, or why. Once there, I sat on a bench and stared at the wall, with the cheers of all those people, I had previously thought to be rooting for me echoing through the air and stabbing at my consciousness.

Nobody spoke to me about it after that, and most steered clear of me, presumably anticipating some physical act of vengeance for having cheered my demise. A few days later we gathered in the gymnasium to watch the final eliminator. Jack was representing our entry against an apprentice from the entry below us.

To be fair, he didn't do badly in the first round, a little frantic maybe, but well ahead on points. However, he tired in the second round. A roundhouse punch, which must have travelled a good six feet, knocked him senseless. I sat watching, knowing I would have easily beaten his opponent, and blaming the Wee Beastie for allowing his dislike of me to overrule common sense.

I looked accusingly across at the Wee Beastie as they helped Jack from the ring, knowing his previous unfairness and bias had cost Jack his consciousness, and me the title. I fully expected him to accept his guilt, or to at least show some remorse, but he just looked at me and grinned.

I remember thinking just how much I hated him at that moment.

After that I gave up boxing. There were no more championships that year and I had lost my appetite for it. Instead of circuit training and sparring I went back to tennis. I spent every Wednesday afternoon and a few evenings practising for the apprentice championships, because we had somehow reached the semi-finals, and were up against the apprentices from RAF Locking. I worked hard at my tennis, because I wanted that winner's medal for many different reasons, every one of which was to do with proving my worth to my adopted father.

In the end we easily beat the Locking apprentices, but lost just as easily to RAF Halton in the final. Nevertheless, as runner-up I got a medal and my name in the in the programme that went with the final passing-out parade. I decided that such a simple distinction would be enough in proving a measure of achievement to the only man I had ever wanted to impress.

It's strange, but when I come to think about it just about everything I did or said or thought during that time was a product of anger or resentment. I held an almost fanatical need to impress my adopted father and somehow prove him wrong. I became introverted, taciturn and unpopular with everyone, and would probably have remained that way, had it not been for a conversation with the Wee Beastie, which occurred just after I had lost the tennis final.

He wandered into the apprentice mess and sat down next to me. I was finishing my tea and staring moodily into the dregs, still fuming from the memory of my patently unfair disqualification. I stood up and made to leave, but he glared at me and said, "Sit down and shut up, you stupid little prat."

I grudgingly sat back down, and then glared across at him.

"Why?"

I had levied the question as accusingly as I dared. He grinned and feigned ignorance.

"Why what?"

"Why did you do it? I would have won that fight. I could have won the whole bloody tournament. Why did you do that to me?"

He nodded knowledgeably as he gave me his answer.

"You would have won it, of that I'm sure. You're a fair boxer, laddie, in fact, you're more than fair, but I didn't do anything to prevent it. You did that to yourself."

I tried a lie.

"I was just trying not to hurt him too badly."

"Bullshit. You wanted to humiliate him and puff yourself up, and you know it."

I had to concede the point, feeling demoralised and dejected and close to tears, but having no intention of ever letting the Wee Beastie know.

"All right, so what if I did? Do you know something, Corporal Campbell? It must be easy for you. You probably win at everything you do, but I never got to win at anything: not ever. That boxing tournament would have been the first time I'd ever won anything in my life, but you couldn't even let me do that, could you?"

Still no sign of remorse, and it had been such a good speech. He grinned and shook his head.

"You honestly believe that by doing what you were doing you would have been in some way winning: making him look stupid and knocking him around for fun? Come off it, laddie. Beating him would have been fine, but you were trying to humiliate him. Now that may be your idea of winning, but I promise you, it's not mine."

I didn't answer him, largely because there was nothing I could say in my own defence. We sat in silence for a few seconds before he explained further.

"Do you remember that day when I found those morons kicking you around outside the pub?" I nodded. He went on. "Let me tell you something. When I arrived I could see the look in their eyes. You couldn't see, from where you were cowering, but I could and it wasn't pleasant.

"What I saw in their eyes was a look of cruelty and contempt, a look of sadism and viciousness. The look most people would have expected from a gang of cowardly bullies taking out their maliciousness and cowardice on someone weaker; someone who, for whatever reason, wasn't able or willing to fight back."

I shrugged my indifference and raised my eyes to the heavens.

"So?"

"So, I'll tell you something else, shall I, laddie? It was the same look I saw in your eyes in the ring that day; and do you know something else? I'd rather see you lying there and getting a kicking, like the cringing little coward you were, than to ever see that look in your eyes again.

"You may not be able to understand this right now, because you're hurt and upset and you think I was wrong. But, as God is my witness, I swear I'd do precisely the same again."

I sat and looked blankly back at him. He stood up.

"In my book you weren't winning that fight, laddie. . . he was."

I clearly didn't believe that, so he leaned closer and stared hard at me.

"Do you seriously think that we set up these stupid little competitions to find the best boxer?" He grinned. "Or the second-best tennis player. . .? Of course we damn well don't. We set up these silly little competitions to discover the true winners; to discover who's got the character, and heart, and the important strengths. We set up these competitions to discover who's got the strengths that a man, a real man, a Royal Air Force man, is going to need during his life.

"I honestly couldn't give a shit about who wins and who loses some stupid meaningless little competition, and neither could anybody else. Not when it all comes down to it, because that's not what it's all about. It never was, and I pray to God it never will be.

"But what I do care about is how they win and how they lose. So you think about that, and I also suggest that some time soon you damn well start growing up and stop pissing everybody off."

With that, he about-turned, stamped his feet together, and then marched smartly out of the mess, leaving me staring into my empty mug of tea-leaves and dregs, and thinking just how bloody impossibly complicated my life had become.

Petrified, propositioned, and posted

The rest of that year flew by. Surprisingly to me, and all who had once known me, I was already some way beyond the necessary speed and accuracy thresholds for the practical telecommunications syllabus, and even my technical and procedural knowledge was keeping pace with most of the entry. In sport, they considered me a good boxer, a fair tennis player, and a good all-round athlete. Most importantly, my popularity had improved, following that painful chat in the apprentice mess with the Wee Beastie. However, and for all the positives occupying my life, there was one seemingly insurmountable problem that remained.

That problem was all to do with my woefully limited knowledge of girls. Many of the others boasted girlfriends, and the majority of those who didn't were intent on improving that sorry state of affairs at every opportunity. A few had even been 'going steady', but not me.

I'd always known that girls intimidated me significantly beyond that considered normal for a young lad's journey through puberty's minefields. Far from helping matters, the voluptuous Anthea Bridges and her basic biology demonstrations had only aggravated the problem.

I knew that I liked girls. I was obsessed by them, but I was so painfully shy that I found it impossible to communicate with them on any but the most superficial and platonic level.

Two events will give you some idea of the problem. The first happened one Saturday evening, when I had been set-up by a friend for a 'blind date' with a girlfriend of his girlfriend.

Although I hadn't admitted it, this was the first time I had been on a genuine date and I was petrified. Jeff, who was experienced in these matters, arranged for us to take the girls to the camp dance. We met them at the guardhouse and escorted them to the dance, with him chattering away to his young lady, and me walking in total silence alongside the friend of a friend. I remember that she was attractive, in fact she was stunning; so stunning that I was tongue-tied.

Poor girl; I didn't say a word to her all the way from the camp gates to the dance, and I still hadn't spoken or offered her a drink or even asked her to dance an hour after that. It wasn't that I didn't want to speak. It wasn't that I didn't have anything to say. It was simply that I didn't have the courage to form the necessary words for any conversation. So she waited and waited for me to say something, and I waited and waited for the necessary courage to present itself.

Unhappily, the necessary courage never did surface, and so she finally put us both out of our misery by accepting an overture from one of the technician apprentices. To give the poor girl her due, she did come back from the dance floor to apologise and explain that she would be going home with him. 'O.K.' was all the approval I could muster in my red-faced shame, as I watched him grinning arrogantly across at me and saw her weak smile fade away to nothing.

I saw him on several occasions after that, but I never saw her again, and so I consoled myself with an all-too familiar litany of excuses: that he had been older, and more sophisticated and experienced. That he probably had a loving family background and properly rounded education and had therefore developed the intellect and self-confidence that came with all of that.

The excuses went on, *ad infinitum* and *ad nauseam*. I conveniently forgot that others in my apprentice entry had experienced similar problems and somehow managed to overcome them.

I later heard that he went on to officer cadetship and they became engaged, but whether they remained together in sickness and in health, or acrimoniously divorced, I never discovered.

There was something I did know, though. I knew that I would always despise the sneering technician apprentices from that day forward, partly because they behaved arrogantly and offensively, with self-assurance beyond egotism or excuse. Mostly, though, because I wished I could have been more like that sneering technician apprentice who stole my first-ever girlfriend.

The second incident, which served to both embarrass me and illustrate my naiveté at the time, was more complex, more harrowing, and significantly more bizarre. It concerned a sweet old-fashioned thing known locally as Albrighton Sally, and occurred when the apprentice entry had just returned from what the Air Force laughingly referred to as 'Summer Camp'. Summer Camp was, in reality, seven days of deprivation and hardship, spent frozen to the bone in malnourished isolation, while camped out along the shoreline of Lake Bala in North Wales.

Albrighton Sally unnerved me. It wasn't that she was aggressive, well not in a punch-your-lights-out sort of way, but she was notoriously promiscuous, and had a reputation for unbridled sexual adventure that would have put the Empress Messalina to shame. I first met her the day we had arrived back from summer camp, around two o'clock on a warm August afternoon.

I was unpacking my holdall when someone called out that something was going on in the field opposite the block. Everyone rushed to the windows to see what all the commotion was, and I followed. That was the first time I saw her, but I had no idea that my first sighting of her and the events that followed would remain as vivid and permanent scars on both machismo and memory.

I'd heard stories about Sally, everyone had heard stories about her, but it wasn't until someone said her name, and someone else crudely confirmed her reputation, that I realised who she was.

She was standing in the field opposite the block, and I have to admit to some confusion, because the notoriously promiscuous female who stood smiling happily back seemed a healthy, good-looking and fresh-faced young woman, and nothing like I'd imagined.

She wasn't stunningly beautiful, but not unattractive either; a trifle on the brazen side of underdressed, but nothing like the ravenous man-eating siren who plundered masculinity at will and bathed in the virgin blood of foolhardy apprentices.

Albrighton Sally was eighteen or nineteen years old, with blue eyes and blonde hair, and was wearing a short red tartan miniskirt and a pale pink blouse, with only the lower buttons fastened. She was standing in the field on the other side of the camp fence, waving and smiling up at us, and so we waved and grinned back at her. One or two of the more vulgar shouted some inane comments, which seemed harmless enough, but as the comments became more risqué, and the wiggling and giggling responses more suggestive, the atmosphere changed.

Suddenly, in the middle of that open field and in front of an appreciative audience of more than fifty sex-obsessed young men, Albrighton Sally began an impromptu striptease.

She began the show innocuously enough by casually loosening one of the two remaining buttons on her blouse and then leaning forward to accentuate the resulting exposure. However, when we greeted that with raucous enthusiasm, she kicked off her shoes and removed the blouse, before unzipping the red tartan miniskirt and slowly allowing it to follow the blouse to the floor.

I never did discover why she did it; for a laugh or a bet, I suppose. Perhaps she'd been drinking, or was simply feeling playful, or maybe all those rumours and the answers to so many of our prayers were true.

Maybe she was a nymphomaniac. I didn't know, and at that moment I didn't all that much care, because I was like everyone else, looking on in wide-eyed astonishment and numb appreciation, while she weaved and twirled in a provocative display of simulated arousal.

That was, I might add, until two sets of scarlet-tipped fingers arrived at the penultimate item of flimsy underwear, and began to play such a disgracefully provocative game of tease and torment that one of her admiring audience found it impossible to remain at a gentlemanly distance. We could hear him clattering down the stairs, clumsily negotiating the individual steps three at a time, while loudly and crudely announcing his intention. That was when all hell broke loose.

Nobody would later own up to being the first person to move, but before anybody had time to identify the culprit, question the wisdom, or even think, the entire apprentice entry followed suit. We stampeded down those stairs like a herd of amorous lemmings, then charged across the road, over the fence and lane beyond, and on into field: fifty young men, with only one thought on their minds, all in frantic pursuit of a wiggling, giggling, half-naked slip of a girl.

Neither could anybody later recall just why we had all suddenly started at once. We may have been sex mad, but were a long way from potential rapists. However, having anticipated, or, more likely, schemingly calculated our red-blooded reaction, the young temptress gathered her clothes and was away, loudly shrieking, as she ran across the field.

Even barefoot and labouring under the handicap of carrying shoes and clothing, she had reached the edge of the first field before most had reached the first-floor stairwell, and could she run. She flew across that first field and easily left most of the apprentice entry floundering in her wake. She negotiated the far fence and then began running across the next field, leaving those few remaining apprentices who foolishly continued the chase some way behind and hopelessly outpaced. . . with the notable exception of one fleet-footed idiot.

As I mentioned, I was an excellent cross-country runner, and, for an insane reason that must have seemed important at the time, was out to prove that to the rest. It wasn't until we started into the third field, however, that I began to compare my own fleet-of-foot position to the ponderous progress of the chasing pack.

And as the others fell farther and farther behind and I drew nearer and nearer to Sally, it slowly dawned on me that I might have to deal with this giggling *femme fatale* without the benefit of their support.

That was when anxiety set in and previously sturdy legs became inexplicably weak.

As we threaded our way through the woods and crossed the third field, anxiety graduated to panic, because I could see that Sally was beginning to tire; or perhaps, more worryingly, beginning to fancy her chances of coping with this loneliest of long-distance runners. Either way, there was no doubt that she had slowed to little more than a trot, and no doubt either that I was going to be alone and unaided when I finally caught up with her.

As we crossed the fourth field, the distance between us was less than twenty paces. The distant pack accepted defeat and came to a halt, and I frantically considered my all too limited choices.

You see, I was the sort of sexual ignoramus who became hopelessly intimidated by the merest smile on a pretty girl's lips. I had regularly turned crimson when the girls at school made double-entendres and laughed at my naiveté, had only been kissed on the mouth once in my life, and hadn't kissed back or had the first idea where to put my hands. I hadn't even known whether I ought to say 'thank you' afterwards.

Yet here I was, a poor, ignorant, foolhardy dupe on the brink of the abyss, or in this case a public alfresco bedding of the most notorious man-eater in the district. The great white hunter without a trophy to his name, hopelessly ensnared in his own stupid trap. The rampant alpha male, about to mount the exhausted female, with no idea of how to begin proceedings, let alone decide exactly what went where and in which order.

I tried to clear my mind as that all-important gap between me and carnal catastrophe narrowed. At this most desperate of moments any soul-searching or self-recrimination was academic. Right now I had more important concerns. Right now I had to do something, anything, to find some way of avoiding this looming disaster. Right now I had to think of something, anything, that might allow me to disentangle myself from this absurd predicament, without the loss of either virgin naiveté or hard-won prestige, or more than likely both.

I considered slowing to an equally unhurried pace, but discarded the idea, because others, although some distance away, were watching my progress and aware of my long-distance running credentials. The second alternative was to stop and allow her to escape, but my already shaky reputation couldn't possibly withstand the fallout from such an inglorious action. Not only that, but I wasn't certain that Sally would take the opportunity, should I choose to present it.

As the pace dropped ever more, and my farcical hot pursuit turned into a comically protracted procession, the knowledge of what the pack and the young seductress herself would expect of me when I finally caught her was filling me with terror.

There was no alternative. Whatever had to be had to be. The dictates of masculinity demanded that I do it. So many million years of mankind's evolution demanded that I do it. The honour of the apprentice wing demanded that I do it. My own self-respect demanded that I do it. Even the wiggling and giggling *femme fatale* herself was seemingly demanding that I do it. There was no other course of action that had come to mind within the time available, or none that offered any lasting credibility. I would simply have to steel my nerve and damn well do it.

So I mentally rehearsed the dastardly plan that would secure this wiggling and giggling prize and confirm my reputation as a callous seducer of sexually provocative women, a man not to trifle with in matters of the flesh. I would kick in with a sudden burst of speed, take her by surprise, hold her struggling femininity in my strong masculine arms, and lay her on the grass. Once there, I would tear away what little remained of that wilfully provocative lingerie, and do what the lady in question and fifty-odd apprentices quite clearly both wanted and expected me to do.

And so I did just that. I took a deep breath, kicked in with a burst of speed, reached out, and, with my voluptuous quarry giggling an expectation that would have tried the celibacy of a monk, I did it. I clumsily rescued that all-important masculine reputation by pretending to twist my ankle.

Sally had been less than a dozen paces away when I suddenly thought up that blessed fourth alternative and fell to the ground. She stopped running, and then turned and stood watching me in bright-eyed excitement and momentary confusion, with her hands on her hips and her breasts threatening to burst the fastening as she gulped at the air and studied my feigned discomfort.

I could only look meekly back at her piercing gaze from my humiliating position, sprawled across the grass like a mortally-wounded stag, hoping that she would laughingly declare an erotic victory over the lot of us and move on.

But she didn't move on. She didn't seem the least bit interested in moving on. Instead, she started to dress, agonizingly slowly, with a mixture of puzzlement and disappointment on her face, while I looked meekly back at her and pretended to massage the soreness from a twisted ankle.

It was just as I began to believe I'd got away with it when everything suddenly took a distinct turn for the worse. Just as I had half-imagined seeing a momentary expression of compassion flitting across feminine features and had begun privately congratulating myself on escaping with dignity more or less intact, I somehow blew it.

I suppose I must have blushed, or failed to meet her eyes, or something, or perhaps she detected something else in my manner or expression that gave the game away. Either way, she studied the deception for a few more uncertain seconds and then smiled.

It wasn't the smile of triumph I had hoped for. It wasn't even a smile of superiority. It was a smile of knowledge, a smile of delicious wickedness; a smile of delight at having discovered someone's most guilty and intimate secret, or in this case the real and lily-livered reason behind my feigned predicament.

"Well now." She purred the comment, while I looked nervously back, like a doomed dormouse under the hypnotic gaze of a deadly cobra. "What's wrong with you then? Lost your nerve, have you, or maybe you've lost something else? Shall we see if I can help you find it again?"

She giggled, and my mouth went dry as she vamped me, and then began unfastening buttons that she'd secured only a few moments earlier.

It occurred to me, as I lay cringing with embarrassment, that her tormenting of this failed seducer might be all that a maiden's honour required; allow her to declare an immoral victory and leave with only my humiliation secured, rather than my honour. However, any hope was dashed as she started toward me, exaggeratedly swinging her hips and running a tongue back and forth across her lips as she moved to only inches from where I sat. Once there, she unfastened the tartan skirt and let it slide to the floor in a frantically intimidating statement of lecherous intent.

I could only lie there with my heart thumping and my mind in turmoil, not knowing what to do and studying the flaunted offering in wild-eyed confusion. I had no idea if she was seriously intending to mercilessly abuse my virgin flesh, or merely perpetuating a convincing bluff. Neither did I know which one of those two diverse possibilities concerned me most.

To my eternal shame and embarrassment, I also remember beginning to tremble; whether this was through fear or anticipation, I'm not prepared to say. All I am prepared to tell you is that for a moment of abject cowardice I did seriously consider abandoning what little pride I had left and running all the way back to camp.

However, when I had come to the shocking realisation that my legs wouldn't move, and had privately conceded that I was about to surrender all naiveté, moral deliverance arrived: in the shape of a dozen or so apprentices who had caught their second wind and resumed the chase.

With the cavalry's arrival now imminent, a would-be seductress stood over me in unhurried contemplation as she re-evaluated the odds and reconsidered her purpose, murmuring seductive sounds and mentally violating me with those piercing blue eyes. I leaned back in petrified submission, and mutely allowed her to do just that, trying not to allow my gaze to fall lower than a gentleman ought; trying also to control the shaking that had started again as I heard her say, "Oh well, I guess we'll just have to finish this some other time."

She shrugged, casually stepped back into her skirt, and daintily refastened that well-worn zipper, while all the time holding me transfixed and mortified in the awareness of my own self-inflicted predicament. Then she slipped into her shoes, gave one last wiggle, and added, "Now you think about what you should have had here today, and I'll think about what I'm going to do to you the next time I see you. But don't think too hard about it, will you, lover? After all, we don't want you going blind before I get back to you, do we now?"

With that said, she wheeled around and sprinted off down the lane, leaving me to study her departure and rue my own inadequacy before clambering awkwardly to my feet and substituting the reality of a wounded pride with the pretext of a wounded ankle.

Presumably because they all felt thoroughly ashamed by their own dismal performances, nobody questioned me too closely and so I didn't offer any explanation, or catch anyone's eye for fear of betraying the guilt. I merely winced occasionally in contrived discomfort as I limped my acutely embarrassed way back across the fields and on to the sanctuary of Fulton Block.

And just as the lady predicted, and just as you might imagine, I have thought about that incident on many occasions since. I'm still not convinced that Sally would have forcibly 'had me' as I lay across the grass in petrified obedience on that summer's afternoon. I'm inclined to think that she was tormenting my wounded machismo with a convincing bluff. Neither was I convinced about her lecherous promise to do heaven knows what in the future, but I never went back into Albrighton. Taking on a bullying group of drunken morons with my newly-acquired boxing and self-defence skills was one thing, but having the notoriously promiscuous Albrighton Sally sexually violate and emotionally abuse me in a pub car park was an altogether different matter.

However, it wasn't all doom and gloom in the weeks and months following that incident, because, for some inexplicable reason, the other apprentices chose to believe my story about twisting my ankle at the critical moment. So I gained an undeserved reputation for being, at the tender age of sixteen-and-a-bit years, the most experienced wayward-wench sorter-out in the entire block. In addition, I achieved the whispered tribute of 'He, who very nearly had Albrighton Sally that day'. I knew the truth of it all, though. I knew that, if anything, it had been the other way around. . . and so, I'm ashamed to say, did 'She, who very nearly had me'.

Culture shocks and cut-throats

They say that schooldays are the happiest of your life, and for a select few there may be some truth in that, but I rarely subscribe to sweeping generalisations and, apart from passing references to Alastair Sim, I have no idea who first said it. You see, as you are by now well aware, I found the opposite to be true. I do, however, believe that when toe-turning-up-time arrives and I look back on a long and largely happy life, apprentice training will number among my happiest memories.

However, that training was coming to an end, and final examinations were looming; not to mention the all-important passing-out parade, which served to mark the occasion. This demanded less time worshipping WAAFs at Wolverhampton Bowling Alley, and more time marching back and forth across the parade ground. It also demanded some frantic revision.

Some people find certain disciplines easier than others, and I was one of the lucky ones. I held no love for teleprinters, but could happily make the necessary speed and accuracy thresholds, and when it came to Morse code I was better than fair. The technical demands weren't a problem, either; nothing to do with being technically gifted; everything to do with the ridiculously low pass and fail thresholds.

Procedure was the problem for me. All those silly little three-letter codes that mostly began with the letters Q or Z and all those other alphanumeric and military acronyms had me so flummoxed that my brain refused to function. I failed the examination the first time; nerves, I guess, or that was my excuse. However, as I did so well with everything else the Air Force called me in for an interview and went through the answers I'd given.

He was a decent guy, the Canadian instructor charged with retesting me. I'd always got on well with him, because he was also my Morse instructor and I'd excelled at that. He looked up as I stood in the doorway, nervously clutching my beret, and then told me to come in and sit down.

"Well," he began, "I guess you take the fur-lined piss-pot, boy."

I knew that he'd say that. It was his favourite expression. I had no idea what it meant, but I'd heard him say it at least three times a week for a year. Everyone laughed when we first heard him say it, why I'm not sure, but since then I'd become sick to death of hearing it. I was glad to hear it that morning, though, because that meant they'd placed the elderly Canadian in charge of my reassessment and I now had a better than fair chance of scraping through.

"ZBM2 means 'I'll be over the target at 0200 hours', does it?" he drawled at me and I shook my head. "No, sir, it means, put on a competent operator." He peered at me over the top of his glasses. "I'd remember it, if I were you, boy; you'll be hearing it a lot. And QRS means 'strike imminent', is that right?" Again I shook my head and gave him the correct answer, and he followed that with another half-dozen or so codes that I had somehow answered incorrectly the first time. Thankfully, I managed to get most of them right the second time, and so he leaned back in his chair and scanned the answer paper, before finding one last mistake. "So FLOT is a naval formation, is it? I must tell the Admiralty." "No, sir, it's Forward Line Own Troops." He half grinned and half sneered at me. "God preserve us when you get out there with them. Go on, get the hell out of here, you little pissant."

I failed to see any connection between his comment and my posting, but when the results and accompanying postings came through, I thought back to that conversation and smiled.

I had made the rank of Senior Aircraftman, the communiqué said. I hadn't passed with distinction, as three others did, presumably because of my failure with that first procedural paper, but I had passed. Most of us had passed out as SACs. A few of the others had passed out as the more junior Leading Aircraftmen, or LACs. Two poor devils failed altogether; they offered them alternative training as cooks or something, but somehow I had passed. I was floating on air after reading my grade and considering my new rank, but it was only when I saw where they'd posted me that I understood the old Canadian's comment about me and those front-line troops.

Theoretically, a newly-qualified SAC telegraphist could be posted anywhere in the world. In reality, though, for the inexperienced, there were three main postings.

The first was RAF Stanbridge, which was nothing more than a tape-relay factory for passing teleprinter messages between the various stations, messages stored on chadded or chadless paper tape. Stanbridge had the largest number of telegraphists and teleprinters operators in the service, and, although nobody in their right mind ever asked for a posting there, the chance of being press-ganged into the communications centre there was high. A posting to Stanbridge held many down-sides, which were mostly to do with monotony, but the upside was a large WAAF population.

The second was an even more monotonous radio-monitoring station. I'm not referring to that celebrated hotbed of dissent in middle-class Cheltenham, in case you were wondering, but another less-publicised station, farther to the north and east. I won't mention the location here, because it may still be in service in some significantly advanced form or other. Personnel assigned to this particular station usually showed an aptitude for Morse code and radio reception during training, and Russian was the preferred second language. Located out in the sticks, and some distance from civilisation and sanity, we tried never to mention its name, reasoning that, like those theories on spontaneous combustion, to consider the name at any length might invoke a posting there.

Third on the list was RAF Tangmere, a once-proud wartime fighter station just to the north of Bognor Regis. Tangmere had all those Boys' Own comic stories to tell of a glorious history during two World Wars, with Douglas Bader and Johnnie Johnson, and the Hurricane and Spitfire, and those incredible few of nineteen-forty, who were owed so much by so many.

As you have probably surmised, Tangmere was my posting. I applied for it because I had only seen the road-show, giving the official version of that fine body of front-line telecommunications professionals, who supposedly formed Tangmere's famous Tactical Communications Wing. I had no idea of the grim reality of the infamous bunch of drunken cut-throats who actually were TCW.

Not believing its luck, or my ignorance, the RAF duly obliged with a one-way travel warrant to Chichester, and I was on my way to Tangmere.

As I travelled south I was looking forward to the experience, but nothing that Cosford had taught me could possibly have prepared me for the culture shock that dear old RAF Tangmere and the Tactical Communications Wing of Number Thirty-Eight Group provided.

To any with a heart for history, there was no doubting the magnificence of those wartime days, but to those with an eye for detail, there was no doubt either that Tangmere was past its best.

Twenty-odd years on from that last squadron scramble, Tangmere's fall from grace had been dramatic. From the faded blue underside of the Spitfire shell parked opposite the guardhouse, to the tufts of wild grass encroaching on the runway from either end. From the rows of prefabricated huts, never modernised or replaced, to the all but disused hangars that stubbornly violated an otherwise empty skyline: giant monuments to a glorious past for those who cherished the memory of nineteen-forty; giant untended eyesores for those who didn't.

They had even downgraded the personnel. All those dashing young fighter pilots in sheepskin jackets, gunning their Merlins through hardship to the stars, had been relegated to a file marked 'bygone age', as had those proud heroes of the 'Battle of Britain', recalled only in black-and-white photographs hung on the walls of the officers' mess and the saloon bar of the local Bader Arms.

Installed in their stead were the dowdy communicators of twenty-five years on, who wore jungle-green combat gear and gunned two-stroke generators and canvas-backed Landrovers.

In the skies above, disenchanted pilots no longer flew Spitfires but lumbering transport planes, and satisfied the thirst for death or glory with monotonous circuits-and-bumps on a damaged runway, before veering away to the west, heading for home and a more worthy stretch of concrete.

Household names like Mannock and Nicolson and Bader and Johnson had given way to the dregs of Royal Air Force humanity, or The Tactical Communications Wing of 38 Group Tactical Support Unit, as the Royal Air Force community of nineteen sixty-six referred to them.

TCW was a law unto itself. The personnel didn't look anything like stereotypical RAF personnel, didn't behave anything like stereotypical RAF personnel, and rarely, if ever, obeyed 'Queen's Regulations', or anyone else's regulations, come to that.

I should add that a smattering of commissioned officers and non-commissioned officers, and one senior aircraftman, collectively qualified as exceptions to this, but, these aside, the rest of TCW were unquestionably the scruffiest, most ill-disciplined, belligerent, notorious, loutish, vulgar, drunken, debauched and altogether undesirable characters in the service.

You see, in those unsophisticated, pre-geostationary satellite, pre-smart bomb, pre-Tomahawk cruise missile days, TCW would be dropped into and ahead of front-lines. Their task was to set up mobile communications links, and relay both enemy and friendly status and location reports to strike forces. In other words, they dumped TCW in at the sharp end as expendable eyes and ears.

In any wartime scenario TCW would have suffered some of the highest mortality rates in the service. However, in peacetime they received all the kudos that went with such dangerous assignments, without too much of the risk, and they milked that kudos for all it was worth.

Whenever members of the wing appeared on regular RAF stations, their arrival would invariably coincide with an alarming rise in cases of insubordination, abusiveness, lewdness, vulgarity and damage to property, individual brawls, mass punch-ups, excessive noise, wholesale drunkenness and the sexual harassment of any susceptible, predisposed, or imprudent females, especially members of the Women's Royal Air Force.

Incidents occurred with such regularity that any areas on visited stations which served alcohol, or where unwary females might be at risk, were always placed strictly out-of-bounds. Many station commandants naively demanded written assurances on behaviour and compensation, while those commandants, without specific written orders from their commander-in-chief, usually banned members of the wing from operating within a ten-mile radius of their stations.

Memories of my first morning parade and roll-call will be forever etched, and may give you some idea of the culture shock that greeted me.

I arrived ten minutes before the published assembly time of 0800, with my battledress trousers ironed to knife-edges, and my tunic boxed and pressed. Both the shirt and collar were new and starched, and I'd bulled my parade boots to a mirror finish. I'd had all those recently awarded badges professionally sewn on to my uniform, in precisely the correct positions. I'd polished my belt buckle and beret badge to such a sheen that they positively glinted in the early-morning sunshine. My head, all but shaved for the Cosford passing-out parade, was still virtually bald. My teeth gleamed white, and my breath was as fresh as a daisy. I'd even manicured my nails.

I stood rigidly to attention and waited for the other forty or so to arrive for morning inspection, and can remember experiencing such an intense and justifiable pride, it bordered conceit.

I was still there thirty minutes later when a Flight Sergeant arrived to open the row of prefabricated huts which constituted my new working environment. Wearing battledress with a faded-green combat jacket over the top, he looked at me and scratched his head.

"Are you all right, lad?" he asked.

"Yes, Flight Sergeant."

"What are you doing?"

"Waiting, Flight Sergeant. For morning parade."

"Are you now? Oh, right, well, in that case, I suppose you'd better wait in here then."

I could see from the skilful application of my peripheral vision that he was making a conscious effort not to laugh. I performed a precise left-turn manoeuvre, and then marched smartly back to the huts and into the canteen. I stamped to attention and then stood waiting for further instructions. The Flight Sergeant mumbled over his shoulder as he left.

"Sit down. I'll be back in a minute."

I may have been naïve, but I wasn't stupid, because I could hear him choking back the laughter as he left. I was obviously the cause of his humour, but for the life of me I couldn't understand what he'd found so amusing. There was no doubting the humour, though, because I could hear him chuckling as he moved on down the row of doors, unlocking each in turn.

He returned to the canteen and smiled to disguise the laughter and blunt the offence.

"Welcome to Base-Comms. I'm Flight Sergeant Foster, but you can call me Chief, everybody does . . . and you are?"

I snapped to attention and gave him my name, rank and serial number. He grinned.

"Straight from Cosford?" I nodded, and stood slightly prouder.

"Yes, Flight Sergeant."

"Do you know something, I had rather suspected you might be. First name?" I told him that my first name was Michael, but everybody called me Mike. He seemed more at ease with that.

"Right then, Mike, sit down and take that beret off, and if I were you I'd unbutton that tunic, at least while you're in here."

"Flight Sergeant?"

"Relax, sit down, this isn't Cosford. The only reason we have a parade ground here is so everybody knows where to find the NAAFI and the airmen's mess, and how best to avoid the commandant's office. The only time we shout around here is when people have a hearing problem. Have you switched the urn on?"

"Flight Sergeant?"

"Chief, call me Chief, for God's sake. Now then, first to arrive in the morning switches on the hot water and brings in the bread rolls. Last out at night switches off the urn and puts the empty bread tray outside. They're the most important tasks of the day, got that?"

"Yes, Chief."

"Now, if I were you I'd relax and have a fag and wait for the water to boil. Mine's tea, strong with two sugars. My mug's got my name on it, and my office is at the end of the row."

"Yes, Chief."

I sat and lit a cigarette while I waited for the water to boil, and then took him his tea. I wondered why I hadn't seen another soul, but when I returned the canteen was thick with cigarette smoke and all manner of odd-looking people. I should add that they obviously considered me to be similarly odd. I should also add that by this time it was gone nine.

Nine-thirty came and went, and still nobody seemed in any hurry to assemble for morning parade. I pushed my way through the throng, made myself another cup of tea, and sat quietly studying some of the faces. I was secretly listening to the conversations and pretending not to hear the derogatory comments about me. Most included the word 'sprog' or the more familiar and descriptive word, first heard during Corporal Campbell's bed allotment on my first day at Cosford.

A scruffy-looking corporal arrived around ten and everyone wandered out to the expanse of concrete that served the dual purpose of volleyball court and assembly point. Nobody seemed in any hurry. They shuffled into three approximate and unequal ranks while he took the roll-call.

A few of them looked hard at me in thinly disguised scorn and ill-concealed hostility, and I glared back at them in defiance. I knew that I must have stood out like a call-girl in a church choir, but refused to allow their scruffy belligerence to intimidate. It seemed that everybody but me sported hairstyles that covered their collars and ears. Most were dressed in mismatched items of combat gear, mixed in with bits and pieces of civilian clothing. Nobody wore regular boots, relying instead on well-worn plimsolls or scuffed and dirty shoes. A few wore muddy football boots, equally filthy tracksuit bottoms, and various coloured football shirts, most of which originated from north of Watford. However there were a couple of Arsenal, and I even spotted what might once have been a grubby looking West Ham shirt, or maybe it was Aston Villa.

At least three still had their pyjamas on; you could see the candy-striped material sticking out beneath their trouser legs. One of them was still wearing slippers. Two were listening to radios. Four others were huddled at the far end, passing a handmade cigarette back and forth. At least half were smoking regular cigarettes and drinking tea. Apart from me, nobody had dressed correctly, including the corporal, and nobody was listening to, or taking any interest in the roll-call.

In the end the corporal ticked off the names of those he could see, and then shuffled back to the canteen. Those who remained continued chattering and smoking. Some started a game of football. A few followed the corporal back to the canteen. Some crept around the back of the huts, climbed over the fence and disappeared. The rest headed back to bed on a roundabout route, which avoided the guardhouse, the parade ground, and the station commandant's office.

That was it: my first formal parade at Tangmere was over. Just what the Wee Beastie would have made of it, I shudder to think. He'd probably have had a heart attack, or certainly have needed a lengthy period of intense convalescence. Nevertheless, for what it was worth, I now belonged to Base Communications Flight of Tactical Communications Wing, 38 Group Tactical Support Unit.

To be fair, I did acquire some new skills during those first weeks and months. I learnt to set up tented encampments, using laced twelve-foot square tents with collapsible aluminium frames as building blocks, and similarly erect and take apart the two-man, self-inflating Igloo tent.

I also learnt to erect varying sizes of aerial mast, cut aerials to frequency, service and repair generators, and use cipher and other specialised equipment. I drove everything from Landrovers to three ton Bedford trucks, even though it would be another four years before I'd take and pass a U.K. driving test, existed on composition rations and camouflaged just about everything.

I joined an unarmed combat group, which met on a Tuesday evening in one of the hangars, and spent time at the firing range, but everything at Tangmere was so different to anything I had previously experienced.

The firing range was a good example. At Cosford a trip to the range was a bi-annual occasion. After an hour of instruction, they'd hand us our own, numbered, cumbersome bolt-action .303 rifle and a set of ear defenders. We would then be given five minutes instruction on what to do, and thirty-five minutes instruction on what not to do, before marching us to the range.

On arrival, each man would be allotted five rounds of live ammunition. Firing would commence on the whistle and end on the whistle. Upon completion, the armourer would check everything from empty magazines to spent cartridges to broken-out rifle parts, before allowing anyone to move. They'd then collect the targets, allot the scores, and we'd clean the rifles and return them to the armoury, before marching back to the block.

At Tangmere we practised when we felt like it. We'd wander over to the range, pick up the first weapon we saw, usually .762 self-loading rifles or 9 millimetre automatics, and then haphazardly pop however many rounds took our fancy. After a while someone would break out the submachine-guns, and we'd spend the next twenty minutes destroying empty ammunition boxes, or trying to cut the heads off man-shaped paper targets. Bullets from the Sterling SMG held so little penetration power, they would happily bounce off a webbing belt at fifty yards, but hit wooden ammunition boxes or paper men with enough of them and the results were devastating.

At the end of the session someone from the armoury would collect everything, and return unused ammunition to storage. That was that; no checks on magazines or spent cartridges, no pass or fail or meaningless grading exercises, no endless breaking down, cleaning and reassembly, and no accounting for ammunition, or not by us. Just turn up, pop away with whatever took your fancy, and then get over to the NAAFI for a well-earned beer.

Not that I had any expectation of using my marksmanship skills in earnest, or not for some time, because I hadn't reached the age of seventeen years and six months, and the Air Force flatly refused to allow junior airmen on military exercises, or at least, not overseas.

However, a quirk of fate came to my rescue, because the wall outside the Chief's office held a board setting out everyone's details. It listed name, rank, serial number, fitness condition, current allotment and schedule of future assignments. For most the details were complex, but for me it simply said 'Junior', but then someone rewrote the list and inadvertently deleted the word 'Junior'.

Had I pointed out the omission there would have been no problem in reinstating me as a junior, at least until the milestone had passed, but of course I didn't. I was bored silly, and desperate to get away on exercise with the rest of them, and so I said nothing and waited to see if anybody noticed the error. Thankfully, nobody did, and so I was allotted to my first overseas exercise.

You see, that was the nature of Tangmere and the Tactical Communications Wing in those early days. Nobody thought to check, because everything was so laid-back. The Wing boasted little discipline, little administration, and little or no formality. Military exercises were taken seriously enough, and would be meticulously planned and precisely delivered, but very little else mattered.

People and places and the perils of exercise

However, if the daily routine and working environment were relaxed, the personnel were more so. Members of TCW were a curious assortment of characters, holding varying skills, varying levels of morality, and differing opinions on all manner of subjects. To a man, they were less than wholehearted, and met the eye as a loosely organised rabble of scruffy and aggressive drop-outs. They cared little for the service, and flouted authority at every opportunity, but to simply dismiss them as that would be to do them an injustice, because many boasted a fair degree of intellect and excelled at their work. On major exercises and in front-line scenarios, TCW always performed well, and occasionally excelled, but I didn't discover that more worthy side until some months after I'd arrived.

During those first months I made some new friends, and assessed the strengths, weaknesses and character traits of many more. However, it wasn't until that mistaken entry on the board and allotment on to my first overseas exercise that I got to know them well. Until then I had only witnessed those less savoury facets of the disgraceful personae they revelled in. I'd not seen the equally admirable personal and professional qualities that most preferred to hide.

"Look, wack, if you saw a hundred-thousand Soviet friggin shock troops charging towards you, wailing like banshees, with blood in their eyes and bayonets fixed, would you really feel more friggin confident if they weren't all in step?"

That had been Joules Carter, a tall Liverpudlian who was to become a good friend in the months and years following that conversation. I remember the conversation taking place on a Thursday night, because that was station dance night. We were standing at the bar, having a beer and discussing my concern at Tangmere's lack of regimentation and discipline. Joules explained why he believed that formal discipline and drill were no longer necessary in an age of mechanised battles, technical warfare and jet-propelled air support.

I can also remember him being vociferous, although he held no interest in the subject, but had been using it as a creative form of diversion while he selected a suitable female for fleeting distraction and casual sex.

The enviably good-looking Joules, I called him, because he was tall, slim, and classically good-looking, with permanently tanned features framed by long straight blond hair, which covered his ears and hung down to his shoulders. As well as an Apollo-like face and bone-structure, he boasted clear blue eyes, which he used to maximum effect by staring deeply and longingly into whichever mesmerised female's unblinking gaze he had just that minute selected.

This invariably caused the helpless creature's jaw to drop, her hands to tremble and her breasts to heave. It also produced a hypnotic effect, which, when combined with his wickedly suggestive smile, would be guaranteed to instantly overwhelm whatever waning hesitance remained, and perish the stubbornness from all known forms of knicker elastic.

Almost all of TCW sported long hair, or at least long when compared to the rest of the armed forces, but Joules' hair was exceptional. It rested on his shoulders rather than his collar. Those who saw him outside the working environment found it hard to believe that anybody could get away with hair that long and still be a serving member of the British armed forces. Then again, most people who saw the enviably good-looking Joules had no understanding of the extraordinary lengths he went to in preserving his appearance.

We would stagger out of bed at 8.30, drag a comb through our hair, wash, shave, and fall into some semblance of uniform, aiming to arrive at work around 9.00, but Joules always rose at 6.30. Although he would spend some time pressing and box-pleating his uniform, starching and pressing his shirt and tie, and polishing his shoes, he'd spend most of that time on his hair. Joules would carefully flatten and tape it into position under a ladies' hairnet, and then pin the resulting wad of restrained locks into place with countless grips and half-a-tin of firm-hold hairspray. Finally, he would precisely position his Air Force beret to hide all trace of those flowing tresses.

The day's end would see the reverse. We would spend the first couple of hours recovering from the rigours of the day by crashing out on our beds, then jump in and out of the shower before heading out for the evening. The enviably good-looking Joules would spend all of that time washing out the hairspray and restoring nourishment and condition to the flowing locks. He'd then carefully dry the restored hairstyle and painstakingly select that evening's outfit, while cavorting back and forth in front of a full-length mirror installed for that precise purpose.

Away from ablutions and electric hairdryers, on exercise or secondment, he would never take the beret off, or not that I saw. That aside, this daily ritual was a twenty-four-five event of mind-numbingly boring repetitiveness. They weren't lengths to which I, or any other sane heterosexual male, would willingly go, and neither was the excessive amount of time spent in front of a sunray lamp at weekends, but Joules didn't see it that way. Joules saw it as the price he had to pay for the sort of chaotic sex life that put just about every other would-be Don Juan to shame.

I could understand girls going for Joules, because he was a good-looking bloke, but I could never understand why they became quite so enamoured, because his chatting-up technique was the corniest and most embarrassingly clichéd I ever heard. However, it was also the most maddening, because that same corny, clichéd and laughingly predictable technique never failed.

You see, I was at a difficult age, secretly ashamed of my chronically virgin condition, and certain in my own mind that all I lacked was a sophisticated and proven chatting-up technique. So I would secretly watch Joules at work, and on one occasion even foolishly copied the maestro.

The weekly camp dance was the place to see his technique at its devastatingly effective best. At the beginning of the evening we would all line up along the bar, ostensibly talking and laughing and drinking, but in reality killing time while we waited for the girls to arrive by camp bus. The young ladies would arrive, drop their coats off at the cloakroom, and then disappear into the 'powder room' for those all-important last-minute adjustments.

With essential maintenance and restorative work done, they would then leave the restroom two-by-two, like wasps leaving the nest. They'd feign lack of interest as they casually paraded their undeniable desirability before us, and chatter nineteen-to-the-dozen about subjects we couldn't begin to understand. Then they'd wiggle away to the dance floor and further arouse our basest of instincts by weaving and thrusting nubile young forms around a collection of handbags.

I always considered this weekly ritual analogous to those old John Ford westerns portraying early American settlers in covered-wagons, heading out through hostile Indian country on journeys to the promised land. We'd be the uncouth savages, staring down on the flaxen-haired maidens from our imagined dominance up on the ridge, drinking deadly firewater in sullen aggression and lecherous anticipation. The nervous flaxen-haired maidens, played by Chichester and Bognor's most nubile of demurely bonneted pilgrims, would defensively wrap inadequate arms around upper torsos in a futile attempt to disguise their desirability, and then, fearing imminent attack, would circle the flickering campfire of patent-leather handbags and await our crude assault.

For the majority, and that included me, this Thursday night ritual was nothing to do with the mating game, or any serious expectation of seducing Miss Right. It was merely an excuse to drink and admire, and bolster self-esteem with unhealthy quantities of Dutch courage, before receiving a thoroughly deserved ration of ridicule and rejection. I say majority, but that didn't include Joules.

He would stand with us, chatting and sipping, as though he were similarly charging the Dutch-courage batteries, but would then suddenly stop and, from that moment on, ignore both colleague and conversation. Sometimes he'd stop in mid-sentence, occasionally in mid-word, while his eyes focused on the answering gaze of whichever young lovely he'd selected from the many who wiggled and giggled and flaunted for his consideration.

Whichever of us he'd been talking to would always grin when they saw those tell-tale signs, and then turn to the other guys and say, 'Guess who's pulled?' The rest would chuckle and follow the direction of Apollo's gaze, to where a sweet young thing would wait in mesmerised infatuation with blushing cheeks, trembling limbs, heaving breasts, and dainty underwear already draped across her ankles.

Well, if she hadn't already physically draped the items in question across the insteps, she might just as well have done, because it only took one look at the helpless creature's unblinking gaze to know that if she hadn't already slipped them off and tucked away in her handbag, she soon would.

With stage one of his regular Thursday night routine performed, the enviably good-looking Joules would saunter over to where she'd be breathlessly waiting to offer her all, and then say, "So what's the score then, babe?"

I kid you not. That was his opening line. He used it without fail, and without fail, whenever I heard it, and I heard it a lot, I would look on jealously, while cringing with a combination of angst and sympathetic embarrassment. It never bothered Joules, though, and it never hindered his immoral Thursday night mission, because, within moments of hearing it, another candidly acquiescent beauty would be out of that dance hall, around the back of the forward comms building, and into the shadows. There she'd remain for between ten and forty minutes, dependent on weather, ground conditions, and the extent of Joules intoxication, with gasps of pleasure on her lips, a groan of indulgence in her throat, and a lunging Liverpudlian Apollo wedged firmly between her thighs.

When I first heard him use that line I couldn't believe that anything that corny could be so effective, but it was. So effective that I decided that if you can't beat them you might as well join them, and tried the same line myself, with sadly predictable results. The sweet young object of my lustful naiveté listened to my opening gambit, and then said, "Dunno, luv, ain't watched the telly tonight. Who's playing?" before adding, "'Ere, 'ope you don't mind me asking, but you see that tall, good-looking bloke with the tight Levis and long blond hair . . . is he a friend of yours?"

John Doggett, on the other hand, was an equally good friend, and another of the many larger than life characters I met at Tangmere, but, any similarity ended there.

Joules was classically good-looking, and faultlessly turned out, with a smile that could charm the birds from the trees and the knickers from a nun, a decent guy and a good friend, but a vain and conceited Adonis, who took an unhealthy pride in his appearance.

John Doggett was anything but that. A hard-bitten and surprisingly knowledgeable Welshman from Cardiff's Tiger Bay, with a stupid grin permanently fixed across a blemished and pock-marked face, John always looked 'high' on something or other, although I never saw him take hard drugs, and reinforced that illusion by wearing an odd assortment of psychedelic and paisley shirts. Somehow, the shirts always managed to clash with his ill-fitting, bell-bottomed hipsters, while his standard Air Force-issue underpants, informally known as 'shreddies', acted as a sort of grubby U.N. peacekeeper between hipster waistband and paisley shirt-tail. John was a good friend and popular with just about everyone at TCW, but some way short of fastidious.

Joules was in his early twenties, and women of all ages flocked around him, hoping to catch his eye and cater for his lust. John was in his early thirties, and women avoided him like the plague, which was just about the only social or communicable disease he didn't contract on a regular basis. I say 'most women', because there was a cross-section of females who did enjoy John, and John enjoyed them. However, if he were financially embarrassed, the lecherous look and answering smile never went any further, because they invariably demanded cash in advance.

That first exercise to Geilenkirchen, to the west of Cologne, was notable for several 'firsts'. It was my first NATO exercise, and the first time I saw TCW at work and in earnest. It was the first time I had been anywhere farther than the Channel Islands, and the first time I witnessed the stupidity of those I had always considered above mistakes; namely, the commissioned officers. It was the first time I had ever flown in an aircraft, well, apart from Cosford, when they gave each of us a twenty-minute stint over the Birmingham chimney stacks in a Chipmunk trainer. It was the first time I had spent an entire night in a bar, and the first time I drank German beer and schnapps chasers. It was the first time I had ever been anywhere where the coinage differed and English wasn't the first language. Most importantly, it was the first time I was ever French-kissed.

We flew to Germany from Brize Norton in Oxfordshire in an Argosy Freighter. The Argosy looked like a sleeker version of the old Beverly transport plane, with twin booms connecting the tail section. I always held a fondness for the Argosy, partly because it was my first experience of flying in a real aircraft, and partly because, unlike the Hercules and Belfast, the Argosy didn't profess to be anything other than a basic and workmanlike freighter.

The journey was uncomfortable and uneventful, and when we arrived at the Geilenkirchen airbase there was good and bad news waiting for us. The good news was that we would sleep in the transit block, in proper beds, with sheets and blankets, instead of having to use our camp beds and sleeping bags. The bad news was that our reputation had preceded us and we were officially banned from all permanent camp entertainment, and any other places where alcohol was served or vulnerable women might be at risk.

I looked from face to face as the Chief broke the news, wondering how such a volatile group might react to the order, which was only a fag paper's width short of slander. To my amazement, they didn't say a word. On the contrary, as we headed down to the bedding store the mood was cheerful and relaxed. I spoke to Doggett, about why nobody in the group appeared in the least bit interested or concerned with the edict's inference. His answer came as a surprise.

"Can't blame them, can you now? It's the animal magnetism, you see. We've got it in spades and the women love it, especially those hoity-toity ones. You see, the RAF's scared to death that some pilot officer WAAF from a well-to-do family is gonna get herself pissed-up and then gang-banged by a bunch of drunken louts in combat gear. I reckon that whenever we're around station commandants must lie awake at night worrying.

"You see, the outcome could be serious; for him and for the Air Force. He'd probably have any future elevation to the Air ranks shelved, and there'd be general media uproar. It could put the cause of women in the armed forces back a hundred years, and then what would all those liberal pillocks up in Westminster do? Multiple couplings across a polished table in the officers' mess is one thing, but they can't have well-to-do young ladies being banged wholesale, and, God forbid, maybe even knocked-up by the hoi polloi, can they now? Well, at least, not inside the camp, not in a place where it's your responsibility. It's a bit of a compliment, when you come to think about it."

I couldn't believe he was serious.

"How on earth could that possibly be a compliment?"

"Well, you see, when the SAS are away on other camps they're not allowed to drink alcohol, in case they get into a fight and kill somebody. It's the same basic problem with us; we're just less vicious and a hell of a lot better looking."

I studied the pock-marked features and bad teeth in the hope that he might be joking. He clearly wasn't, and so I came to the conclusion that dear old John Doggett came from a different planet, and this was a conversation going nowhere. I finished making up my bed, and then got the transport to the communications centre, intending to check out the shift roster.

They'd positioned the communications centre with the rest of the tented encampment, on the far side of the airfield. It comprised around twenty, twelve-by-twelve tents laced together to form one large tented area. The watch was twelve hours on and twelve hours off, then twelve hours on and thirty-six hours off. This gave us a fair amount of free time to explore and relax, but the twelve hour stints dragged, and were less than ideal.

Being my first exercise, and given my relatively tender years, they assigned me to the least important duty in the centre: a point-to-point dual simplex teleprinter, which in plain English means that we had one teleprinting machine for transmission and another for reception. They'd hooked it up on a couple of fixed links, which ran between us and the forward comms site on the other side of the airfield. It was hardly used, because, unless aircraft were taking off or landing, people could almost shout to one another over such a distance, and just about anything was more efficient than simplex manual teleprinting.

However, it was good experience, because most used the field telephone, which ran along the same conduit. This meant that an unnecessary link, using all but obsolete technology, became even more unnecessary and even more obsolete, and left me with little to do. I was able to wander around and see what went on.

Johnny Haynes was in charge of booking and routing signals, which demanded that he check the original for accuracy, and then decide the best route and medium for transmission. We called him Johnny Haynes rather than his real name, which I never discovered, because he came from Fulham, the same area of West London as a former England soccer captain of that name.

I had never taken that much notice of Johnny Haynes, because we had nothing in common. He was quiet, drank soft drinks, and preferred building model aircraft to chasing girls. I wasn't, and I didn't. He knew his way around a communications centre, though, because booking-in signals was one of the most important tasks, as I was about to discover. I wandered over to chat and see what he was doing, and found him talking to a young Flight Lieutenant, who had brought in a signal.

"I sorry, but I can't accept that, sir, not in that condition."

Johnny Haynes held out the signal for the Flight Lieutenant, who bristled and said, "Of course you can. What's wrong with it?"

I say 'young', but the Flight Lieutenant had to be seven or eight years older than me. He just seemed younger.

"I can't tell the threes from the eights, the Os from the zeros, the fives from the Ss, and the zeros from the sixes...sorry, sir, it's not clear enough. It'll need redrafting. You see, it's a strike request, which usually comes in to here over CW or RT, and they're usually double-checked and typewritten when they're received. Sorry, sir, CW's a Morse circuit and RT's a voice circuit."

The young officer snatched at the signal and began reading. He was clearly not amused, and equally clearly not going to allow a mere SAC to fob him off, especially one who spoke to him as though he were an imbecile.

"Well, it's obvious . . . these are zeros, these are threes, this is an eight, that's clearly a five and that's a six. For God's sake man, try using your bloody initiative for a change."

He tossed it back on the desk and glared triumphantly. Johnny Haynes picked it up and studied it again. To give him his due, and despite the Flight Lieutenant's arrogance, he preserved the same even-toned façade of calm bureaucracy.

"And you're the originator of this are you, sir?"

"Well, of course I'm not."

"But as the messenger you're willing to take responsibility for interpreting the time and coordinates on an air-strike request, are you, sir?"

Referring to him as a messenger did not sit well on such lofty shoulders.

"Don't be so bloody impertinent. Look here, Airman, it came into headquarters over the telephone, because one of your bloody circuits was down. I'm just trying to do you a favour. Now, for God's sake stop prevaricating and just send the bloody signal; and hurry up with my stamped copy. It's marked Immediate, you know."

Johnny didn't bat an eyelid.

"I can see that, sir. They mostly are, but unless you're willing to take responsibility for interpreting these figures, I can't send it, or not like this."

Since his arrival at the centre, the young officer had suffered varying states of indifference, anger, arrogance, frustration and rage. He had been about to add apoplexy to that list when the Chief, who had been quietly listening, wandered over and intervened.

"Good morning, sir. So, what's the problem, Johnny?"

Johnny Haynes had been about to answer, but the young officer interrupted.

"I'll tell you the problem, Flight Sergeant. This airman is being rude, uncooperative and thoroughly insubordinate. Now I want this signal processed immediately, and I want something done about this man's attitude."

The Chief didn't hesitate. He glared at Johnny, then relaxed and smiled an apology at the Flight Lieutenant as he handed him a ballpoint pen and a blank message form.

"Yes, sir, of course, sir. Now, if you'd care to redraft the signal so we can all read the numbers a little more clearly, we'll send it straight away, sir."

"Oh, for God's sake. Look, it's only a bloody exercise, man." Then, when it became clear the Chief wasn't going to budge, he added, "Give me the pen. God knows what people like you are going to do if there ever is a real war."

"Thank you, sir; that's good of you."

The young officer grudgingly accepted a seat, and sat down to redraft the signal. The chief watched him for a moment, and then turned to speak to Johnny Haynes.

"And you apologise to the officer for wasting his time. And send that straight away. Oh, and make sure the Flight Lieutenant's name is clearly printed underneath his authorisation signature."

"Yes, Chief."

"Good, good. Then, if the coordinates are wrong and we send a squadron of fighter-bombers into Soviet-occupied East Germany, we can tell Reuters, Tass and the News of the World precisely who issued the order that started World War Three."

I wish that I could have frozen that moment, because as he doubled back to headquarters with the unsent signal in his hot little hand, the look of horror embossed in crimson across that Flight Lieutenant's face was priceless.

Beside the suddenly red-faced Flight Lieutenant, there were several other, mostly junior, youthful and inexperienced officers we only saw once. One Flying Officer arrived at the commcen entrance with a recently received signal. His copy of the signal was indistinct and the print faded. The teleprinter ribbon obviously needed changing. Johnny Haynes had been about to apologise for the mistake, when the young Flying Officer demanded we send another signal, asking the operator at the other end to press harder on his keys. It's true, I swear to goodness.

Another similarly wet-behind-the-ears Pilot Officer was obviously feeling homesick. He appeared at the commcen entrance with a newly drafted signal in hand.

"I want you to send this immediately." He then, a little less authoritatively, added, "By telegram, to a private address in Lincolnshire. You can send telegrams, can't you?"

Johnny Haynes was on a tea break. The Chief was standing in.

"No problem, sir. We'll send it to the MOD in Whitehall. They'll pass it by inland telegram."

The Chief looked at the signal and smiled quietly, and so I glanced over his shoulder. I won't disclose the name of the lady, but the text read . . . 'Happy Birthday, darling. Missing you like mad. Home soon, Love Geoffrey'. There were two Xs at the bottom, presumably kisses.

"I shouldn't do this you know, sir."

The young officer gave a weak smile.

"Well, perhaps not officially, but it is her birthday today. Can't you make an exception, Flight Sergeant. I would be most grateful."

The young officer seemed such a pleasant and modest type. The Chief relented.

"I'll see what I can do, sir."

With that he took the signal, stamped it, and handed the young officer the second copy. He then placed the top copy at the bottom of a pile of other signals, similarly awaiting processing.

""What are you doing?"

"Sorry, sir, they're precedence signals, to do with the exercise. We have to send them first."

"What do you mean . . . have to?"

Suddenly, a more recognisable and arrogant 'sprog zobbit' had replaced the inoffensive young officer. The Chief flashed a caution, which went unheeded as the young officer began to rant.

"Her birthday's today. I want it sent now. That's an order."

To give him his due, the Chief did try to explain as he thumbed through the pile of signals.

"Look sir, these are all immediate precedence, and these are priority precedence, and those at the bottom are routine. I understand the urgency and I'll try to get to yours as soon as I can."

The young officer obviously had a great deal to learn, and, from the look on the Chief's face, little time in which to do so. He snatched at the signal, scrawled the word 'immediate' across the precedence box, and replaced it on top of the pile. The Chief looked wearily at him.

"You don't have the authority to do that, sir; you need to be at least a Wing Commander."

By this time a small crowd had gathered to watch the fun. Partly because of that, and partly because he was a jumped-up little twit, the young Pilot Officer found it hard to back down.

"And I'm telling you, Flight Sergeant, to stop being obstreperous and obey my orders."

In all the time I knew the Chief I never saw him lose his temper, and this was no exception. He picked up the signal, screwed it into a ball, and casually tossed it into the nearest waste bag. Then he leaned across the table, fixed the young Pilot Officer with an unwavering stare, and said, "Fuck off, will you, Geoffrey . . . there's a good officer."

They'd erected a beer tent alongside the mess tent, a vast and uninviting place that sold tins of Heineken and Amstel and packets of nuts and crisps. The only time we risked the place we found it full of administrative staff and the usual local station loudmouths. Station loudmouths were a little bit like the old prohibition 'gang-buffs', or 'asexual friggin groupies', as the enviably good-looking Joules called them. One or two would appear at every exercise, wearing combat jackets, which they claimed to be from a former death-or-glory life. They'd try to impress us with how tough they were, and how much they knew about everything deadly and dangerous.

Some of us, new to large-scale military exercise, hadn't experienced anything like this before, and so we sat listening in amazement. Thankfully, the worldly Doggett came to our aid. He recommended we avoid such people at all costs, and so we set off toward the lights in the distance.

The road from the main camp gate to the local village was as straight as a die, and about three miles long. This was fine on the way there, because you were reasonably fresh and relatively sober, but a nightmare on the way back, because you invariably weren't. It was an essential journey for visitors, though, because the local village boasted a bar called Mama's.

I can't remember Mama, although I must have seen her, because, as well as being the owner, she looked after the takings, managed the staff and controlled the customers. Customer control was essential in Mama's, because forces personnel packed the bar, and the bar stayed open twenty-four hours a day. It was essential, too, because Mama had two daughters, who also worked in the bar. It only took one glance at the blonde curvaceous and capricious Sonja and her younger sister, the dark seductive and mischievous Edith, to understand why I had failed to notice Mama and why this bar was so much more popular than the rest.

Sonja and Edith were classic examples of how women always do, always have, and always will effortlessly control men without any need for aggression or competition. They were two wiggling, giggling, curvaceous and beautiful young women, who loved being women, loved being feminine and flirtatious, loved men, and loved men to love them. They were also determined young women, in total control of themselves and every man they met along the way.

Between them, they managed and manipulated every pair of hungry eyes, every pair of wandering hands, and every lecherous mind in the place. They were certainly in control of me, or I should say, the young, sensuous, Edith was in control of me. The blonde-haired Sonja had more sophisticated fish to fry than a naïve and blushing sprat of a senior aircraftman.

Sonja spoke fluent English, and was reasonably fluent in several other languages, but the younger Edith spoke little English, other than that necessary to do her job. In fact, Edith offered no verbal communication, other than German and a few words of Pidgin English. However, at nineteen going on thirty-five, that dark-haired young temptress could communicate the erotic intent behind a provocative wiggle or flashing-eyed smile in a dozen different languages.

She first wiggled and smiled that impish provocation at me as I walked into the bar on the first night, and I was instantly smitten. So smitten that I spent the rest of that night, and most of the next two, waiting for an encore. I would watch her as she flitted from table to table, studying every giggle and wiggle, until she relented, put down the tray, took me by the hand, led me outside and around the back of the bar, and kissed me on the mouth.

No one had ever kissed me on the mouth before. Well, apart from Susan Creech, one night at a party, but never someone as sexually provocative as Edith, and never like that. She shoved me against the wall, moulded her body to mine, forced my lips apart, and began exploring my mouth with a squirming and mischievous tongue. I stood, unable to move, trying to fathom how anything so presumptuous, intimate and ostensibly disgraceful could feel so wonderful.

I wasn't certain at the time, or have any wish to tell you precisely what happened during the ten minutes or so I spent forced up against that wall around the side of Mama's Bar, but after ten glorious minutes she whispered 'auf wiedersehen', smoothed her skirt, adjusted her blouse, and slipped quietly back through the side door into the smoke-filled bar. I also remember that it took a further fifteen minutes of restoring composure and form before I was in any condition to return.

It was to a less than subtle roar of approval that I did finally return, offered by comrades who had assumed rather more than the truth. However, it took three more days and nights before I came to realise that the fiercely erotic Edith wasn't as hopelessly in love with me as I with her. Three days and nights of sitting in the corner, sipping at my beer, and seeing a mischievous young beauty slip in and out of that same side door with a succession of similarly infatuated young men, before I finally understood. And so I took my battered ego and broken heart, and gloomily decided that I would have to look elsewhere for my first adult love and my next youthful experience.

Instead of Mama's Bar, I started taking the bus across the border, to Heerlen in Holland, in that little pouch of land that looks as if it should belong to Belgium. I made for a discothèque and bar in the centre of town, a place that didn't have the beautiful Edith to torment my youthful infatuation, that didn't cause drunken tears to well up, that didn't invoke jealousy, and wouldn't leave such a naïve and inexperienced young heart so badly broken.

However, young hearts are like young limbs, they mend quickly. Two weeks later I climbed aboard the Argosy and left my first ever military exercise, a significantly wiser young man.

But I will never forget the beautiful and sultry Edith's impish smile and seductive wiggle. I will never forget those electric ten minutes of erotic discovery and frantic excitement, and I will never forget the pain I felt watching her and her beautiful blonde sister Sonja, boosting trade and breaking hearts at the fabulous Mama's Bar.

Go east, young man, go east

The rest of that year involved a constant stream of military exercises. I travelled everywhere from the Hudson Bay Lowland, one of the coldest places I have ever known, to the officially hottest place on earth, the Sahara Desert.

Sadly neither of those two constants involved erotic young women with intertwining limbs and flickering tongues, but in April of the following year, I got the news that I had been eagerly anticipating since my arrival at Tangmere.

We were off to the Far East, to the Malay Peninsular and a place called Penerak, where we were to spend three weeks in the jungle under canvas, with only water and composition rations for nourishment. On our side in the war games to come would be the Gurkhas. Against us would be the Australians and a then relatively unknown outfit called the Special Air Service.

At the time I knew little about the fighting credibility of our opponents, but the allotted forces secretly pleased me, because I had heard something of the Gurkhas. People said they were tough and capable, and the best jungle fighters in the world. I'd not heard all that much about the SAS, though, and what I had heard had been sketchy third-hand information.

You see the SAS was the least of my worries, because images of survival in the Malayan jungle unnerved me more than anything. I had visions of giant pythons swallowing undersized Gurkhas whole, and of king cobras and poisonous insects crawling into my sleeping bag, while a billion mosquitoes sent me into a delirium of madness. Then there were thoughts of hungry leopards and man-eating tigers waiting to ambush me from overhanging branches, and wading through deadly snake-infested swamps, before having to burn the leeches from my skin with a cigarette. All in all, it was not a pleasant or comforting picture that I was mentally painting.

But the silver lining draped around my cloud of apprehension was the acclimatisation period. This was a two-week 'Jolly' before we went into the jungle, and another week when we came out, billeted in the transit block at Seletar, one of two major RAF stations on the island of Singapore.

Singapore today is a thriving metropolis of high-rise buildings and modern commerce. It bears favourable comparison with any financial city centre in the world, and should be applauded for such a feat of social and economic transformation. However, in those days there was nothing modern and sober and efficient and, let me be honest, downright boring about Singapore. In the sixties, the island of Singapore was everything a young man could dream of.

But the jungle clouds were darkening, and that Singapore silver lining was becoming fainter, because everyone was now boasting about previous battles with the Special Air Service, or SAS, as in the first syllable of Sassenach, as it was more usually and knowledgeably pronounced. What they were saying was not good news. It seemed the SAS didn't always play fair, in fact they never played fair. According to the lads, it was no good pointing an SMG or SLR and saying 'Bang, you're dead'. Because, knowing you would be holding an unloaded gun, or at best a gun loaded with blank ammunition, he would simply kick you where it would do the most damage and tell you to go away in short, jerky, sensual movements.

On that first Far Eastern exercise we flew to Singapore on a Britannia. On later trips, for reasons of goodwill and safety, they upgraded us from turbo-prop Britannia to the VC10 jet, but on the first few occasions it was a twenty-two-hour flight, in conditions that would give deep-vein thrombosis to a tin of sardines. We were, however, mostly young, all relatively fit, and all looking forward to the wonders of the Orient. So the journey, as with the exercise itself, was treated as a minor inconvenience in our continuing search for leisure and pleasure. Despite the straightjacket of a seat, I'd been about to nod off when somebody shook me by the shoulder. I looked up and saw Rory Walters holding out an upturned beret brimming with Singapore dollars.

"If you want in to the sweepstake, it's two dollars."

"Sweepstake? What sweepstake?"

"Gonorrhoea sweepstake."

"The what?"

"Are you deaf or something? I said the gonorrhoea sweepstake."

"What's that?"

He shrugged his shoulders and looked back matter-of-factly as he answered.

"Simple enough idea. Everybody sticks two bucks in the hat. First one who gets a dose takes the pot. Doc's gotta confirm it, mind you; can't just start dripping and expect to claim the money. You in or not?"

"Uh, yeah, yeah, sure."

In truth, I wasn't at all sure, but my entry into the sweep was all part of a clever plan to disguise the true extent of my sexual naiveté. I decided two dollars was a small price to pay in preserving that façade, and handed it over, only to have my already slender odds extended still further.

"What if nobody gets a dose?"

"Don't be fucking stupid. We're going to Singas." He looked wistful as he added, "Although I don't know why any of us bother, 'cos Doggett wins it every time."

"Doggett?"

"Oh yeah; it's odds-on." He leaned over his shoulder and spoke to one of the others. "How many times in a row has Doggett won it now?"

A chorus of voices answered.

"Four."

"Four, and it's a racing fucking certainty that this trip it's gonna be five."

"Why?"

"Because Doggett always goes down Syph Alley as soon as he gets there. It's the same every time." I must have looked bemused, because he explained further. "Syph Alley; runs along the back of Bugis Street. Nobody in their right mind goes there, except for Doggett, some retarded rockapes, and a few of the hornier good old boys off the U.S. Fleets.

"Oh yeah, it's your first trip, isn't it?" I nodded weakly. "Well, keep well away from Syph Alley. There's more cases of syph down that one badly-lit street than anywhere else in the world."

"But I thought you called it the gonorrhoea sweepstake?"

"Gonorrhoea, syphilis, who cares?" He shrugged his shoulders. "Even paid out on a bloody good dose of NSU once."

"Which presumably went to Doggett?"

"Oh yeah, it's the same every time. He's gotta be odds-on."

"So how do you know it's not the same dose?"

Such a simple thought had obviously not occurred to him.

"Bloody hell, that's a thought. You might have something there. Hey, Mel. Got a bloke here reckons Doggett might be conning us; reckons it could be the same dose that never clears up."

There was a pause of a few seconds before a voice called back.

"Possible, I suppose, but how the hell do we find out?"

I looked on down the plane to where Doggett had been listening and was now openly glaring at me. He climbed out of his seat, ambled down the aisle to where I was sitting, glared again, and growled out in a voice that had clearly once boomed out from the valleys.

"Don't be fucking stupid. If that was the case it would have dropped off by now, wouldn't it?" The glare relaxed. "You want me to lob it out and show it to you?"

A cacophony of nos greeted the offer. Doggett smiled, broadly and knowledgeably, and then ambled back to his seat, while the sweepstake organiser shrugged his shoulders and nodded in reluctant acknowledgement of the assumptions logic. I felt I'd handled the matter reasonably well, hiding my naiveté behind a well-considered question, but, before I had time to enjoy my new-found celebrity status, blew what little credibility had been so cleverly and cautiously amassed.

"So why don't you go down to Syph Alley as well . . . beat him at his own game?"

I should have quit when I was ahead. He disparagingly viewed my ignorance and sneered.

"Look, prat. We're not trying to get a dose. Most of us, well most of us, apart from Doggett, are trying their level bloody best not to get one." He sneered again and moved on down the plane, and I shrank back into my seat in red-faced embarrassment as I heard him say, "Dumb fuck."

We first staged at Bahrain, which didn't bear mention, but the next stop was Gan, the RAF's major Far-East staging post, set among the Maldives.

The Maldives, as we now know, are a collection of languid and picturesque atolls lying in the middle of the Indian Ocean and protected by coral reefs. Today, half the western world has been on holiday to the Maldives, but in those days they were all but unknown. Gan suddenly appeared on the left-hand side of the aircraft as a miniature tropical paradise; a shock of green, trimmed with white gold, ringed by turquoise, and set in a deep-blue ocean. It was the first genuinely beautiful, tranquil and unblemished island I had ever seen.

Gan's inhabitants included a few hundred men, each on a nine-month secondment, and a few thousand fruit bats that had the annoying habit of dropping out of the trees and on to passing heads. There were a few million tiny frogs, the hopping variety, and one woman who worked as a Red Cross nurse and was fiercely protective of 'her boys'.

To any sexually liberated young women who might now be reading this and suddenly considering life with the Red Cross on Gan, there were two further and essential qualifications. The first was all-round medical competence. The second was that any interested female had to have reached her seventy-fifth birthday prior to applying.

Frankie Aps was one of the less endearing characters at Tangmere, a fast-talking Londoner from the leeward side of Battersea Bridge. I referred to him as Frankie Aps, because of his favourite catch-phrase, which he used with monotonous regularity. He was a greasy, nasty little man, who took delight in embarrassing wives and girlfriends with crude remarks and inappropriate questions. By now you may have gathered that he wasn't one of my favourite people. He immediately asked where they had billeted the lady.

"Any port in a storm."

He'd announced his intent in true-to-form style, while somebody who clearly didn't know him had incredulously answered, "For God's sake, you can't be serious. She's well into her seventies. What are you, some sick pervert?"

It fell to the worldly Doggett to place a paternal arm around the young man's shoulders and lead us to the bar.

"Now then, my boy, if I were you I should forget all about that, at least until we reach Singas. Come to the bar with the rest of us, and let's all have a bloody good drink."

"But. . ."

"But me no buts, boyo. This is the island of Gan. Here you either drink or wank. There are no other choices worth considering. Now I had a damn good wank on the plane, so right now I reckon I could do with a bloody good drink."

Frankie Aps seemed unconvinced.

"Well, I reckon somebody's gotta be giving her one."

Doggett raised his eyes to the heavens as he led us to the bar.

"So much to learn and so little time. Just take it from one who knows, boyo . . . that is not a port in a storm; that is a dry dock in the blistering heat of the midday sun."

Aps was clearly sceptical of Doggett's motivations.

"You just want to win the sweepstake. You're frightened I might beat you to the money."

Doggett smiled, as if in reminiscence.

"All that you will ever catch from dear old Auntie Florence, over there in sick quarters, is a mouthful of abuse, a knee in the groin, and a bloody good clip round the ear. Now then, my boy, if you're determined to try out any port in a storm you can come with me tomorrow night. I shall show you ports that even the brave Odysseus would not have dared to enter."

Frankie Aps looked around uncertainly, while those who knew pulled faces of distaste and shook their heads in a well-meaning effort to dissuade him from any such foolishness. For once in his short and senseless lifetime wisdom got the better of him.

"No, it's OK. I reckon I'll manage by myself, thanks all the same."

Doggett grinned that same knowledgeable grin, and then ordered up a beer from the nervous-looking islander who had the misfortune to be on NAAFI bar duty that night.

"You may of course please yourself, my boy, but your unwitting loss is my most salacious gain. Two half-litres of Tiger, please, my good man."

The hapless barman answered apologetically. "Only pints, I'm afraid, sir."

"Then I shall take two of those, and a further large clean tankard, plenish'd fairly with an excessively large vodka, and another to follow. Although, on second thoughts, perhaps you'd better make it two to follow, if you would be so kind?"

We watched in silence as the barman poured the beer and haphazardly measured the vodka from a litre bottle into a tumbler. He clearly hadn't understood, because Doggett then ordered him to up-end the tumbler into a second pint jug and follow that with two further haphazard measures. The barman wisely chose to save any further wasted effort by handing over what remained of the bottle to a clearly delighted Doggett. It fell to me to ask.

"Tiger? What's that then?"

Doggett instantly waxed lyrical.

"It is a taste of the Orient itself; a glimpse of what lies beyond the horizon. It is nectar of the finest kind, my boy, a brew of the most sublime ale, to savour and worship, and then savour and worship again. He held the glass tankard up to the light. "Allow me to say this most wondrous product of the noble Tiger brewery is a shower of gold, a demure and magnificent spending, copiously issued from the harlot of Singapore's most sumptuous and bountiful loins."

I suddenly wished I hadn't asked, while Frankie Aps was now foaming at the mouth. To be truthful, I wasn't at all sure whether he was considering Doggett's vulgar description of the beer, or the aged Auntie Florence over there in sick quarters. Doggett had been right in his fulsome praise of the Tiger brewery's own, though. It was the best draught beer I had ever tasted. I was savouring the first pint when the Chief arrived back from the airfield and wandered into the bar.

"Hold it, you lot. You can forget about stopping over for a couple of hours, 'cos they're putting us up in the transit block until tomorrow. So you can all slow down and take it easy, because you've got the rest of the night to drink yourselves into a stupor."

"Why's that then, Chief?"

"Brit's gone U/S. They've got to ship the spares out from Changi. So make your way over to the transit block when you're ready. ETD, nine a.m."

The announcement received a mixed reception. Most smiled good-naturedly and considered the prospect of a night spent under a tropical moon, downing a few pints of Tiger beer. Doggett toasted the great god of aircraft airworthiness. Aps looked disappointed. The rest determined to make the best of the situation and set about the Tiger brewery's finest with some alacrity.

It must have been seven or eight hours later, around 2 a.m. when they finally conceded defeat and closed the airport. To be fair, they had little choice, because there were bodies everywhere. Frankie Aps never did find his 'port in a storm'. They found him folded over some picket fencing outside sick quarters, with a lecherous smile on his face and his trousers around his ankles.

There were bodies just about everywhere: in monsoon ditches, on roads and pathways, outside the commandant's office, down by the cinema, and strewn across the airfield. Most embarrassingly, they found some sprawled across the main runway. In fact, the only place where thirty-eight group bodies were notably absent was the transit block.

Draught Tiger beer, it seemed, was a significantly more powerful brew than your average pint of brown and mild served up at the Eastgate Inn. That, coupled with the balmy conditions and vodka chasers, had disabled to such an extent that they couldn't rouse most of those located.

I had been one of the lucky ones. The beer had similarly affected me, but I'd passed out in the NAAFI bar, and that was acceptable. They poured mugs of coffee down my gullet and ordered me to join the airfield search, led, unbelievably, by the still guzzling and clearly inebriated Doggett.

They put on the airfield and runway lights to aid the search, and I have an enduring memory of the drunken Welshman as he staggered from side to side on an approximate journey down the centre of the runway, stopping every few yards to hitch up his trousers, shield his eyes from the sodium lights, and swig from a litre bottle of vodka, while calling out between belches, "Come along, children, come to Mother."

Finally, and blessedly, even the indomitable Doggett conceded defeat, as he sank to his knees with the inevitable stupid grin fixed across pock-marked features. He would later claim that it was not the effects of fourteen pints of Tiger and a litre or so of vodka, but a natural reaction to the potential loss of valued comrades and the emotional strain of it all. Either way, it allowed us a well-earned break, and so we sat down alongside him on the runway.

With some admiration, we watched him take one last, and to my mind foolishly ambitious swig from his second bottle of vodka, before looking up to the stars and crying out, "God, I love this place!"

He then spent some further moments of reflection in that same kneeling position, swaying from side to side, and softly humming the chorus from *Men of Harlech*, before gathering his resolve, rallying his troops, and negotiating the runway on all fours.

Eventually, after a combined belch and fart of sufficient strength to have registered on the Richter Scale, he gustily expelled such a quantity of vomit from the cast-iron stomach that the resulting pool stretched across the runway and caused others to follow suit.

With that unedifying but clearly essential function performed, the plucky Doggett heroically tried to stand, and for a couple of suspended seconds it even looked as though he'd make it. But then his legs gave way and, amid a spontaneous round of drunken applause, Thirty-Eight Group's favourite son collapsed in a pool of his own vomit and was carried off to the transit block.

Amid much muttering and grumbling and a good many hostile glares, we finally shipped out from that once unspoilt and idyllic tropical island, at just after 1400 hours on the following afternoon, our delayed departure being nothing to do with all the kerfuffle delaying the spares consignment, or the airfield's closure, but because that was how long it had taken to locate everybody, get them sober enough to stand, and then somehow negotiate the Britannia's steps.

It was dark when we arrived at Changi, the other main RAF station on Singapore. I staged through Changi not long ago on a trip to New Zealand, and found a major modern international air terminal. However, in those days it was somewhat less than that.

Changi had a terrible history of internment, deprivation, and the abuse of British prisoners during the Japanese occupation, which began early in nineteen forty-two and only ended with the surrender of Japan in

September of forty-five. There was no sense of history in our thoughts, though, as we shuffled out of the Britannia. All we cared about was finding somewhere to sleep.

My enduring memory from that first night was the smell. It enveloped me like a heavy cloak of perfumed warmth, a glorious aroma of heat and humidity and wood smoke, and all manner of exotic fragrances. It was a unique and splendidly-evocative bouquet that I grew to love, and, just as I never tired of Singapore, I never tired of breathing in that wonderful aroma.

There were so many reasons for my love affair with the old Singapore. The people were overwhelmingly friendly and welcoming and gentle, the men often agitated, but always polite, the children enchanting and always smiling, the women dainty and delicate and quite, quite beautiful. The countryside was full of interesting places and the city more so. Down at the harbour everything was bustling and frantic, with the quayside crammed with all manner of interesting vessels, returning from or en route to all manner of interesting places.

In the city, and some of the busier villages, the people appeared as a cosmopolitan army of colourful ants, scurrying from place to place as they went about the daily business of survival. All talking at nineteen-to-the-dozen as they moved: Chinese, Malay, Indian, African, European, American, Australian, Japanese, and so many other nationalities, all crushed together in that wonderful multicultural melting pot which was Singapore.

In old Singapore there was no denying the poverty, and all that seem to go hand-in-hand with such an entirely unnecessary state of affairs. However, there was also so much culture and colour and interest and excitement to both engage the population and captivate the traveller.

During the day, parts of old Singapore City were quiet; well, apart from the traffic, which was a nightmare. But during the hours of darkness, the place was magical.

The beggars were there, of course, twenty-four hours a day, sitting in the gutter alongside children maimed or dismembered in an attempt to appeal to our 'western consciences'. To many in the Far East and other parts of the world, begging was and is seen as an honourable profession, but I can think of nothing less honourable than the harming of a new-born child, especially to guarantee a meagre income through a lifetime of disability spent begging in the gutter.

Outside of the city you could see the huts and shacks of impoverished families, dotted across the landscape like corrugated sheds on an inner-city council allotment. Each with more than their fair share of people to shelter, and more than their fair share of misery to hide. But there was so much more to Singapore than the street beggars and the poverty.

In the local villages the *machan* stalls displayed wonderfully-smelling food, offered by smiling proprietors who always managed to eke out a living, no matter how lax the hygiene and how unwholesome the fare. Along every village street you would find the same colourful scattering of shops and stalls, run by similarly-agitated shopkeepers who rarely found a customer. If you ventured into the city and along the crowded walkways, there were always colourful stalls and colourful characters, and this was never more apparent than along Change Alley.

I will never forget my first visit to Change Alley and my first ever Singapore taxi ride. It had been on the day following our arrival, and I went into the city with the enviably good-looking Joules. He had been to Singapore many times and knew it well. We walked up from the regular taxi stand at Jalan Kayu and flagged down a 'pick-up' taxi, a cheap method of travelling, which allowed the driver to 'pick-up' anybody else who might hail the taxi on the way. A 'pick-up' taxi could save a good percentage of the fare, but it was an economy that I bitterly regretted making.

We had only travelled a mile or so when I saw an elderly woman crossing the road sixty or seventy yards ahead. Now, forgetting serious road accidents, where the driver is driving too fast or a child dashes out from behind a row of parked cars, we've all seen people cross the road at silly times. An exaggerated braking, a heavy hand on the horn, a few choice words, and we all go about our business, but on this occasion I swear our taxi-driver put his foot on the accelerator.

Whether he hit the wrong pedal, or was too busy scouring the sidewalks for fares, or whether he was simply a homicidal maniac, I know not, but the car hit the poor woman at speed. The impact threw her up and over the bonnet and on to the roof, where she remained for a few moments before sliding to the ground and lying in agony by the roadside.

She had obviously broken both legs, but what internal injuries she sustained I couldn't say. One of the locals sent for an ambulance. Our taxi-driver flagged down a passing taxi.

"You go with him."

The driver seemed unconcerned by the poor woman's condition. He waved for me to get into the second taxi, but I stood my ground and shook my head, incensed by the criminal recklessness of his driving and the sheer callousness of his subsequent behaviour and attitude.

"No chance, mate, I'm giving a statement to the police. You're a bloody lunatic. They should lock people like you up."

"No police. No police. You go with him. You go with him."

The agitation was clear, but I stood my ground.

"No way, I want to see the police."

"No police."

The words had come not from the taxi-driver, but from the woman on the ground. Joules took me aside and explained.

"Forget it, mate, and get into the other cab."

"Forget nothing. You saw what happened."

"Look, the driver probably hasn't got any insurance, the cab's probably unlicensed, she's probably here illegally, and you're a bloody foreign invader who shouldn't be here. And in case you've forgotten, this is a pick-up taxi, and that's illegal, too. Now get into the friggin cab."

I glared at the driver and then grudgingly moved towards the second taxi, but before I'd moved two paces the first driver called out to me.

"You give three dollars."

"What?"

"You give three dollars . . . part fare."

I won't bore you with the precise terms of my reply, or a precise account of my actions. Suffice to say that they had to coax the driver back from where he had hidden, behind the counter of the nearest *machan* stall. By this time a crowd had gathered, and they didn't look happy. Joules apologised profusely, handed over three dollars, pulled me away, and hissed, "Look, we're not taking on the whole friggin village. Get this into your thick skull, you moron: this isn't your country, it's theirs, and they're not interested in your stupid opinions or your half-baked western values. If they say no police, then it's no police. Now just shut the frig up and get into the cab." He nodded to the second driver, who had been studying me with a nervous look on his face. "Seven dollars, into the city . . . Brit Club. OK?"

"OK, John."

Probably for the first time in his entire taxi-driving career, the second driver didn't argue or even try to negotiate. He just blurted out the words and nodded furiously as he cautiously eyed my still-smouldering wrath. He climbed back into the driver's seat and we headed off and into the city. My first ever taxicab ride on the island of Singapore was over, and my second underway.

There were no further accidents or incidents, but when we arrived in the city my humour still hadn't improved. We headed to the Britannia Club bar for a swift beer and some calm, and then wandered out and into the city, heading for Change Alley.

Change Alley didn't disappoint. As we turned into the alleyway and shoved our way through the crowd, the scene of sheer pandemonium was astonishing and the noise deafening. There were the traders, fighting with each other and the world as they peddled trinkets to rich and poor alike. There were policemen and street pedlars, street entertainers and buskers, crooks and cheats, hustlers and swindlers, pickpockets and tramps, and foreign tourists by the boatload. Along Change Alley, on any given afternoon, one could see the broadest cross-section of humanity, from the poorest waif to the wealthiest wife. Unfortunately, it was two of those same individuals, bartering over a carved wooden figurine, who dragged me into my second confrontation of the day.

Since that day in Albrighton when I walked back to camp with my head bowed, and in all of my adult life, I have suffered from the same problem. I have never been able to tell the difference between the time to stand and fight for principle and fairness, and the time to shut my mouth and walk away. It is a trait I blame the Wee Beastie for; well you've got to blame someone. It is also a trait that has drawn me into innumerable scrapes and arguments and fights over the years, and cost me friends and colleagues and so many career moves I've lost count. This would prove to be another example of that same pig-headed stupidity.

The woman was English, in her late twenties, I guessed, obviously well-educated, well-spoken, and well-to-do; one of those classically good-looking women who look like they've just stepped off the cover of an extortionately priced glossy magazine. You know the type: heavily made-up, at two in the afternoon, with expensively-streaked blonde hair, and designer sunglasses, and faultlessly-tailored clothes clinging precisely to cosmetically sculpted contours, looking and sounding like the same million dollars that undoubtedly once belonged to an elderly husband.

I instantly, and probably unfairly, pigeon-holed her as unapproachable: a porcelain-featured beauty who would reject a penniless and handsome young stud, no matter how lasciviously he drooled, but happily succumb to a wealthy geriatric, no matter how uncontrollably he dribbled.

She was arguing with a young Chinaman, or he looked Chinese to my inexpert eye. Dressed in a pair of threadbare khaki shorts and a tattered Coca-Cola tee shirt, he sat on a plain wooden stool behind an upturned tea chest and carved wooden figurines with a short clasp-knife. He had the completed carvings laid out on the tea chest in front of him. The porcelain blonde had obviously taken a fancy to a figure of a dragon, beautifully crafted and rampant, and carved from a block of dark hardwood. She clearly intended buying it, because she was holding the dragon in one hand and eight Singapore dollars in the other.

The young man wanted ten dollars for the article, not eight, and even though that was less than a tenth of its U.K. high street value she wouldn't budge from her original offer of eight. I stood and watched them bartering for a couple of minutes, partly because I found it interesting, and partly because that faultlessly-tailored skirt was so beautifully cut and so wonderfully close-fitting.

Finally and reluctantly, the young man dropped the price to nine dollars, but flatly refused to reduce it further. She pretended to sulk and stamped her foot, and repeated her demand that he let her have the carving for eight dollars. He refused, and so she pouted and stamped her foot again.

Then her friend arrived, an equally beautiful and sexy lady, who struck the same arrogantly seductive pose as she stood waiting, looking like an auburn-haired clone of the beautifully tailored blonde. When I saw them together, I thought, it's no wonder we look alike to the Chinese, but I can also remember thinking that no matter how beautiful they might be, I didn't much like them.

The auburn-haired friend was impatient to be elsewhere. She asked the porcelain blonde to get a move on, but the blonde refused and once again held out the eight dollars, like a spoilt child whose doting parents always mistook petulance and tantrums for individuality. The young man explained to her, in his best pidgin English, that the article had taken him almost a day to complete. She seemed unmoved by that, and continued to hold out the four notes. It was then that I stuck my oversized nose in to where it was clearly neither wanted nor needed.

"Here, for God's sake, have a dollar on me."

As I somewhat extravagantly dropped the money on to the tea chest the auburn-haired clone stepped back and the Chinaman looked bemused, but the porcelain blonde turned and glared.

"And just what the hell do you think you're doing?"

I answered her in my best outraged proletariat.

"I know it must be great fun for you, squabbling with a peasant over some unwanted coins lying in a silk purse at the bottom of a designer handbag, but I need to get by. You see, I have to get back to work, obviously unlike you, and this guy needs to get on with earning his living and feeding his family. Oh, and I do realise that filling the belly of some malnourished baby, lying in a shack outside Jalan Kayu, is of no interest to you, but surely a dollar can't be that important?"

There was plenty of room to pass, but I'd added that bit for effect. I left the lone dollar on the tea chest and started to walk away, feeling hugely self-righteous and enormously pleased with my little speech. Little Miss Petulant dropped the rest of the money on to the tea chest and then started after me, complete with newly purchased trophy. She was clearly still furious, but not enough to offer to refund my money, I noticed.

"I said, just what the hell do you think you're doing, and just who the hell do you think you are? And how dare you speak to me like that?" I stared a wilting indifference back at her and then started to walk away, but this was obviously a woman used to getting her own way, and equally obviously not used to suffering criticism. "You mentioned Jalan Kayu. Are you stationed at Seletar? What's your name and rank? Come on, I demand that you tell me. I'll have you know that I'm on excellent terms with the Air Commodore there."

That was just what I needed to hear. Of all the dames, in all the alleyways, in all the world, I had to pick one on intimate terms with an officer of air rank. For once, self-preservation got the better of me. I kept walking and said nothing. If only others had done the same the whole sorry episode might well have passed without further incident.

"I gotta be honest, babe. From where I'm standing, I'd have to say that old Air Commodore's getting the best of the deal. No wonder they have to drive him everywhere. So tell me, babe, how does a guy get to be on excellent terms with a dynamite chick like you?"

That had been Joules, of course, in typically overt and embarrassingly clichéd fashion. He'd been crudely and blatantly admiring the unmistakeably feminine figure beneath that tailored skirt, and being less than helpful in the process. I noticed that Jules always stressed the Liverpool dialect whenever any female was in earshot. He claimed it helped him to score, which could have had something to do with the then unparalleled popularity of Messrs Lennon, McCartney, Harrison and Starr. I comforted myself in the knowledge that at least he hadn't said 'what's the score then, babe' but I guess there was still time.

The porcelain blonde glared up at him as though he'd just crawled out from under a rock, while he smiled his most alluring and provocative smile back at her. For an instant she relaxed the frown, and I thought I'd detected a spark of interest, but it quickly faded and I saw something I'd not seen before, or since: the flat and unequivocal rejection of Julian Carter by a mature, heterosexual female.

"The two of you are together, I presume. Now I wonder why that doesn't surprise me. Well, I'm not having people like you insulting me in public, so come on, I want your names." When it was clear we had no intent of telling her, she stamped her foot for the umpteenth time that afternoon, in that same well-practised display of petulant frustration. "I'll find out, you know, I can promise you that. I'll find out, anyway, you see if I don't, and when I do. . ."

Joules appeared singularly unimpressed by the threat, and singularly impressed with everything else, but if his chatting-up technique was archaic, his putting-down technique was Neanderthal.

"You don't have to go to all that trouble, babe. If you're looking for a quick bang you just have to say so and I'll be happy to sort you out. I mean, let's face it, babe. . . vertically, you look like sex on a stick, but I bet no one's ever nailed you to the dirt and given you a seriously bloody good seeing-to in your entire spoilt and pampered friggin life."

I still hadn't said a word, but Joules clearly didn't take rejection well. More to the point, he was showing his indignation by being more and more offensive, and less and less helpful, with each successive Liverpudlian syllable.

With crudely worded insult delivered, he shoved me into a waiting trishaw and we left her standing at the side of the road, simmering and speechless, alongside her auburn-haired friend, who seemed similarly taken aback, but was nonetheless grinning from ear to ear.

He told the trishaw driver to peddle us over to the Hong Kong bar and we disappeared into the traffic. Once underway, we changed the destination, though, just in case the porcelain blonde might decide to follow us with some of those friends in high places she had spoken of.

"What the bloody hell did you say all that for?"

I hadn't spoken during the journey, largely because, as a suicidal trishaw rider weaved in and out of the busy traffic, I had been too terrified to speak. When we finally arrived at some sleazy backstreet bar with a name I can't remember, I paid the cyclist and let the enviably good-looking Joules know that I was less than happy with him. He loudly protested his innocence.

"What the frig are you talking about? You're the one who decided to pick on God's lieutenant's friggin leg-over, and you were the one who started it all, remember? What was all that social conscience crap about designer handbags and babies' empty bellies? I was just being a mate and giving you moral support, that's all."

Butter wouldn't melt, but I was having none of it.

"Moral support? Is that what you said? Are you being serious? For Christ's sake, Joules, I may have started it, and I reckon I had a perfect right to, but we kinda lost the moral high ground when you offered to shag her."

He nodded happily and then grinned broadly back at me.

"I wasn't being greedy. You could have had the other one. I'll tell yer something, I reckon that little red-head would have been more than up for it. She looked like a right little goer. I reckon she'd have blown the pair of us out in bubbles, if we'd asked her nicely. Anyway, like I said before, I was just backing you up, wasn't I?"

"Bollocks, you were just trying to get your leg over."

He shrugged matter-of-factly and spoke to me over his shoulder as we headed on into the bar.

"D'yer blame me? I'll tell yer, if I had done, that stuck-up little madam would have been too busy learning to walk again to have complained about you. I might have even got you yer dollar back. Mind you, she was a looker, wasn't she? What a babe. It was worth a dollar just to see those lips pouting up at you, and did you see that arse? That arse was friggin magnificent."

He shrugged his shoulders and sighed in lascivious reminiscence. When we reached the bar, he said, "Two Tigers, wack," in his best scouse. The man behind the bar passed over two bottles. Joules theatrically raised his bottle high, and said, "A toast, I think. To that arse . . . To that magnificent friggin arse."

For the first time that day I couldn't find anything to argue about.

Jungle warfare, and bar-room skirmishes

I loved Singapore, especially at night. At night there were market traders by the dozen, selling garishly illuminated, cheap and cheerful produce at cheap and cheerful prices. There were thieves and pickpockets, and beggars and pimps, and street girls by the truckload, but for all that, or perhaps because of all that, the place was magical.

Nowadays I have the wisdom of hindsight and age to temper the youthful enthusiasm I once held for the old Singapore, but at the time I was no different to any other young man, choosing not to see the poverty and suffering, only seeing the potential for selfish enjoyment.

The Bugis Street crossway was the place to be, or certainly after ten o'clock at night. It was said that if you hadn't seen the dawn come up over Bugis Street, you hadn't lived. We'd descend on the place, mob-handed because it was safer, and then sit and drink and chat with the transvestites, known as Kai-Tais. Not that I'm any surer of the spelling now than I was then.

Many of the Kai-Tais were disconcertingly beautiful, and well-educated and fascinating to talk to. We would sit and discuss all manner of subjects with them, from politics to music, and from the meaning of life to the latest Hollywood movie. They would then lighten the mood by telling us amusing tales of Bugis Street and the many colourful people they had known.

They would tell risqué tales of disorientated travellers who had so easily fallen for the deceptive beauty of the Kai-Tais: graphic accounts of lonely men, thousands of miles from home and loved ones, men who had salved that loneliness with a few brief hours of tenderness and passion in the company of a beautiful and delicate Singapore flower.

They would describe the rugged good looks of boyfriends past, and show us photographs of smiling faces, and we would chuckle and scoff at the naiveté of handsome red-blooded young heterosexuals who had declared their love and spent their lust in the subtle glow of a candlelit boudoir, or the confusing gloom of a discreetly lit apartment.

Sometimes they'd talk at length of the men behind the smiles, men who had left the next morning, none the worse and none the wiser for the experience; men who had vowed to return and declared their devotion with love letters and tokens of affection. Men from the four corners of the globe: young men, ordinary men, naïve men, in love with a fantasy. Men who would hopefully never return to the island, and never discover the truth of the beautiful Singapore flower they once knew, or the special distinction of a love they once unwittingly shared with another man.

I must confess I loved those nights of laughter and risqué tales and intrigue, and became addicted to them. As each nightly Bugis Street cabaret rolled on, I found myself increasingly embroiled in the fun and vibrancy of it all. I would talk and drink and laugh and joke, seeing the bustle, and hearing the noise and the chatter, listening to the arguments, and watching the fights, and meeting and greeting so many different people, from so many different places, all gathered on a simple illuminated crossway in a little-known corner of South-East Asia, forgetting our troubles, and whiling away the hours of darkness in the most splendid and decadent of fashions.

Almost every night during that two-week acclimatisation period you would find me in the thick of it all, chattering drunken nonsense to the pseudo-intellectuals at four in the morning, or playing noughts-and-crosses with the street urchins for fifty cents a game, soaking up the atmosphere and seeping into the crowded canvas of the special place that was Bugis Street. Seeing it all and hearing it all as I watched the world going around and waited for the dawn to appear.

However, although I spent most nights during that first two week period along the Bugis Street crossway, it wasn't to Bugis Street that I first headed. That first night I had more important issues on my mind: an outstanding agenda item, going all the way back to Albrighton Sally in the field that day. It was an item of importance, one that demanded renewed courage, a steeled resolve, and the long-anticipated loss of something I held no value for whatsoever . . . my virginity.

Tonight was the night it would finally happen. I'd made up my mind. Tonight was the night when I would leave all that embarrassing naiveté behind me, and become the 'man of the world' I had always wanted to be. Tonight I was going to get myself seriously laid.

I left the rest of them at the Tokyo Bar, which had an unwholesome reputation for the sort of education I was seeking, but was a little too public. I headed instead to the New Zealand Bar, because I had been told that this bar wasn't hugely popular, because it was off the beaten track, but was just about as sleazy and disgusting as any bar on the island.

I remember feeling the cooling air as the trishaw sped through the balmy Singapore night en route to the New Zealand bar, and must admit to a degree of youthful exhilaration, partly at the prospect of spending an evening at such an infamous location, and partly at the charting of unknown sexual territory. It was sometime later, though, after I had arrived and paid the fare, that I began to assess the reality of that uncharted territory and lose my nerve.

She must have seen me standing there, looking anxiously up at the neon sign and hopping from one foot to the other, because she sashayed over, took my arm, guided me to the door, and said, "You wanna drink, John?" Then, when I failed to answer, "We go in, you buy me drink? OK John? We have good time, I be good to you . . . you see."

Within a minute and thirty seconds of my drunken arrival, she had introduced herself, banished my indecision, herded me through the door and across the floor, and negotiated her percentage with the bar manager. A minute and thirty seconds after that, she had manoeuvred me into a booth, shoved me against the wall, ordered drinks and snacks from a giggling accomplice, unzipped my fly, awakened my sleeping ignorance, coaxed my senses from dulled to delirium, and discovered the precise location of my wallet.

The she in question was young Malaysian girl, whose name I instantly forgot, but whose face and charm I never will. She was a delightful and consummate beauty, with daintily expressed vulgarity and well-practised, fluttering fingers that swiftly and expertly overcame the anaesthetic mischief of excessive alcohol to incite a visible lust from beneath my nylon zip-fastener.

I was captivated, and she knew it, chattering sexily and constantly, and only releasing my bewilderment to order more drinks from the bar. However, each time she completed that expensively frequent and clearly important chore, her fingers appeared more than happy to resume my temporarily suspended education.

And so I sat transfixed, in a heady mixture of lust and delight, watching her delicate and mischievous smile, and breathing in the-never-to-be-forgotten aroma of peppermint and garlic.

I can still picture every last detail of her beauty, still hear each and every daintily expressed vulgarity, still recall the blissful memory of every delicate electric caress from those dainty fingertips, and every bolt of surging adrenaline that coursed through me.

I remember, too, those desperate moments of sheer, blind panic as her heated breath sent goose bumps down my neck and encouraged my own fumbling exploration higher. And while lilting tones encouraged, insistent feminine fingers guided my own to where a naïve and trepidant young man nervously caressed and silently marvelled at the delicate perfection of the female form, realising at least a part of the magnificent truth which would be destined to motivate his every waking moment for the next fifty years. (Well, hopefully.)

I can also recall that same divine creature offering her all to me, in whispers that sent shocks of excitement through my teenage imaginings. I knew that whatever else life might hold, it couldn't possibly get any better than this. I knew, too, that those husky syllables of absolute temptation were just about the most wonderful thing that anybody had ever said to me.

"You want fuck me, John?" She had squeezed the words into my ear, and I felt a surge of sexual adrenaline. "I know a place, good place, special place. I give you best jig-a-Jig in Singapore. Extra special rate for good-looking man like you, John. No short time. I like you, I like you lots. You come with me now; fuck me all night. You want fuck me all night, John?"

Of course I did. I was frantic to do just that, but I still didn't have the first idea of how to set about the chore, or what sophisticated carnal knowledge or athletic expertise she might reasonably expect. So, just as I had on that warm summer's afternoon in a Staffordshire farmer's field with a half-naked Albrighton Sally, I lost my nerve at the crucial moment.

It was a familiar and all too depressing pattern of events, which began with my heart thumping against my ribcage, and then moved on to my legs feeling weak and my hands shaking uncontrollably. However, my retreat was even less glorious than on that memorable afternoon, because this time there was no obvious excuse, and my humiliation was so much more public.

I mumbled some feeble words of capitulation about the night being early and my friends waiting, and then dropped an obscene amount of my hard-earned Singapore dollars on the table, repositioned a hugely disappointed appendage, adjusted my clothing for decency, and fled from the scene in confusion, leaving much laughter in my wake, and the high-pitched cry of, "You still cherry boy, John? Extra special rate for cherry boy. Come back, John. Come back. You fuck me. I give you special cherry boy rate. I make you man, John; I make you man."

I could still hear those words stabbing into my consciousness long after I had reached Bugis Street. I can still hear them now, those cruel and shameful words of public humiliation. They reverberated around the crowded bar, out through the open doorway, and on into the Singapore night air, directing everyone's attention to my youthful countenance, advising the world of my virgin condition, and invading my consciousness with the awful truth of my own wretched naiveté.

The shame of it all was almost too much to bear. Yet again I had panicked, as absurdly and embarrassingly as I had on that balmy August afternoon. Yet again I had fallen at the last hurdle. Yet again I had let a golden opportunity slip from my grasp and, instead of negotiating the insignificant price of my long overdue entry into manhood, had allowed a beautiful, delicate, and shamelessly willing creature, and an oh-so-desperately awaited opportunity to elude me.

I doubt anyone could possibly understand just how much I hated myself at that moment.

Around a dozen bottles of Tiger and a couple of hours later, with colour and courage temporarily restored, I returned to the same bar, only to find her gone.

A couple of guys who had witnessed my earlier debacle explained.

It seems the young beauty had watched my frantic departure, then slid into an adjacent booth, slipped the hemline beyond the bounds of decency, smiled that same garlic- and peppermint-laced smile, and negotiated a peculiar form of group discount with six drunken fusiliers from the Welsh Border Collies, or some such other largely Druid regiment of foot.

And so I once again headed back to Bugis Street, in embarrassed and sad contemplation, a wiser man, a more confident being, a more experienced sexual sophisticate. Sadly, though, still the same unsullied young virgin who had arrived in Singapore almost a lifetime before.

That two week acclimatisation period had been wonderful, with colourful nights that seemed to go on for ever, and extravagantly lazy days, with nothing to do but eat and sleep and swim and relax. Now, though, that was over, and the military exercise was about to begin.

We hopped over to mainland Malaya in a Charlie One-Thirty, otherwise known as a Hercules transporter. Many thought it the most versatile aircraft in history, but I always thought it the most uncomfortable transport plane in service, apart from the Beverley. You see, a Hercules would take off from uneven surfaces, around a football pitch length, and, if that wasn't enough to shatter the nerves, pilots didn't so much land it, as drop it from a great height and stop on a sixpence.

The ride was always made doubly uncomfortable because TCW boasted active paratroopers, and we often carried large quantities of equipment. Consequently, the exercise planners only allotted planes that were equipped for such sheer insanity and lowly cargo.

Our Charlie One-Thirties were usually fitted with metal seats, running along either side of the fuselage, with safety strapping, or more often netting, providing stability and security at either end of the flight. Vehicles and other heavy equipment, which shifted alarmingly during turbulence and the aircraft's famed short take-offs and landing, filled the bulk of the interior.

The take-offs and landings were simple enough. In the absence of strapping, you clung to the netting until your fingers went blue, closed your eyes, prayed to whatever God you worshipped, and waited for a badly-tethered vehicle or technical cabin to splatter you against the fuselage.

You see, with non-commissioned ranks, the Air Force only ever catered for the lowest common denominator. As parachute drops only involved expendable men with drained faces and white knuckles, who were never there to endure the uncomfortable and nerve-wracking landings, the Air Force saw little point in wasting money on fittings. Neither did they see the need to pander to an unappreciative and uneducated clientele of erks and hoi polloi.

I am sure that many, having just read the drained faces and white knuckles bit, can't believe that jumping out of an aircraft could ever frighten a macho parachutist. I am equally sure that many believe that modern-day parachute jumping is a doddle, performed by everyone from aged grandmothers to dare-devil thrill seekers. So, allow me to enlighten you.

Jumping from a static line ain't the same as skydiving. Forgetting that there may be people trying to kill you, the standard military chute is cumbersome and difficult to manoeuvre; or it was then. Not only that, but the drop is often just a few hundred, rather than thousands of feet. This means, if the main chute doesn't open, the 'chutist will be scraping himself off the ground before he has time to realise the problem, pull the cord, and allow sufficient descent for the reserve chute to fill.

Secondly, apart from large areas of Salisbury plain and a couple of fields outside Abingdon, the drop zone is often uneven, and sometimes jagged and hostile. Thirdly, there are the problems associated with having a damn great canister hanging between your legs during descent. Lastly, there are all the dangers inherent in stick jumping: everything from candlesticks of silk that refuse to open, to tangling with other 'chutists, to droopy-loops of static line flapping alongside the aircraft and just waiting for some poor sod of a para to jump through and hang himself.

Which is why paras have more to worry about than the way they're facing, or cushions, or legroom. So much so that if they see anybody sitting alongside with anything other than an ashen face and white knuckles, they will steer clear of that individual, and should the individual somehow muster a smile, they will refuse to jump with such an obviously deranged lunatic.

But back to my cramped and uncomfortable seat on the Hercules, which was now on final approach at a temporary landing strip a few miles inland from the Strait of Malacca. The pilot dropped us on the grass runway from fifty feet, and then slammed on the brakes and reverse thrust, so severely that I had marks on my neck and down one side for over a week. It took an hour to restore the circulation to my fingers, but at least we were down and I was still in one piece.

Everyone filed out of the back of the plane and took a look around the jungle clearing. We had brought a fair amount of specialised equipment with us, and the rest was already there. To one side the temporary motor pool comprised a couple of three tonners and a dozen Landrovers. There was a pile of jungle green twelve-by-twelve canvas tents, a couple of technical or KT cabins, and a stack of composition rations. Last, but not least, a couple of nervous-looking Gurkha riflemen stood guard over an armoury of SLRs and SMGs stowed beneath camouflage netting.

I was stretching my limbs and restoring circulation, when I saw it: a Mirage jet, from the Royal Australian Air Force, coming straight for us, at no more than a few feet above the trees.

It fascinated me, because I'd never seen a Mirage that low or that close, and so I took a moment to study it as it swooped in, buzzed us, and then turned away. At the risk of sounding like a music hall act, I won't say it was low, but I could see the pilot mouthing the words 'Pommie bastards' at us. We gestured and shouted back as the fighter screamed low over our heads, and then watched as the pilot pulled the aircraft into a steep climb before heading away to the west.

"That's it. You're all dead. You're all dead."

He was a British Army Warrant Officer, I could see that much from the insignia; short of stature, slight of frame and narrow of mind, but I had no idea where he had come. He was obviously not directly involved in the war games, or not as a player, because he carried a clipboard and wore an armband marked in red with the word UMPIRE printed in bold letters. He wore an immaculately pressed battledress, with an immaculate SD hat, immaculately starched collar and immaculately knotted tie. An immaculately buffed webbing belt and immaculately bulled boots with mirror-finish toecaps completed the apparition. Lastly, and obviously to demonstrate his immaculate authority, he carried the obligatory pace-stick tucked immaculately under and at precisely ninety degrees to his upper left arm.

All in all, he would have been more at home parading his pint-sized perfection along the Mall, rather than a Malayan jungle clearing hundreds of miles from civilization, but he seemed oblivious to the incongruity. His only concession to the dangers of the jungle was a pair of immaculately wrapped puttees to seal the gaps between trouser legs and gleaming boots.

Most of us looked blankly at him, a few grinned good-naturedly, someone sniggered, and a couple of comedians fell to the ground, feigning death throes and clutching imaginary wounds. For his part in this slightly-bizarre confrontation, the pint-sized Warrant Officer continued to rant.

"What on earth were you lot thinking, just standing around like that? Why didn't you run for cover when you saw the aircraft? You do know you've just been killed, don't you? Well that's it. It's all over. I'm not joking, you know. I'm deadly serious. You're all going to have to head back to wherever you've just come from. I'm sorry, but that's all there is to it."

"Fuck off. We've only just got here."

That had been Slim Hollister, a Cornishman from Penzance, who was an affable twenty-stone member of Base Comms, and one of the most experienced among us. For a concerned moment, I seriously thought the pint-sized Warrant Officer would have a heart attack. His eyes bulged and his face went bright red as he considered the comment. Then he began to splutter.

"Fuck off. Is that what you just said to me? Fuck off?"

He had expressed his disbelief and outrage in a strangled scream, directing both question and hostile glare at the affable west-countryman. Slim ignored both. The gentle giant turned his back on the spluttering features, nodded to the aircraft, and said, "Come on, guys, this lot won't unload itself."

The spluttering Warrant Officer was beside himself with rage. With two undersized legs going at nineteen-to-the-dozen, he raced across the grass to confront the affable Slim. This confrontation was comical in itself, because Slim was six-foot four, twenty stone bone-dry, and in complete control of his faculties. A thankfully now only a reddish-pink around-the-gills Warrant Officer was five-foot seven in his shiny boots, eight stone dripping-wet, and literally shaking with rage.

"Did you hear me, soldier, did you hear me? I asked you a question. Now then, did I hear you just tell me to fuck off or not? Did I, did I?"

Slim looked suitably bored as he gazed down and into outraged features.

"Yeah. Oh, and incidentally, I'm not some bloody pongo . . . I'm RAF."

"What do you mean? I don't . . ."

Slim pointed to his shoulder and the shabby blue beret rolled up inside the epaulette. The RAF cap badge was buckled and tarnished, but almost garish when viewed against the combat gear's jungle green. A brief study of the pompous Warrant Officer's confused features confirmed that such unexpected and unwelcome information simply didn't compute.

"R.A.F? R.A.F? What do you mean, R.A.F? What are you people doing here? You're not supposed to be here. Who are you? Where are you from? Why are you here?"

Somebody chose to further enlighten him.

"Thirty-eight Group, mate."

He was off again, the tint fluctuating between red and redder, as he digested and processed the information before wheeling around to address whoever had spoken.

"Mate? Mate? I'm not your mate. Bloody insubordinate rabble. I am a warrant officer in this man's Army, and you call me sir. Do you hear me? You call me, Sir." He had obviously remembered something relevant, because he furrowed his brow and said, "Hold on, wait a minute." He carefully consulted his clipboard, "You're not supposed to be here; you're supposed to be over at Penerak."

The last time that so many barbs hit their mark, the military exercise had been Agincourt.

"Get away." "Are we really?" "It's lucky we brought some transport." "I knew it began with P." "He may be a short-arse, but he can still see over a clipboard." "I told the pilot to turn left at Hong Kong, but he wouldn't listen." "Thank God you were here, we could have starved to death."

The pint-sized Warrant Officer failed to see the humour.

"Don't you take that tone with me, you insolent bloody rabble. Anyway, you can't go now, because you're all dead. I've got it marked here on my board, and that's the end of it."

It fell to the enviably good-looking Joules to explain the logistical and economic facts of military-exercise life to the alternately confused and spluttering features.

"Look, wack, we're Thirty-Eight Group, and if we don't get to Penerak at some time today, unload, get the commcen up and running, and start communicating with all those poor bastards out there by first light, there'll be no friggin exercise; just a bunch of pongos running around the jungle with their dicks in their hands, and some seriously pissed-off strike aircraft flying around in ever-decreasing circles and firing missiles up their own arses.

"Now if that happens, it will mean that someone," he nodded pointedly, "will have to explain to SEATO that they just blew thirty million friggin dollars on an exercise that didn't happen. All because some friggin Aborigine fly-boy flew over the wrong landing zone at the wrong time, and some pongo meathead sent the main field communications centre back to Singapore."

An outraged Warrant Officer bristled at the insubordination, but then became lost in thought. You could almost see the wheels going around as he assessed the potential fallout from this. It was the affable and generous Slim Hollister who offered a solution.

"Look, pal, from where I was standing that Aussie pilot timed his run all wrong. He overshot the target. I reckon he must have missed us by a good hundred yards or so. What do you think?" He winked and smiled as he offered the olive-branch. "I'm sorry. What do you think, sir?"

Somebody else chipped in.

"Yeah, typical bloody Aussies. Just like their pace bowlers. Never could get line and length right, well, not at the same time, anyway."

The undersized Warrant Officer was still deep in thought, obviously wondering how he could disentangle himself from what was rapidly turning out to be a fiasco without in some way losing face. He finally glared at the enviably good-looking Joules, and said, "How come your hair's so long, soldier?"

"It's airman, not soldier, and the judies like it that way, Wack."

"I don't care who likes it, it's a disgrace, an absolute disgrace. You're to get it cut. Do you hear me, you 'orrible little man. And you don't call me wack, you call me sir, do you hear me?"

We could all hear him, loud and clear, even the 'orrible little man', who was in reality six-foot, three inches tall. I couldn't believe my ears. Despite his self-inflicted predicament, the pint-sized Warrant Officer was behaving like a caricature from *The Army Game*. It was the less than subtle Frankie Aps who mimicked the comment and started to snigger.

"'Orrible little man?' Is that what he just said? Did you hear that? He's gotta be having a laugh."

Slim tried to pour on the oil. He shook his head in disapproval and motioned for Aps to shut up, then turned to the once-again pink-around-the-gills Warrant Officer.

"Sorry about that, sir,' he said. "So can we get on with unloading the aircraft now, uh, sir?"

I had to feel sorry for the beleaguered Warrant Officer. He stood in indecision for some further moments, studying each of us in turn and shaking his head in disbelief at the collective scruffiness and insolence that stared back at him. I had to agree with his overall impression, though, because we did look like a rabble, particularly when compared to his immaculate presentation. Unfortunately for our pint-sized and pompous Warrant Officer, he had painted himself into a corner. There was no easy way out, other than to either risk the considerable wrath of the South East Asia Treaty Organisation, or humiliatingly capitulate. He wisely chose the latter.

"Get out of my bloody sight, you scruffy-looking rabble."

Two hours later, with convoy loaded, we did just that. The convoy consisted of the two three-tonners, packed with masts and canvas and radio gear and generators and composition rations. Three Landrovers behind them, with technical cabins attached. Four Landrovers leading, with most of us piled in. Four more slotted in toward the back, with the balance of the party and more equipment, and the two nervous-looking Gurkhas guarding the weapons and bringing up the rear.

Which was fine, because our main problem wasn't the loading or sequence of vehicles. It wasn't even that we had positioned our most experienced jungle fighters and guides at the rear, with enough firepower between the two of them to defend Singapore. The problem was that Frankie Aps had somehow managed to install himself behind the wheel of the lead Landrover.

Now Aps had shown himself to be an insensitive oaf on more occasions than I care to recall, and the fact that we allowed a moronic and inexperienced point-man, without so much as a driving licence, to lead our convoy through hostile jungle terrain spoke volumes for the rest of us. At best, it was poor judgement. At worst, it was sheer lunacy.

In mitigation, we did have Slim Hollister sitting alongside him with the map, a compass, and a degree of common sense. Unfortunately, Slim wasn't the man behind the wheel.

Of course Aps immediately began driving far too fast along the uneven jungle track. It was too fast for an experienced driver on a decent surface, let alone an idiot whose only experience of driving had been chasing rabbits across Tangmere airfield at night. He drove so fast the remainder of the convoy, having their speed governed by impact-sensitive, high-tech equipment cabins and lumbering, fully-laden Bedford three tonners, was unable to keep up. They soon began to lose sight of the lead Landrovers, which wasn't good news for those lagging behind without a map.

On the upside, however, it probably saved us from a multiple pile up when Aps suddenly swerved off the road and hit a tree.

"It wasn't my fault. It was that fucking snake."

We were surveying the damage to the Landrover, which wasn't good. Neither were the various injuries to the moronic Aps, a bloody-faced and disgruntled-looking Slim Hollister, and three of the four guys who had been sitting in the back of the Landrover. Slim had been lucky, he'd got away with cuts and bruises to the affable features, but Frankie Aps had a broken arm. The three men who had started off in the back of the Landrover and finished in the front, had numerous cuts and abrasions, two broken ribs and a broken collarbone. An incredulous voice asked, "What snake?"

Slim Hollister glared across at Aps, and then shook his head in anger and frustration.

"Bloody idiot was zapping cobras. I told him not to. I told him to slow down and stop being stupid, but he wouldn't listen. I hope it's a compound fracture. Serves the little shit right."

Rory Walters chipped in.

"OK, so maybe he was going too fast, and maybe it was a stupid thing to do. Let's face it, everybody knows he's a wanker, and as thick as two short planks, but I still don't see why he had to swerve off the track like that."

Frankie Aps tried to defend an indefensible position, only to turn it into a hopeless one.

"Wasn't my fault. The bastard moved."

We suddenly realised what had happened. It fell to the enviably good-looking Joules to sum up our collective opinion.

"I don't believe it. You utter prat. You total friggin tosser."

The problem was that we had been travelling through thick jungle in the middle of the day. The winding track, which led from the airfield before crossing the tracks leading south-west to Penerak and north-west to Kuala Lumpur, had been the only place where the rays of the sun had penetrated an otherwise densely populated undergrowth.

Now snakes of all kinds love to lie out in the warmth of the sun's rays, and so you would find dozens of them curled up in the middle of the dirt tracks. Passing drivers would rarely notice them, because if they were quick, and the driver travelling at a sensible speed, they could slither quietly away. However, if for some reason that didn't happen the unfortunate creature would often be sadly, but unceremoniously, squashed.

Cobras aggravated the problem, because the kings are so much bigger than other snakes, with some stretching to eighteen feet. Not only that, but as they heard the drivers approach, they would do as cobras habitually do when threatened. They would rear up in the middle of the road and open the cobra's famous hood, providing a tempting target for an idiot with a lethal weapon, or in this case Aps and the front of a Landrover travelling at speed.

Ignorant, stupid, senseless, immature, cruel, unnecessary, moronic, contemptible and sad are some of the many adjectives that come to mind. Hindus might add, blasphemous. However, in Aps' case one could add absurd and insane, because one of the cobras had reared up in the centre of the track as it heard Aps approach, before realising discretion to be the better part of valour. As the snake hurriedly retreated to the safety of the undergrowth, a fool and his Landrover followed.

You see, Aps being Aps had been so caught up in his moronic objective to squash as many snakes as possible that he swerved to catch the retreating reptile and promptly lost control of the Landrover. The result of that little moment of madness was four casualties and a written-off vehicle, while a fleeter and wiser king cobra lived to boast about it to his grandchildren.

What made matters worse was that, because Aps had been charging along like a lunatic in his efforts to decapitate cobras, we had lost contact with the three-tonners and the Landrovers pulling the technical cabins. Not to mention the other four Landrovers behind them, and the two nervous looking Gurkha riflemen with the weapons cache.

The Chief calmly put everything into perspective when we finally limped into camp.

"So let me recap, lads. Just so I can fully understand this before I have to explain it to the Wing Commander. Four hours ago you landed safely at the temporary airfield. You loaded up the trucks, formed into a column, and travelled here to the communications centre site. En route you sustained four casualties, three of them serious enough for a casevac, wrote off a Landrover, lost half your men, all your equipment, two three-ton Bedford trucks, seven other Landrovers, three KT cabins, the armoury, and the two Gurkha riflemen guarding it. Is that right, or have I missed something?" Somebody nodded. The Chief exploded. "You only had to travel twenty miles."

It was a disconsolate looking Chief who reported the sorry state of affairs to the Flight Lieutenant, and two even sorrier looking men who subsequently presented themselves at the Wing Commander's tent. We sat around waiting for the inevitable fallout, which came some minutes later when the Chief returned looking sheepish.

"How did he take it, Chief?"

"The Wing Commander said that perhaps he ought to wire Hereford and tell them not to bother sending the SAS to attack us. He said we'll probably all be dead long before they get here. Then the Flight Louie reminded him that we couldn't do that, because we'd lost all the communications equipment. I think, all in all, you'll find the Wing Commander's not best pleased with you."

The Chief started to walk away, but then turned back toward us and said, "Oh, and by the way, the Wingco also said that he'd received a field telephone call from operations headquarters. Something about a bunch of long-haired yobs dressed in RAF berets and combat gear who'd had a quiet chat up at the airfield with a Warrant Officer from the same headquarters. The Warrant Officer levied a formal complaint, and requested we bring charges against the long-haired yobs for insubordination and refusal to comply with a direct order. He also claimed the long-haired yobs used the terms 'fuck off' and 'pongo meathead' . . . Nice one, lads."

It seemed our immaculate pint-sized Warrant Officer had undergone a further narrowing of mind and decided to make an issue of it. At that moment our future looked decidedly bleak, but just as the Chief began to walk away the answer to our prayers arrived. To be precise, two three-tonners, three Landrovers pulling KT cabins, four more Landrovers and two nervous looking Gurkha riflemen. As they rolled into camp, the Chief shook his head and grinned.

"You lucky bastards," he said.

"Look, he was being a prat, Chief. He wanted to send us back to Singas."

Slim Hollister had blurted the mitigation. The Chief looked quizzically back at him.

"Who did?"

"The friggin pongo meathead."

That had of course been the enviably good-looking Joules.

"Why?"

Slim related the tale of the Mirage and of the arrival of the pint-sized Warrant Officer, while the Chief listened carefully. At the end of the explanation the Chief looked pensive, weighing up the arguments and counter arguments for some moments.

"If you shower can manage to get this place operational, and that means everything up and all the radio checks completed before twenty-one hundred, I'll have a word with the Wingco, OK?"

Unsurprisingly we didn't hang around, and were in fact up and running, with all checks completed, thirty minutes early. When the chief returned, he brought the Wing Commander with him, who congratulated us on our speed and efficiency.

"Oh yes," he said, "and as for that unfortunate incident over at the airfield. . . On the record, I have to say the RAF will not tolerate insubordination for any reason, especially when directed at officers from other branches of the service. You would do well to remember that." He started to walk away, but, as he reached the entrance to the commcentre tent, then added, "Off the record, I have to say well done, lads, but let's try not to make a habit of it, OK?"

It was a popular Wing Commander who floated out of the makeshift commcentre, with a cacophony of cheers and a sycophantic thank you, sir ringing in his ears. Now all we had to do was survive the perils of the Malayan jungle, the Australian armed forces, and the SAS on a diet of composition rations and half a canteen of water a day for the next three weeks.

The Wing Commander's popularity wasn't unconditional, though. The next day a contingent from field catering arrived and set up facilities next to the officers' quarters. They also installed a makeshift shower, which was slightly galling because we didn't have a sufficient ration of water each day even to wash our faces. It wasn't until that first lunchtime, however, when I came to witness the true extent of the great divide that exists between RAF officers and other ranks.

At the time, I was sharing a dead tree-stump with a colony of ants, and nervously eying a rustle from an adjacent bush. I was eating lukewarm tinned-meat stew, which I'd heated myself, scraped off the blackened base of a billy-can with the screwdriver attachment from my Swiss Army penknife, and then hooked out with a folding fork. While swallowing the chunks, I looked across the clearing to see our noble commissioned officers, sitting down to a full three-course luncheon, served on a long trestle table. Covering the table was a spotless white tablecloth, with white linen napkins, silver cutlery, water jugs, bread rolls, and all the necessary condiments precisely laid out.

Expertly cooking the officers' meals were two chefs, complete with white-jackets, chequered trousers and toque hats, presumably seconded from the officers' mess in Seletar. White-jacketed waiters were scurrying around the table and plying their silver service skills, for the sole benefit of those same officers.

As the mouth-watering aroma wafted across the clearing to where I sat, the incongruity of it all reminded me of a scene from a *Carry-On* film. At any moment I half expected to see a rotund Joan Sims get an inquisitive python up her skirt, or hear an emaciated Kenneth Williams saying, 'No, don't do that. No, stop mucking about.' But, instead of listening to a feminine shriek followed by a lecherous Sid James' chuckle, or hearing one of the endearingly camp Kenneth Williams' catchphrases, all I heard was, "How's it going, chaps?" Followed by another voice saying, "Well, it's clearly not ideal, sir, but I suppose we'll survive."

Bastards.

The Gurkhas kept themselves to themselves. They didn't say much to us, and we didn't say much to them. After the first four days our officers followed their lead. Although that was more to do with us not being able to wash, rather than any conscious decision to send us to Coventry.
The duty roster was iniquitous, but sensible. We handled everything communications, and when off shift during the hours of daylight, would also chip in with guard and patrol duties. The Gurkha riflemen, of which there were about thirty, would take a share of the daylight guard and patrol duties, but handle all guard duty and camp security during the night.

Although this meant us working double shifts in the commcentre, and then grabbing a few hours sleep before going out on patrol or 'standing-to' in fox-holes around the perimeter, I didn't mind. The time went faster that way, and didn't allow any opportunity for boredom. More importantly, it meant I didn't have to run around the jungle at night.

Although the Gurkhas were largely uncommunicative, they were good at what they did. They took their duties seriously, had an unsurpassed reputation for courage, and a similar reputation as some of the best jungle fighters in the world. On those odd occasions we did acknowledge one another, they seemed personable enough. However, if nature called after the hours of daylight, it was wise to make as much noise as possible, because they would see you before you saw them, and if they thought that you were the enemy. . . well, as I said, they did take their work seriously.

But if potentially-homicidal Gurkhas were a hazard, the SAS was reputedly more so. I say reputedly, because until then everything I had heard about the SAS had been rumour. They hadn't even officially been confirmed as the enemy, but that didn't stop the rumour mills.

The first rumour to hit the camp came at the beginning of the second week. It came in over the RT, or radio-telephone, from K.L. or Kuala Lumpur during an unauthorised chit-chat. It said the SAS were close by, because a pongo sprog-zobbit, otherwise known as an inexperienced officer, had stupidly tried to capture two of them. Surprisingly, he had sneaked up on them and held them at nine-millimetre gunpoint. Unsurprisingly, they had ignored his spoken commands and the weapon's threat, approached him at speed, and cracked his skull. It also claimed they had left him lying there, but that he was now out of danger and recovering in hospital up in K. L.

The story may have been true, but I doubt it. Not because they wouldn't happily incapacitate a sprog-zobbit in such a way, but because it is unlikely that such an inexperienced man could have surprised them in the first place.

Rumours were now spreading like wildfire. Stories included everything from an affirmation the SAS never went on exercise with empty weapons or dummy ammunition, to an affirmation that they would never play dead unless they were dead. More rumours assured us that their hand-to-hand skills were extraordinary, and almost always lethal. More still claimed they would start any action with stun-grenades, rather than the more usual and benign thunder flashes. One even claimed they would be under orders to incapacitate anybody not already incapacitated by the early shock tactics who might be stupid enough to get in their way.

However, when the unprincipled and black-hearted devils did finally attack, the reality was less blood chilling, but just as impressive as anticipated. That experience, and experiences of other exercises around the world similarly involving the SAS, left me with an enduring and unsurpassed admiration and respect for their abilities.

The first warning, which set everybody's nerves on edge, came from an unidentified source. I had my suspicions about that source, and a regimental headquarters not a million miles from the river Wye was top of my list. However, no group formally claimed responsibility, and nor would any group afterwards admit to origination. The coded signal had come in over the WT, or wireless-telegraphy circuit. SEATO Headquarters passed it under an 'Immediate' handling classification, which was the second highest for speed of transfer. They addressed it to the Wing Commander, and classified it 'Secret', which was the second highest for security.

I knew precisely what information it contained before anybody else, because I had received the signal and subsequently decoded it. Most of the lads also knew before the Wing Commander, because, as well as being responsible for the WT and signals decoding, I was also a blabbermouth.

The signal was both clear and succinct. According to 'intelligence' received, they had scheduled the SAS attack for that night. It advised us to take all possible precautions, to protect the communications centre and ensure continuity of information transfer.

The Wing Commander didn't bother to call us together for a briefing. It was obvious from the dog-eared condition of the signal that finally reached him under the valueless cover of a brown envelope, that everybody in camp had read it before him. However, the Gurkha commander called his men together for a briefing, and they didn't look happy.

Suddenly the smiling brown faces were gone and an altogether more severe detachment of Gurkha warriors had replaced their friendly colleagues. They were now nervous, and wary, and even less communicative than before. As darkness arrived to heighten the tension, the atmosphere worsened. Suddenly, the after-dark Nepalese chatter around camp was gone. Suddenly, the fun and camaraderie was gone. Suddenly, it was serious business, and all those stupid rumours we had exaggerated and dissected and then exaggerated again began playing on our minds.

It was no good telling yourself this was just a game and we were only playing at war. No good telling yourself that they were on your side, and wouldn't seriously injure you. Suddenly we started to understand a fraction of the fear that terrorists and other hostile forces must feel when confronted with the SAS. For them it must be terrifying; for us it was irrational and foolish, but nonetheless worrying for all that. As I 'stood-to', and nervously poked the SLR's barrel into the blackness, I understood how powerful irrational fear stoked by rumour and exaggeration can be.

There were several false alarms during the evening and early part of the night, with people jumping at shadows and hearing all sorts of noises. Everything was imagined, from armies massing in the jungle to aircraft dropping parachute brigades, and helicopter gunships dropping black-suited night fighters on to the commcentre roof. However, the first cry of genuine alarm went up around two a.m. and pandemonium followed.

It seemed an SAS guy had appeared at the commcentre entrance seconds before. He simply said 'hi there' to the guy on duty, and then casually tossed a small parcel on to the officer of signal's desk. The attached note read: 'This is a bomb. You have just been blown up'.

And that was it. That was all we saw of them.

Despite the forewarning, and us at our most vigilant. Despite having some of the best jungle fighters in the world alongside, soldiers similarly warned, and even more vigilant than we. Despite having a superior knowledge of the terrain and the camp layout, and despite having just about everything else in our favour, they had slipped through our defences and planted that make-believe bomb. Then, in the middle of all that uproar and pandemonium, they slipped out through our ranks and disappeared. Nobody saw them come, and nobody saw them go.

I understand that for you, sitting reading this, it must be difficult to appreciate just how impressive a feat it had been. To those brought up on a diet of SAS survival techniques, Iranian Embassy sieges, winged daggers, 'who dares wins', and general media saturation, it may not seem remarkable. But to me, in that place, at a time long before they had begun to achieve a fraction of their current celebrity status, it was nothing short of awesome.

Suddenly I realised just how inadequate we were, and just how poorly trained and inexpert we were by comparison; how outclassed we had been, and how pathetically ineffective we would be against any top-flight special forces outfit, let alone the best. We believed ourselves a relatively tough bunch, and would happily prove it to anyone who troubled us, but compared to the very best we were nothing more than a poorly-prepared and ineffectual bunch of amateurs.

The Gurkhas had similarly failed, at night and in the jungle; as did so many, reputedly tough outfits I met on later exercise, in other scenarios and other parts of the world. The Royal Marines, the Parachute Brigades, some of the toughest, best trained, and most distinguished infantry outfits from around the world. They were all tough and brave and strong and deadly, and many of them battle hardened. You would undoubtedly want them on your side in any serious conflict, rather than pitted against you. But what I saw from the SAS that night, and during the years that followed, transcended mere toughness, and bravery, and fighting ability, and conventional battle worthiness. What I saw then and later was something very special indeed.

Although it may have been gloom on more than one level as we switched off the generators and cut communications, it wasn't all doom. That make-believe bomb had knocked us out for twenty-four hours, according to the war games adjudicator, which meant we had twenty-four hours to kill before resuming duties. That meant a free day, and that meant a trip to the beach.

Not that it had started out that way, because we looked at the map and found a river just short of the beach. A river suggested fresh water, which would allow us to wash. As you can imagine, two weeks in the Malayan jungle humidity without the benefit of fresh water for anything but a mouthful of tea, had severely strained the boundaries of presentation and personal hygiene.

And so, while a group of faultlessly-dressed officers settled down for an elegant full-English breakfast at their own 'private club in the clearing', we set off for the river. A couple of sullen-looking Gurkhas, still acutely embarrassed by their inability to guard a simple canvas tent, watched us go. We arrived at the river, piled out of the Landrovers, and instantly decided against washing in the cool fresh water; not because of any slovenliness or laziness, but because it was almost impossible to find a cupful of water not already occupied by snakes.

There were tens of thousands of them in that river; in fact, the whole river seemed alive with them. I don't know what species they were, but they were mostly dark brown, between two and five feet long and probably deadly. We steered clear and headed instead for the beach.

The beach, though, was wonderful; in fact, more than wonderful, it was heaven. The sand was soft and powdery and clean, with coconut trees swaying in the breeze, the water brilliant blue, clean and sparkling, and so clear that you could see the ocean bed from a hundred yards out to sea. Thomas Cook would have given his right arm just to put a picture of that beach on the cover of one of his brochures. Miles of soft sand and clear blue ocean, without a soul in sight, set against a background of jungle greens and soothing browns, basking beneath a cloudless blue sky. All in all, it was a tropical paradise and an advertising executive's dream.

Five or six Malaysian children appeared from nowhere shortly after we arrived, and began selling coconuts and pineapples for a few cents each. I remember lying out on the sand under the heat of a sun tempered by a cooling zephyr, and eating fresh pineapple the like of which I had never tasted before or since. I also remember thinking that all this place needed for me to desert, build a hut on the beach, and go back to Mother Nature, was a leggy blonde with a grass skirt.

There was one moment of minor concern, when a few of the guys cornered a baby shark in the shallows. Slim casually enquired if anybody had seen the baby's mother in their travels, and added that she had to be around somewhere. The exodus from the water was instantaneous and comical.

That lazy day spent with half-a-dozen smiling brown-faced urchins and the great TCW unwashed on that magnificent beach across from Penerak was one of the most memorable of my life. It set me up for the rest of the exercise, and provided a warmth of reminiscence that has lasted half a lifetime. It was just about the most pleasant and therapeutic day I ever spent, and, give or take a leggy Bounty-bar blonde or two, just about as close to heaven as any man could wish.

When it was over and we headed back to camp, I looked back to see the palm trees swaying in the evening breeze, the sun receding, and a group of happy little brown-faced children waving and smiling their goodbyes. I remember vowing to return, but I never did. Not because I didn't have an opportunity, but because some memories are so wonderful and perfect they are best left that way.

The rest of the exercise was an anti-climax. The shadows held no pint-sized warrant officers. The sky held no foul-mouthed Australians in Mirage jets. The SAS, understandably, didn't see the need to trouble us again. The Gurkhas returned to smiling and chattering, and the commissioned officers continued to shower, dress well, eat well, and complain about everything.

It was something I often noted, of those RAF officers press-ganged into Thirty-Eight Group. They invariably behaved as disgruntled fish out of water. I appreciate they knew nothing of telecommunications, and less of combat and survival, but, instead of swallowing their pride and learning something new, they chose to be aloof and disenchanted. They rarely seemed happy about anything, especially those with pilots' or navigators' wings stitched across their chests.

I suppose a fear of the 'Admirable Crichton' syndrome inhibited their thoughts, and I'm sure that many of them considered playing cowboys and Indians with us to be beneath them. I can see their point, but if they had just swallowed their pride and asked, or appreciated all the wonderful sights and sounds and characters and incidents along the way, their lives would have been so much richer. Then again, maybe there's an element of sour grapes in all this, because there was never a chance in hell of me rising to such dizzy heights, and so perhaps I'd better leave it there.

As the aircraft took off and I clung to the netting for dear life, I thought a lot about all that had occurred during the previous weeks and months. I also thought back to my grandmother and her lecture that day, when she had talked about my finding something to be good at.

I thought, if life truly was a series of checks and balances, then I could begin to fill in a few of the boxes. I could survive in the jungle, as well as in life, albeit with a little help from my friends. I could do my specialist job reasonably well, and I was beginning to get on with all sorts of people, from all walks of life and all parts of the world.

I studied some of the people who shared that life, seeing the dirty faces and filthy clothing, and listening to the even filthier language that breached the aircraft's drone. Laughing and joking with them, as we contemplated another seven nights in Bugis Street.

There had been bad times, of course. Times that, unlike the stereotypical cannon fodder we undoubtedly were, we rarely complained about, or even recalled unless pressed. Mostly, though, there had been good times, and fun along the way, and my grandmother had been absolutely right in her generous prediction. I had found something I was good at, and now I did belong. Maybe it was to a bunch of punch-drunk, foul-mouthed, and even fouler-smelling cut-throats, who sat in a military no-man's land somewhere between complete soldiers and complete arseholes, but I'd found a niche of sorts, and, contrary to all predictions, I was truly happy.

It takes all sorts

It was a strange phenomenon, and something of a simple truth, that while publicly denouncing Doggett, most of us held a sneaking admiration for the man. Some even held a reluctant fondness for that permanently grinning countenance of self-induced stupefaction and pock-marked irreverence. To the uninitiated, he appeared as foul-mouthed and uncouth, frequently diseased, morally bankrupt and utterly degenerate, but Doggett was also a fascinating character. There was no denying that he was a social leper and unashamed bigot, and perhaps, a tad more endearingly, the only truly unrepentant Male Chauvinist Pig I ever met. However, John was also a good friend and, despite all appearance to the contrary, a decent, albeit seriously flawed, human being.

For the modern emasculated male in this sanitised, pressurised, and politicised twenty-first-century world of ours, it only requires a man to use the plural 'women', with eyebrows raised, for the MCP or misogynist accusation to be levied. Opinions that a man of Doggett's perspective might voice on feminism or post-feminism, or any other aspect of female emancipation, would undoubtedly result in questions in The House and the ritualistic burning of phallic-shaped effigies on Brighton Beach. But in those marvellous bygone days of mini-skirts and machismo, when a set of fluttering eyelashes routinely brought grown men to their knees, Doggett's philosophies on amoralism and the fair sex were something to hear.

I remember sitting in the Eastgate Arms one night in nineteen sixty-eight, when he was waxing lyrical about being 'a man's man', as Doggett preferred to call it. Not that he wouldn't have revelled in the MCP title, but pre-nineteen-seventy, when asked if a remark was 'germane', we assumed the question concerned relevance rather than female passivity.

Interested to know why he showed neither embarrassment nor remorse for his bigotry and multitude of politically-incorrect sins, I asked him about it.

"So why do you do it all, John?"

He proceeded to attack the pint with some gusto, taking a large gulp of the demon brew, before grunting an answer through the froth.

"Do what?"

"The constant boozing and whoring and that. You're an intelligent guy. Why do you do it?"

He shrugged his shoulders and then leaned back as he rested his pint of Eastgate's finest on a decidedly rotund belly, and a pair of oversized feet on the table.

"Because that's me, isn't it? That's what I like doing. It's who I am, and who I wanna be."

I feigned astonishment.

"You consciously decide to get pissed every night of the week, and have it off with clapped-out hookers instead of regular women, or WAAFS and WRENS?"

Again he shrugged, but then smiled philosophically.

"You pay 'em all, son," he answered. One way or another, you pay 'em all, but with my way I'm in total control of both the emotional and financial sides of my life."

"Come off it. You're always borrowing money. You still owe me a tenner from last month."

"Well, of course. If you're fool enough to lend it, I'm more than happy to take it. Show me a financial adviser who wouldn't recommend you to take an interest-free loan if you could get one."

I have to admit he had a point there. I hadn't ever thought about it like that.

"But why all the booze? I mean, we all like a drink, but . . ."

"Why the hell not? I get pissed as often as possible, because I happen to like myself when I'm pissed. I think that I'm OK, and life feels pretty good; well, a hell of a lot better than it feels when I'm sober, that's for sure."

"But other people think that when you're drunk . . . well, you must know what they think."

I had been treading lightly for fear of causing offence, but needn't have bothered. If there was one thing about Doggett beyond dispute, it was his honesty, especially in self-analysis.

"Yeah, of course I know. They think I'm a waste of space, but that's only 'cos they're not drunk enough. If they were, they'd be too busy having a good time themselves to worry about pigeonholing me. You see, boyo, other people's opinions of me aren't my problem, never were and never will be. Their opinions of me are their problem. You should remember that sometimes."

I smiled, in acknowledgement of my own emotional complexities and insecurities. He went on.

"Far as I'm concerned, if they've got bloody great corks stuck up their arses, they should get out more; screw a few hookers and climb into the bottle next to mine. It's a comfortable existence and the view's not bad. In fact, I can thoroughly recommend it."

"Sure, but why do you have to go with prostitutes all the time?"

"Prostitutes? Now there's a very middle-class word."

He grinned across the table at me and took another swig at his pint. Doggett understood something of my adopted middle-class background. He also understood something of the inverted snob who inhabited, or should I say inhibited, my being. He could see that he'd got to me again. My indignant response merely confirmed his tongue-in-cheek victory.

"So what do you want me to say?"

"I couldn't give a flying fuck what you say . . . why should you?"

"OK, so why the whores? Why not ordinary girls with ordinary lives? Why not girls looking for sensible relationships, girls who like ordinary blokes; blokes who feel the same way they do?"

"God preserve us. Don't you understand anything about me? I'm not looking for a sensible relationship. That's the last thing I'm looking for. I'm just looking to get as pissed as possible, as often as possible, and as quickly as possible. After that, I'm looking to get my leg over the first woman I find who's not entirely repugnant . . . and who's willing to sensibly negotiate, of course."

I knew that Doggett's threshold of repugnance was short of the norm, but didn't argue.

"But why always with hookers? Why not with somebody who might care about you?"

"Well, you see, that's the best part. Whores don't care if you're drunk or sober, as long as you can afford the extra time. She'll always be nice to you, as long as you've got a few quid, and she'll never disappoint you, because you won't have any expectations to begin with. She'll never screw your mate behind your back; she'll do it openly. More often than not, she'll let you watch. She'll never get a headache, and she'll happily share her friends with you. . . if you can afford it."

"If you say so, John."

I held my hands up, assuming my half-hearted agreement would end the matter, but he had obviously considered the subject at length.

"You don't need to take out a mortgage to get a hooker between the sheets. You never have to ask her dad's permission. You don't even have to be pleasant to her mum; well, not unless you're looking for a threesome. She'll never expect you to do the washing-up, or follow her round the shops. She'll spread her legs at the drop of a fiver, and once you've handed over the readies, the only time that she'll open her mouth is so you can put your dick in it. She'll never ask you to respect her in the morning. She never has a wrong time of the month, never has a headache, never asks for her LPs back, doesn't mind if you shag her flatmate, knows her way around your scrotum better than your own right hand, and she'll come as often as you want her to."

I tried to be as subtle as he had been blunt.

"You don't perhaps think they might be faking it? The coming as often as you want, I mean?"

The question seemed to amuse him.

"They always fake it. That's the whole wonderful point of humping hookers. I prefer it that way. If I thought that one of 'em wasn't faking it, or was getting too serious or emotional, I'd probably be too eaten up with remorse to get it up. Anyway, I'd fake it too if I was them.

"You see, that's the beauty of paying up front. It's conscience-free humping. It means you can put all those worries about whether she's having a good time, and whether you're bigger or smaller or better or worse than the last bloke out of your mind. Instead of all that guilt and repression, and earning points out of ten, you can just get on with having a good time. Then again, to tell you the truth, I've never bothered to ask any of them about it, so I'm only guessing."

"So, why haven't you? Perhaps you should."

A temporarily preoccupied Doggett sat studying his glass. He held it up against the light to check the contents for sediment and clarity. Apparently satisfied, he returned to the subject matter.

"Why haven't I what?"

"Asked for their opinions."

"Because I'm not paying them for their opinions, am I? Don't get me wrong. I'm sure they've got opinions, but I'm not interested in them. Why should I be? If women want to share opinions, they should share them with each other; that's what we have to do. They're not interested in helping me tune my old six-fifty, or in guessing the weight of the barmaid's tits down at the Selsey Tram, or in letting me know the latest score from Cardiff Arms Park. Why should they be?

"It's the same with all this understanding-women shit that everybody's getting so hung up about these days. It's total bollocks. Mankind's being hung out to dry by a bunch of spineless bloody cretins, who are only sucking up to women in the hope of getting their end away. Well, that's not for me, and as far as I'm concerned, it's not for any man. All I ever ask from a woman is that she deals with the birth control bit, washes her underwear on a regular basis, and keeps her bloody opinions to herself. I'm entitled to ask that, just as she's entitled to ask me to hand over the going rate in readies before we start, and let her know when I've finished."

My jaw was dropping by the syllable. I joked back, hoping to make a point.

"What about cooking and washing-up, and the laundry and ironing? You're entitled to that?"

"Yeah, well of course, that goes without saying."

He had pretended not to see the joke. I persevered in my role of devil's advocate.

"But doesn't it worry you, the fact you're just paying them, and may not be pleasing them? I mean, isn't that all part of making love. . . the sharing and the giving and the caring?"

"Fuck me sideways with a loofah. What the hell goes on in that mind of yours?"

"Come off it, John. You know what I mean. Don't you like the idea of sharing the important things in life with someone you care for, someone who cares for you?"

He seemed genuinely indignant at that.

"I share a lot. I'm not tight. You ask anybody. I'll share a beer with mates. I'd lend you my last quid, if you needed it. I'll always cover your back when we're out there. Anyway, I'm sharing now, aren't I: sharing the experience of twenty years of screwing women, sharing it with you?

"And what about some of these bloody women doing a bit of sharing for a change? What about them doing a bit of giving? I mean, does a woman share anything when she gets on her back? Course she doesn't. She gives you nothing more than you're giving her. Most of the time, she puts a hell of a lot less effort into it than you. In fact, when I come to think about it, most women don't put any effort into it at all, especially the good-lookers. Yet, for some reason, blokes think they've gotta constantly worry about whether some little bird-brained scrubber is getting off on time."

I had nobody but myself to blame for this. Not that our one-sided conversation wasn't amusing, but it was becoming repetitive. However, the beer was going down well and Doggett was in full flow. A couple of elderly men sitting at the bar and still wearing raincoats had abandoned their game of cribbage. They turned to listen. As ever, the worldly Doggett didn't disappoint.

"No, mate, they've got us all by the balls and we don't know it. Think about it. If she doesn't come, for some reason, it's always your fault. Go on, think about it, it's true, but if you don't come, it's never hers, is it? Oh no, it must mean that you're half-pissed, or impotent, or a faggot or something. If you don't spend half-an-hour working her up and giving her complimentary orgasms before you start, then you're a selfish bastard who's got no interest in anybody but himself. But you try asking her to spend five minutes of her precious time on a spot of oral encouragement or structural reinforcement, and it's either, 'what kind of a girl do you think I am?' Or else it's, 'what's the matter with you, then, can't you get it up?' And if you don't spend half-an-hour afterwards telling her how grateful you are and how much you love her, you're a heartless bastard with no romance in your soul."

"Hear, hear."

One of the elderly men at the bar had mumbled the endorsement. Not having the necessary experience to argue with any conviction, I shook my head in feigned disbelief and raised my eyebrows to the heavens. Doggett rose instantly to my clumsily presented bait.

"Oh come on, be fair now. If some little scrubber's been on her back more times than a one-armed boxer, it's never her fault, is it? Oh no, it's always somebody else's problem. I can hear them now, making excuses for the little tart, saying things like, 'Poor kid, she didn't have much of an upbringing, it wasn't her fault. Her father's a right sod; nobody ever helped her to understand'. Or else they'll say, 'It's so sad, so unfair, because all these bloody men are just using her.'

Forget the fact your poor old widget's red raw, because she just spent the last hour-and-a-half jumping up and down on it. Or else they'll say something like, 'She's just looking for someone to love and going the wrong way about it. Nobody ever told her that the only thing men are interested in is giving her one . . . well, men are all the same, aren't they? Absolute bastards.'"

More interruptions from the geriatrics at the bar.

"You've got to admit he's got a point there, son."

"Yeah, they say that; they do. I've heard 'em; heard 'em too bloody often, I can tell you."

The two heads at the bar were now nodding vigorously, and I was in the minority. That's the trouble with feminists. They're like policemen, or is it the buses? There's never one around when you need one, and then two come at once. An encouraged Doggett crudely amplified the point.

"We're always portrayed as the bastards. The little scrubber's probably sucked the juice out of more meat than an Oxo factory, but the moment you ask her to clamp her giggling gear around your little bit of gristle that's conveniently forgotten. Suddenly you're another callous bastard, taking advantage of a poor defenceless little creature. No, mate, as far as I'm concerned, it's all totally unfair. Why the hell blokes like you put up with it all is a bloody mystery."

"So you reckon that's what it's all about then? You reckon its men who are the victims?"

"Bloody right, and it's high time that we started fighting back. I mean, let's be fair here, women constantly remind us that they're doing us a favour by just lying there and getting seen to. So great; thanks for the favour, Blossom. Wham, bam, thank you, mam, same time next week and bring your sister. You see, that's the way all men should be, more like me, I mean. I worry about getting on with my end, and I leave whoever's just slipped her knickers and my hard-earned readies into her handbag to worry about her end. That's fair, isn't it?"

More interruptions from the bar.

"Bloody right it is. Good for you, lad, good for you."

"Too bloody true. Wish I'd had the sense to do the same forty years ago."

The two geriatrics were beginning to annoy me. I ignored them, and defended on the back foot.

"You can't mean that? I mean, come on, John . . . love's not like that, you know it's not."

He thought about that for a few seconds, and then said, "I couldn't tell you, because I never got screwed up by falling in love with someone that badly. But there's something I do know. It's not like that with hookers. It's different; more even-handed, more honest. There's less bloody hypocrisy, and more enjoyment.

"With hookers, and strippers too, for that matter, you shell out a few ackers and they come across with the goods. If you don't like the look of the goods, you take your money and your inclinations and you go and trade them somewhere else. No hard feelings and no harm done.

It's free enterprise at its best. It's Harrods for humping. It's what they set-up the Hudson Bay Trading and East India companies to achieve. It's Robert Clive and Charlie Clore and Cecil Rhodes. It's five thousand years of man and womankind's commercial history, all rolled into a fifty-bob short-time. It's what made this nation great, and I'd never want to change any of it."

"But haven't you ever been, even slightly, in love . . . at school and that?"

He smiled a whimsical smile and took another swig of his pint.

"Yeah, I suppose I was once . . . I'll never forget her, that's for sure."

I nodded encouragingly, fully expecting him to relate a tender tale of schoolyard romance with a sweet young thing in pigtails and gym knickers. It only went to show how little I knew him.

"She was the first hooker I ever went with. She was the first woman I ever went with."

He took a further swig, and then smiled again in obvious reminiscence.

"I was only thirteen. I didn't have a clue what went where, but I'd counted out all the pocket money I'd saved, and I was bloody sure I was gonna get me money's-worth.

"Her name was Mary, and she was something else." He looked up as he reminisced. "God, was she ever something else. She wasn't an attractive girl, mind you; not by any standards, even mine, but she was fantastic.

"Monumental Mary, they all called her. She had a seven-o'clock shadow across three chins, and thighs that could have squeezed the life out of an infantry regiment. She had a pair of tits that hung down to her waist, and an arse that looked just like a couple of white rhinos on the job. But don't go thinking she was flabby, because she was in beautiful shape, well, at least, beautiful shape for a woman of her age. My old man told me about her."

I looked quizzically at him. For once, he almost looked embarrassed as he explained.

"He decided she'd make a better fist of it than any stories from him about the birds and the bees. He was bloody right. He said she worked at the steelworks during the day, then hung around Tiger Bay at night, looking for a bit of business. Don't get me wrong, she wasn't any cheaper than the others, charged a few bob more than most, but I went for it 'cos my old man said that half-an-hour with Monumental Mary was worth a lifetime with some of the smart-looking crumpet with their little tight arses and Marks & Sparks knickers. That's why I went with her."

"And what happened?"

"She took my money like a shot. One minute I had two ten-bob notes in my hand, the next they were gone. We went along one of the docks and did it on a stack of pallets."

"In public? Didn't that put you off?"

"You're joking. Given a long enough run-up I could have pole-vaulted that whole stack of pallets, and her with it. Anyway, bollocks to that. I'd just shelled out three months of my hard-earned pocket money. I told my old man about it when I got home. I think he was pleased."

I was beginning to have serious reservations about the fitness of Doggett's father for any form of modern or socially responsible parenting, but said nothing and asked instead, "And was it worth it?"

I saw the eyes light up as he considered the question.

"Was it bloody ever. We did it twice, but she only made me pay for once. Jesus, she was good. She even saw me safely home afterwards. Well, it was getting dark by that time, and she was a bit worried about me. Heart of gold, old Mary had. I reckon being with her was just about as close as I ever got to being in love. God, what a woman! Monumental Mary. Two-hundred-and-forty pounds of shiny skin, sweaty crevices, and Lily of the Valley. . . I wonder where she is now."

I must have given him an old-fashioned look, because he grinned and said, "Well she may not have been all that pretty to look at, but she was spectacular. Sure as hell beat the shit out of three months of Gob Stoppers and Sherbet Dabs. I've never wasted a penny on a packet of sweets from that day to this."

"But they keep giving you the clap, John. The hookers, I mean. What I'm trying to say is, well, you don't get that with decent girls. You know, the serious relationship kind, the marrying kind."

"Oh, don't you now? I could tell you about a couple of housewives I know in Bognor Regis, who'll give you a bloody good dose just by sneezing on you."

I do believe that Doggett had intended the story as a joke, but it only served to act as a prompt for more facile interruptions from the bar.

"I reckon he must know our old ladies, Ted. D'yer reckon we ought to start charging him?"

"Naw, if he's seeing to our old ladies, I reckon he ought to be charging us."

Doggett smiled an unnecessary encouragement, and I sat looking on in mild disbelief, while the two of them continued to laugh and wheeze at their own inane commentary. I decided the only sensible response was to ignore them and returned my attention to Doggett.

"Maybe, but they have to be the exceptions."

"Yeah, I suppose you're right, but decent girls wouldn't do the things I pay hookers to do. And what's a jab in the arse and fourteen days of minor discomfort compared to a lifetime of nagging?"

"Listen and learn, son, listen and learn. There speaks a man who knows, I can tell you."

I ignored the advice from the bar, but there was no answer to that last question, or none that I could think of, and so we sat and drank our beers in silence. When we had finished our pints, Doggett ambled over to the bar. He chatted to the geriatrics and bought each of them a half-pint of mild. When he returned with two fresh pints, we each took a measured swig before he said, "So what do you wanna be, then?"

"What do you mean?"

"Well, this is what I wanna be. What you see before you is what you get. SAC Doggett: usually pissed, mostly clapped-out, and always cheerful. So what do you wanna be then?"

I shrugged my shoulders.

"I don't know, John . . . honestly, I don't."

"Then why can't you just be whoever you are?"

I thought about that for some moments and suddenly felt miserable.

"I'm not sure I even know what that is."

"Do you care?"

"Yeah, I do. It's funny, but I do care."

He again looked hard at me, and then smiled ruefully.

"Well then, let me tell you something. If you ever find yourself asking any question of that nature, and if the answer doesn't come to mind immediately, here is what you do . . .

"Instead of sitting there, and worrying about something you can do nothing about, you say 'bollocks to it', as loud as you like. Then you get yourself seriously pissed, and well and truly seen to by a couple of the roughest-looking scrubbers in town. I'll look 'em out for you; it's no trouble.

"The next morning, you wake up, sober up, wash your face, clean your teeth, shampoo your dick, and then nip down to sick quarters and get yourself a shot of penicillin. Then you commit the whole experience to memory, and make a mental note to ask yourself again in a fortnight's time."

"A fortnight. Is that how long it takes to clear up?"

"After the jab, it's just tablets; it's not a big deal."

As desperate as I was to gain the necessary experience, it wasn't at any price.

"I don't think I wanna get a dose, John, thanks all the same."

"You haven't listened to a word I've said, have you, my boy? Oh well, all I can say is that it's your loss. Cheers."

At the other end of the scale, and at the risk of the 'sour grapes' accusation, I do feel a need to further mention the commissioned officers. This is not because of any deep-seated resentment, but because these people held such sway over my life during that time that not to discuss them would be remiss. I had no problem with the genuine fly-boys, who were usually pleasant and well-rounded individuals. Those who galled were invariably administrative officers and former pilots and aircrew, who, for whatever reason, were no longer allowed to pilot or navigate aircraft.

I have no idea what the academic selection criterion for the commissioned ranks is today. In those days, the difference between proud acceptance of the Queen's Commission and relegation to the ranks of hoi polloi, was two 'A' level GCEs. I suppose it has to be more rigorous today or, on that basis and given the year-on-year improvements in the government's 'A' level pass-fail ratio, today's Air Force would boast fifty officers to each enlisted man, but I digress.

Now, if you look long enough and hard enough, you can disprove any rule. However, while accepting that premise, those commissioned officers I met slumped into one of three categories.

At the bottom of the scale, the junior officers were mostly young, invariably arrogant, often stupid, remorselessly self-opinionated, and fell into one of three sub-categories: chinless wonder, snob, and inverted snob. Those who made it through the RAF's own form of executive puberty and joined the middle ranks, i.e. those with ranks including and on either side of squadron leader, were usually sensible, pleasant and well-mannered. Most held enough knowledge and experience to temper any underlying arrogance or snobbishness, and the wisdom of relatively-mature years to combat the inherent stupidity of youth.

Those officers above wing commander, in other words, anybody with scrambled egg on their peaks, were considered all-knowing and all-powerful, but as I only ever saw them on parade grounds, or in chauffeur-driven cars, I couldn't confirm or deny this. There is, however, no denying that the leap from thin blue line to thick yellow piping was significant.

Knocking the chips from those thin blue lines was a pastime we revelled in, and I like to think we contributed in some small way to officer development. By the time a group captain's single layer of scrambled eggs loomed large in the career gun-sights of an impatient wing commander, he would have survived countless baptisms and assumed a hard-earned recognition.

Officers of such seniority commanded a healthy respect from all, and usually got it, but every once in a while an exception that proved the rule would raise its ugly head.

"Well that's it, they're out, they're damn-well kicked out, and bloody good riddance, I say."

That had been one of our noble young ultra-thin-blue-lined pilot officers, making his opinion of the SAS abundantly clear. He dropped his voice to a whisper.

"Do you know what they did last night? Do you know what they had the bloody nerve to do?"

"No, sir; no, I don't."

We were in the middle of yet another military exercise, and yet again the SAS was the opposition. Unusually, on this occasion, we were in the UK, thirty minutes flying time from our base. The deadpan response came from the Chief. He knew what had happened the previous night, as did we, but he wisely decided not to upstage the over-excitable young man. For his part, the young Pilot Officer told his tale of daring-do in an agitated whisper.

"They only had the damned effrontery to break into the officers' mess last night."

"No, I don't believe it! They didn't, did they, sir?"

"Oh yes, Flight. I was there; we were all there."

"Well that's not on, sir. That's outrageous. What did they want? Something to eat, I suppose."

As I listened to the Chief gently winding him up with a succession of puerile comments and ridiculous answers, I did feel he might be overplaying his hand.

"Well of course they didn't want to eat. Don't be ridiculous. Why would they want that?"

"Well, they've got to eat some time, haven't they, sir? Perhaps they thought the food would be better in the officers' mess than the airmen's mess."

Somebody sniggered. Luckily the young officer failed to hear it.

"Well, yes, that may well be so, but they'd hardly break into the officers' mess to get it, would they? Well, not right in the middle of dinner. Not with everybody still there."

"No, sir, I hadn't thought of that. You could be right there. So, what exactly did they want?"

Bursting with excitement and an overwhelming need to tell somebody about his terrifying ordeal of the previous night, the young officer blurted out, "Officers; that's what they wanted. They wanted officers."

The Chief was aghast.

"Surely not for . . . you don't think. I mean, not for . . . you don't mean . . . for sex?"

"Well, of course not. I didn't say they wanted that. I just said that they wanted officers. For goodness sake, stop being so bloody obtuse, man!"

The young Pilot Officer suddenly sensed the potential for ridicule. He eyed the Chief cautiously, before taking a rapid sweep around the commcentre tent to check on the rest of us. Reassuringly, nobody seemed interested in what he had to say. More than that, they appeared oblivious to his presence as they concentrated on individual and clearly essential tasks.

What the young officer didn't know, but should have known, was that a field commcen, about to undergo a morning watch change, was rarely such a frantic place. What he didn't notice, but should have noticed, was that every back turned toward him was shaking uncontrollably.

"Well, I suppose that would have been the ideal place to have gone then, sir."

"What?"

"The officers' mess . . . It's the ideal place to find officers, sir."

This time the chief had overplayed his hand. The resulting glare of suspicion was immediate.

"I don't know if you find this amusing, Flight Sergeant, but I can't see anything funny. As far as I'm concerned, they had no right to be there, but then to behave like that was just outrageous."

"Yes, of course it was. I'm sorry, sir. So, what did they want the officers for, sir?"

"Hostages, of course, and they took them too; they've still not handed them back. It's just not on, not on at all. The Commandant said so."

"Ah, so the Commandant was there as well, was he, sir?"

"There? I'll say he was there. He was the first one up against the wall . . . they had him pinned there, right in the middle of the dining-room; threatened him and everything."

"Well then, they're obviously out of control, sir. That's clearly unacceptable behaviour, especially when they're in the officers' mess without permission."

"Yes, that's what the Commandant said. He's banned them from the exercise, and not a moment too soon as far as I'm concerned. He said he'd set the dogs on them if they weren't out by tonight, and he means it. I was with him when he said it . . . and he wants his men back."

By this time the commcen seemed eerily quiet, not because of any sudden downturn in workload, but because those on watch had been unable to control the laughter and had slipped outside to explode. The Chief's expression of concerned interest didn't waver as he said, "What men would these be, sir?"

"The officers, of course; those I spoke of. Weren't you listening? I told you, they took them with them, bound and blindfolded. Took three of them, one from each branch. They took young Neil Simpson, our junior liaison officer . . . well, he was before they took him."

"Well then, it should be some good practical experience for him, sir."

"No, I don't mean . . . He's not trained for hostage negotiation and all that, he's trained for . . ."

The excited whisper died away as he watched the Chief carefully processing the only signal received in the last half-hour. The NCO painstakingly stamped the envelope and restored any faltering composure before returning his attention to the agitated face before him.

"Oh well, I suppose it doesn't matter what he's trained for, but we haven't seen him since. He was sitting next to me when they burst in. It could have been me; we hadn't even finished dinner."

"Well, I just hope they don't torture him too badly, sir."

"They wouldn't dare." A nervous glance confirmed the possibility. "Would they?"

By this time it was clear that even the poker-faced Chief was having trouble not laughing as he casually turned away from the earnest expression and mischievously added, "Oh yes, sir, they're known for it."

"Good God."

Until then, I couldn't tell if his lucky escape had left the young officer relieved or disappointed by his lack of celebrity, but suddenly his relief was clear. I do, however, wish I could have been a fly on the wall in the officers' mess that previous evening, because the SAS had been having fun with everybody's favourite target . . . the junior officers.

Severely criticised by the camp Commandant a day or so earlier for apparently taking the exercise too seriously, the SAS responded by raiding the officers' mess. Held against the wall of the mess at knifepoint, the previously talkative Commandant had wisely kept his own counsel. He watched them take the three junior officers hostage and said nothing, but after they'd gone recovered both courage and garrulity and flew into a rage. Within minutes of their departure from the mess, he had officially banned them from the station, poor, misguided fool that he was.

For their part, as that particular Commandant's nemesis, and our regular officially-sanctioned enemy, the SAS quite rightly saw the officers' mess and their three junior officer hostages as legitimate targets. For the duration of the exercise, the camp had been classified as a war zone. As far as the SAS were concerned, that included the officers' mess and everybody in it.

A furious Commandant hadn't seen it that way. The following morning a high-level telephone call to Hereford preceded written confirmation the SAS were no longer needed. The confirmation signal went further. It demanded the immediate return of the three officers and an unreserved apology from the SAS. Unsurprisingly, he received no such assurance or apology. Then, an enraged Commandant made an even more foolish error. He naively threatened that if Hereford didn't withdraw its men within twenty-four hours, he would let the dogs loose on the airfield.

Nowadays, nobody in his or her right mind would dream of doing anything so foolish as to threaten the regiment with dogs, or anything else, for that matter. Nowadays, everybody is more than aware of their abilities. However, in the sixties, few people, even among members of the regular armed forces, knew just how good these guys were. Better informed than most, we sat back and waited for the fun to begin.

As ever, the regiment didn't disappoint, and on the following night the Commandant received his answer. It came via the obligatory make-believe bomb tossed into the commcentre, and the sabotaging of our generators, leaving us unable to even switch on a light bulb, let alone send a signal. Most telling and downright embarrassing for all concerned, though, was the theft.

They discovered it the next morning, when the military police went to feed and exercise the dozen or so vicious Alsatian police dogs held in kennels at the back of the guardhouse; the same dogs a furious Commandant had threatened to set on the SAS. When the duty policemen arrived they found every kennel open, and every animal gone.

Panic resulted. A red-faced Commandant was told, and a frantic and hugely embarrassed team of military police searched the base.

Fortunately for everyone's blushes, they found the missing dogs, barking and bemused but otherwise unharmed, tethered to stakes in the centre of the airfield. Also left were three bemused junior officers and a note for the Commandant, left by a group of men who had more than proved their point, and who must have laughed themselves silly all the way back to Hereford.

The spoils of war

Nineteen sixty-eight was undoubtedly the most interesting, significant and memorable year of my life, or my life until that point, and for so many different reasons. I travelled extensively and grew both physically and emotionally. I discovered much about the world and its peoples, and ever more about myself. I spent six weeks in the Western Australian Outback during a series of long-range manoeuvres, which were little more than exercises in boredom incurring lengthy periods spent alone and manning a mobile WT circuit. However, despite the monotony, I came to appreciate some of the beauty and scale of the Australian continent. I also came to understand the dangers of being inexperienced and alone, on such terrain, and the need for basic human contact.

I volunteered for just about everything far-eastern, and regularly flew in and out of Changi. I also spent more time up-country in Malaya, this time farther north beyond Kuala Lumpur. As well as my continuing love affair with Singapore, I developed a similar affection for another South-East Asian country, and an enduring love for the gentle humility of its people. Many of those people I will forever recall with fondness, and while my heart will always belong to Singapore and its vibrancies and colour, a part of me will always belong to Thailand.

However, I'm getting ahead of myself. Before I came to sample the delights and wonders of Thailand, I had a rather sensitive exercise to complete.

The sensitivity was nothing to do with tactics or procedures or codes and documents, or even the latest technology. It was to do with our presence, because we were British forces, officially at peace with the world, about to begin a military training exercise for the South-East Asia Treaty Organisation on a warring nation's base, along the margins of a bloody and tragic conflict.

"Sorry about this, chaps, but they've got some priority traffic coming in from the north-east, and so we're going to have to delay putting the old kite down for a while."

The Charlie one-thirty pilot doing the Biggles impersonation was an aged flight lieutenant, complete with handlebar moustache. He had kept us entertained during the flight with a succession of bad jokes, as well as snippets of interest on landmarks, current locations, and other relevant and irrelevant details, delivering each announcement with the same arguably comical affectation.

Most of the guys groaned each time the voice on the tannoy interrupted the aircraft's drone and their much-needed sleep, but I enjoyed it. However, I must admit to mild annoyance when he explained his reason for correcting an earlier announcement about our expected time of arrival.

"I've been up since six. I don't believe this."

One of the guys had voiced the majority view. I answered, "It's all right for you, at least you got some sleep. I haven't been to bed for thirty-six hours."

"Well whose fault's that? If you stayed away from Bugis Street and all those bloody freaks and weirdos that hang out there, you might get some sleep once in a while."

That had been Dave Tate. Despite the holier-than-thou posture, I had always got on well with him, but we had never become close friends, because Dave had a long-term and serious girlfriend called Jenny, who worked nights at the local petrol station. Dave and Jenny were deeply in love and committed to each other, and that commitment was all-consuming. So much so, they spent every spare moment of his free time, and her working hours, in the stockroom at the back of the forecourt kiosk. It was only when Dave was on exercise that the petrol station managed to show a nightly profit and the man himself managed to catch up on sleep.

"Is this the guy who can't keep his eyes open without popping a couple of bennies every hour? The same guy who'd rather have some nymphy little petrol-pump attendant wrap herself round his dick and shove a shot of Redex up his arse than get some sleep?"

I had made the unsubtle retort, good-naturedly. He grinned.

"Well at least I can remember her name in the morning. At least I don't feel the need to screw anything and everything just 'cos it's got tits and a pulse."

I blushed like crazy and said nothing. Dave misread my reaction, assuming it was a silent admission of guilt, rather than shame at the persistence of an embarrassingly virgin condition.

We stayed in that same holding pattern, two hundred kilometres north of Bangkok, for the next twenty minutes. We were waiting for clearance to land at Korat, a U.S. Air Force base on the Khorat Plateau. Korat was only seventy miles from the Cambodian border and not much farther from Laos. Just how close we were to the main conflict didn't fully sink in, though, until the pilot explained why we had to wait. A group of F105 Thunderchiefs was returning from that day's mission over Hanoi. Many were in poor shape.

It was only after we landed and filed out of the back of the one-thirty that we came to see just how churlish and selfish our grumbles were, and how lethally effective Hanoi's anti-aircraft defences were. The condition of the Thunderchiefs that had made it back, and the condition of some of the other F105s that limped in after we landed, was sobering to say the least.

We came to know some of the pilots during our three-week stay at Korat. To a man, they were straightforward and decent guys. To a man, they were generous and fun-loving. To a man, they were full of life and scared of death, and to a man, they had a philosophical contemplation of death's inevitability that was one of the most harrowing phenomena I ever witnessed.

The mortality rate for a 105 pilot over Hanoi was high, too high, and so it was not anticipating peace and home and loved ones far away that dominated their lives, but a cynical contemplation of an impending death. I spoke to some of them about this and that and the war. They each left me with the impression that it was death, and not the end of the war, that was an inevitable fact of tomorrow, or the day after, or the week after that. Whether that fate was days or weeks away was of little consequence, because, to many of them, life and survival was merely a reprieve, granted by a whim of fate today, and revoked tomorrow.

If a pilot made it to fifty missions the resulting party was unbelievable. If he made it to one hundred missions the resulting party would light up the Khorat Plateau. But, to my mind, those parties were nothing to do with celebration. They were hysterical reactions to a freak of chance, a morbid acknowledgement that the odds against dying on tomorrow's mission were now reduced.

There are already so many books and articles and films portraying the horror and futility that was Vietnam, and I am in no way qualified or have any wish to add to those works. However, Exercise Ramasoon, on the Khorat Plateau in central Thailand in nineteen sixty-eight, showed me a side of human nature that I hadn't seen before. It gave me a better understanding of life and death, and the tenuous threads that links the two, and of mankind's ability to cope with the most desperate circumstance. It was an experience that was educational, remarkable, and seriously disturbing.

There were only a dozen of us on the Korat base, with a further dozen working farther north at Leong Nok Tha, a token presence, if you like. It was, however, a token appreciated by our U.S. hosts, and the most vivid memory of my time there was the American's overwhelming generosity and hospitality amid, what was for some of them, a life-or-death struggle.

By this time I was something of a veteran. I had been on numerous exercises, and was considered a fully-fledged member of the team. But I only knew of far-eastern warfare British style. I only knew of spartan tents, camouflaged alongside a jungle clearing; of dried and tinned food, with condensed milk and powered tea. I only knew of heavy jungle-green combat clothing that fitted where it touched; of nights of boredom manning a Morse circuit, or sitting alone in my tent, perched on a canvas camp-bed supported by steel rods and protected by mosquito netting.

I didn't understand jungle warfare American style, and Korat was the first time I saw an alternative to war by attrition and stealth. It was also the first time I came to realise just how vast the American resources were, and how poorly funded we were by comparison.

The first and most obvious difference was the clothing. Our clothing was practical and hardwearing, but abysmally scruffy. The boots were cumbersome, and padded out with thick uncomfortable socks. The jackets rarely fitted, and the trousers were worse. The shirts were khaki and shapeless and needed a green netted cravat to camouflage the contrast and keep out the rain. All uniform material was coarse and shabby, and the cut non-existent.

The Americans always looked immaculate. Their uniforms were beautifully tailored, and the material finely woven. Combat gear was similarly tailored and similarly immaculate.

Another glaring disparity was the food. Our food consisted of composition rations, carried around for months on end in dog-eared cardboard boxes, heated over open fires or small individual tin stoves, and eaten only when ravenous. The American food was splendid.

Because of an anomaly in the rankings, the Americans considered us equivalent to junior NCOs, and therefore demanded that we eat in the NCOs' mess. There, the food was wonderful, with not a tin of processed cheese or an oatmeal biscuit in sight. The meat was always lean and tender and beautifully cooked, the salads crisp and colourful, the milk full and cold, and the juices varied and fresh. The sheer quality and variety of food and drink on offer in that place would have put the Connaught to shame, but it was the barbecues I best remember.

They organised the first as a special welcome. We showed willing and wandered along, expecting a frugal affair with a few black and malnourished sausages and a couple of tins of under-strength beer. You can imagine our surprise when we found a dozen chefs lined up behind a forty-yard-long trestle table, serving succulent steaks and all manner of other meats and fresh vegetables, with each cut of meat specifically prepared to individual preference.

A huge square of tables offered fresh salads of every description, and freshly-baked bread. At either end, twenty-foot-diameter paddling pools were filled with ice and tins of every conceivable beer. But if the expanse of barbecue staggered me, the entertainment left me flabbergasted.

After the barbecue, they took us over to the Enlisted Men's Club. In truth, it had been a long day and we would rather have slept, but went along because it would have seemed impolite not to. However, the scene that greeted us was incredible, and more than worthy of a few hours lost sleep.

There must have been between two hundred-and-fifty and three hundred guys crammed into that hangar of a room. They were whistling and cheering and hollering and decidedly the worse for wear, or alcohol, or whatever. Fussing around them and catering for their every need, fleets of young waiters and waitresses offered drinks and cocktails. A second army scurried from table to table clearing the debris, while attractive young women dressed in fishnet stockings and bunny-girl costumes served cigarettes and candy from trays hung around their necks.

A sickly smell of something aromatic wafted across this scene of pandemonium, a smell I would not instantly identify until a later posting closer to the Lebanon. On stage, a five-piece rock band played the latest sounds, and a troupe of scantily-clad girls danced different routines for each number. As well as the music and conventional cabaret, a bevy of attractive strippers took to the stage and bared their desirable alls to recorded music after each live music or cabaret session.

Contrasted with the scene of devastation and death that had greeted our arrival, this was surreal, and to my first impression almost irreverent. I kept pinching myself and telling myself that this was a war zone, and that people were dying. . . wholesale, and every day.

If this had been a British front-line airbase somewhere in the middle of nowhere, there would have been a couple of twelve-by-twelve tents laced together, an aged gramophone playing scratched seventy-eight recordings of Vera Lynn or Eddie Calvert, and a faded picture of *Playboy*'s playmate of the month glued to the tent flap with bodily fluid. If we were lucky, there might even be a half-empty barrel of Double Diamond propped up against a webbing belt in the corner, but this place was unbelievable. It was like some vast Florida vice club, rock concert and drinking den, all rolled together and then hidden away in the middle of South-East Asia.

I have to say the GIs and USAF people were marvellous. In the time I was there they didn't once allow me to put my hand in my pocket to buy a drink. Few Americans in the EM club had any idea why we were there, or what we were doing, but it was almost as though they half-expected some form of announcement about British involvement in the war and this was their way of showing appreciation. Not that I'm labouring under any illusion that our paltry contribution would have made the slightest difference to the outcome of that particular conflict, but I guess the Americans figured they had never lost a war involving the Brits, either as allies or enemy, and presume they looked on us a delegation of scruffily-dressed good-luck charms with odd accents.

Fortunately, for sleep and our general physical well-being, the work was undemanding. It consisted of a single voice circuit and hourly voice checks, with live traffic being almost non-existent. Housed in six-man huts with comfortable beds and curtains on the windows, we found the USAF had assigned us dhobi women, who turned out to be three charming and shy young girls from the local village. They came in early in the morning, and cleaned and washed anything not previously hidden, including bed-linen, trousers, jackets, berets, and on one occasion a pair of expensive suede shoes. They returned them the following day, irreparably turned up at the toes and suitable only for the feet of a pantomime Aladdin or oversized pixie.

Those three young dhobi girls were captivating. They spoke little English, and were shy and giggly and feminine and enchanting. I came to look forward to their daily visits, not because of any lecherous motive, but because they were sweet and gentle and natural and beautiful. You see, even in the late sixties, the street girls of Bangkok were infamous, so much so that we had arranged a two-night excursion to the capital to see for ourselves. However, such a reputation does a grave injustice to Thai women, because the overwhelming majority of unmarried Thai women were dainty and innocent and chaste; chaperoned courtships were the norm, and any suitor's wish for a Thai lady's hand demanded patience, gentility, and the constant respect of her and her family.

The war was never far from our minds, though, because we could hear the aircraft taking off in a constant cycle, and hear the regular explosions from the north as pilots jettisoned explosives before landing damaged aircraft. If we needed reminding, the immediacy of the conflict was brought home to us a few days later, in the early hours, while I was on watch at the commcen.

It had been a boring night, similar to every other, sitting in a brightly lit room, with only one telecoms circuit demanding hourly radio checks. I had been on watch with Dave Tate and a fiery little Irishman, unsurprisingly named Paddy, who was running the circuit. Because of the brightness, Dave took the camp bed outside, and was trying, as he often did, to get some sleep. I wandered outside to take in the night air and smoke yet another in a constant chain of cigarettes.

The first sign of anything wrong should have screamed a warning, and would have done to anybody with first-hand experience of such matters, because the sky suddenly went from jet black to bright orange. However, instead of hitting the deck, I stood tall and looked around, with my eyes wide and mind marvelling, like a five-year-old child at a fairground. Then the blast hit me.

Although not of enough strength to flatten me, it knocked me a couple of steps back and spilled Dave Tate from his camp-bed. This was not by the force of the blast, although I didn't tell him that and he afterwards used an embellished story as a party piece. It was because I had trodden on the edge of his bed while steadying myself and tipped him out.

He picked himself up, dusted himself down, and then said, "What the fuck was that?"

Whatever Hollywood might have us believe, those funny one-liners never come to mind at a time like that. Instead of holding my stomach and saying, "I'm sorry; I do beg your pardon," in inimitable Dudley Moore style, I simply said, "Bomb, I think."

"I know that, but where the fuck did it come from?"

"I dunno, but I wish I had a weapon."

And that was it. That was my first reaction. At any second I expected the air to be putrid with cordite and the screams of ten thousand Vietcong shock troops sweeping across the plains of Khorat in a horde of savagery. I had visions of them forcing us back with sheer weight of numbers, and engaging hung-over and desperately outnumbered British and Americans in hand-to-hand combat. Instead, all I saw was lights, and all I heard was sirens, dozens of them.

It seemed, a Vietcong unit had evaded the Cambodian border patrols, sneaked across country, infiltrated the base and sabotaged the bomb dump, around three hundred yards away. They had brought the ground war into the backyard of the US Air Force and unintentionally brought some appreciation of what the residents of Hanoi must have suffered to my limited understanding.

A distinct sense of fear went through me in the immediate aftermath of that explosion, fleeting but undeniable. Worse, though, was the impotence I had felt at not having the means with which to defend myself, or not knowing which way to run, or where to take cover, or how to deal with any subsequent explosion or threat. It was, I have to imagine, only a fraction of the fear and impotence that those ordinary people of Hanoi must have experienced on just about every night of their lives.

All in all, we had been lucky. There had been casualties, but only one fatality, a local Thai, working night shift at the dump, and the cruel irony of that didn't escape me either.

Two days later we completed our part in Exercise Ramasoon. The important stuff was about to begin, because the reward for those weeks of monotonous work, exhilarating play, harrowing experience, and all-round sterling diplomatic effort was R&R, two hundred kilometres south, in Bangkok.

We arrived at the Grand Hotel and checked in, two to a room. I had no idea why they had put us up in hotel rooms. I assumed it was a reciprocal arrangement with the Americans, a token of generosity that I was happy to make the most of.

I shared a room with Dave Tate, and that suited me. I intended spending the next forty-eight hours out and about, sampling the delights of Bangkok. I assumed Dave would use the two nights of luxury to catch up on sleep and further charge the stamina batteries in preparation for his return to Jenny and the rigours of the petrol station stockroom, but he was about to shatter that assumption. He wandered over as I was preparing to head out for the night, and casually asked, "Where are you going tonight?"

"We're meeting at a place called the Villa Club . . . Upmarket joint with a cabaret and that."

"Plenty of women?"

"I dunno, I suppose so. Why? Do you wanna come?"

Knowing Dave's devotion to Jenny, his answer surprised me.

"Might as well, I suppose."

I looked closely at the feigned nonchalance.

"What? You wanna come, too? Out and about in the sin capital of the world? I thought you didn't wanna mix with all the freaks and weirdos? Why the sudden change of mind?"

He shrugged.

"Can't hang around here all night and every night. Too much of a drag. Thought I'd see what was what. Thought maybe I'd come with you and see what all the fuss is about."

"Jenny hasn't dumped you, has she?"

"No, nothing like that."

"Then what?"

He looked uncomfortable, in fact, more than uncomfortable, he looked embarrassed; in fact, more than embarrassed, he looked downright guilty. Suddenly it all came gushing out.

"Look I've got to tell somebody 'cos this is driving me mad. You see, something happened back there. I think I might have to split up with Jen."

This was intriguing.

"Why? What the hell happened?"

He slumped down on the edge of the bed, and bowed his head in misery and contrition. I anticipated the worst, but then listened in amusement as he blurted a confession that wouldn't have registered as a misdemeanour on most sixties couples' fidelity scales.

"You remember that dhobi girl at Korat? The beautiful one, who always said '*Mâi pehn rai*'?"

"They were all beautiful, and they all said, '*Mâi pehn rai*'. That's all they ever said, well, that and '*Sa wàt dee*'."

Sa wàt dee was a formal greeting or farewell, said with the palms touching and a slight bow of the head. *Mâi pehn rai* was pure U.S. of A., or it was then. You said *Mâi pehn rai* with a shrug of the shoulders. Today's translation is the spontaneously shallow 'you're welcome', which, when combined with 'have a nice day' and 'you're the man', surely rank as one of the three most puerile expressions ever devised by reputedly intelligent beings. The literal translation of *Mâi pehn rai*, according to everything American in the sixties, was the equally detestable, 'No sweat'.

Dave went on with his confession, and I tried not laugh as I studied his expression of abject despondency and heard the misery pouring out of him.

"I mean the little one, the shy one who was always giggling. She was beautiful, wasn't she?"

I nodded as I recalled the three dhobi girls assigned to our hut, and especially the little dark-eyed beauty with the impish giggle.

"They were all beautiful, mate, every one of them, especially her. Why, what's the problem? You didn't?"

"No, nothing like that. It's just that, well, look, don't say anything to anybody, 'cos they'd only take the piss, but I think I fell in love with her."

It was difficult to stifle the laughter as I saw he was in earnest. Rather than risk further upsetting him, I looked out of the window and said matter-of-factly, "Get in the queue; everybody fell in love with her. Paddy used to dream about her every night, and then wake up with a hard-on every morning. That's why she was always giggling."

"No, you don't understand. I don't mean I fancied her. I mean I fell in love with her, really in love. I think she felt the same, 'cos she was always smiling and sending messages with her eyes."

I suddenly felt some empathy for his condition. She had been beautiful, there was no doubt of that, almost to the point of perfection, and I'd come close to the same fate. For me it had been a fleeting infatuation, but Dave was seriously smitten and in emotional turmoil. He went on.

"It sounds stupid. It sounds pathetic, I know it does, but I can't stop thinking about her, and I don't know what I'm going to do about it. I mean, if I am in love with her, how can I be in love with Jen? It's not possible, is it, not with two of them, not at the same time?"

It wasn't a question I was in any way qualified to answer. Instead of spouting hollow words of wisdom, I posed a question of my own, hoping to lighten the sudden gloom that had descended.

"So you thought you'd solve everything by coming out on the town, boozing and whoring with the rest of us? You haven't spoken to Doggett, have you? He hasn't been giving you advice?"

"No, why?"

"Oh nothing; just a thought."

He had no reason to see the humour in that, and clearly didn't. I studied his misery and decided to be more sympathetic.

"So why do you want to come out with us? What's that gonna solve? You don't drink, well not all that much, you don't like nightclubs, and you never looked at another woman after Jenny, well, until now. Why fuck everything up over a girl you've just met, haven't shagged, haven't even kissed, can't talk to, and probably won't ever see again?"

"Because I need to know."

"Know what?"

"I need to know how I feel and that; about her, and about Jen. We were thinking of getting married next year. I need to know if it's just because I'm away from home and lonely, and that it doesn't mean anything, or if I should scrub round getting married because I want other women. I'm not like you, I never had it off with anyone but Jen, and so I don't know how it feels. You know what I mean . . . being with someone else and that. If I'm thinking of getting married, I have to be sure. I do, don't I? I mean, what do you think?"

"Christ, Dave. How old are you?"

"I'll be twenty in November."

"Well, you're a fuck sight older than me, so why are you asking me for advice? I'm not the burning bloody bush."

I wished I hadn't asked, because the resulting gush of admission seriously embarrassed me. If proof were needed, it also showed just what a consummate liar I had become since Cosford.

"I know that, but you know all about women. I don't."

I favoured him with one of my old-fashioned looks, but he stood his ground.

"It's true. You've been shagging women for as long as I've known you, and you never stayed with any of them. I heard about that time you screwed Albrighton Sally in the field, and then dumped her straight after. They said she was always hanging round camp, asking about you. Everybody reckoned she'd fallen in love with you, but you never got hung up over her or any of them."

I tried not to blush at the memory of that afternoon's debacle, recalling a vision of the all-but naked and terrifyingly promiscuous Albrighton Sally as she towered over me and made clear her equally terrifying intent. I recalled the injury I had feigned, and the lies I had told, and my unwarranted elevation to the rank of junior rake, but I wasn't aware the rumour-mongers had exaggerated the story to such an extent. I had similarly been blissfully unaware of any later efforts by the notorious lady to make good her lecherous promise of that afternoon.

I thought about it, and decided that I was still no more courageous or informed than I had been in the field that day. I smiled as I saw Dave's earnest expression and considered his back-handed compliment. The knowledge of my unfounded notoriety pleased me. It similarly pleased me that such an irrelevance as the truth hadn't managed to get in the way of a good rumour.

"That was a long time ago, mate."

"Yeah, maybe it was, but it still happened and it never bothered you. You're not like me, you don't care, you never did. I mean, look at the Pink Panther."

"What about it?"

"Everybody knows that you've screwed your way through just about every one of those little dolly birds over there. They say you only have to look at them and they start getting 'em off."

The Pink Panther was a typical sixties coffee bar, sited along the seafront in Bognor Regis. It was a place where I spent far too much time. Some of the girls who worked and chatted there were attractive, and I had enjoyed strictly platonic affairs with two or three of them. However, it seemed the 'everybody' to whom Dave referred had confused me with the enviably good-looking Joules. Perception, it seemed, was ninth-tenths of the law of barrack-room gossip, or certainly the law of any barrack-room gossip involving me. I decided to try a touch of honesty for a change.

"Let me tell you something, shall I, Dave. I was just sixteen that day in the field with Albrighton Sally, and all that got screwed was my ego. As for the girls at the Pink Panther, all I can say is that you don't want to believe everything you hear, mate, 'cos most of it's bullshit."

He obviously didn't believe a word of it, while I reasoned that, however noble the cause, too much honesty of that sort could be bad for my hard-won reputation. Instead of any further and possibly damaging revelations, I changed the subject.

"When was the last time you ate?"

"That's just it. I can't eat, haven't eaten properly for days. I'm just not hungry, and on top of that I'm knackered. I've had trouble sleeping for the last three nights."

I figured if Dave Tate had trouble sleeping the problem was serious.

"Well, let's go and get something to eat, and maybe have a few beers. After that, if you still want to come out on the town, we'll do the Villa Club, or whatever it's called, and then we'll see what happens . . . but only on one condition."

He looked quizzically across at me.

"What's that?"

"Jenny hadn't better find out that I took you out on the town in Bangkok. If she ever does or, God forbid, you get a dose, she'll come looking for me, and we'll both be singing soprano."

He mustered a weak smile, but agreed, and so we wandered out of the hotel and along the busy streets. We stopped at a café and ordered food and beer. I made do with a sandwich and a couple of beers, but a suddenly relaxed and ravenous Dave tucked away three platefuls of spaghetti bolognese. He washed them down with six or seven beers, and all in the space of an hour. Confession, it appeared, was as good for the appetite as the soul.

After that we jumped into a trishaw and headed over to the Club. The Villa Club turned out to be a relatively sophisticated nightclub: American style, with subdued lighting, button-back seats, formal waiting staff and a quality cabaret. It was still early. The others hadn't arrived, and so we chose a large table, set out in front of the stage. I took an uneasy look at a worse-for-wear Dave Tate as he weaved drunkenly towards the table; so, for that matter, did the management. I saw the manager speak to a waiter, who warily studied Dave before coming over to me and saying, "He drink too much?"

I smiled unassumingly.

"No, nothing like that. He's just got himself a bit worked up and emotional, that's all. He's O.K. I'll look after him, don't worry."

"You no American?"

"No, no, we're British forces, we're both British forces."

"You got American dollar?"

"Sure, American dollars, bahts, Singapore dollars... anything you want."

Suddenly a beaming smile had replaced the look of mistrust.

"We like British, British OK. Your friend want coffee?"

"No thanks, just a beer. We've got some friends meeting us here; more British."

The beam widened even further.

"More British, good, good. We get lots American G.I., no British; British no problem."

"*Mâi pehn rai*, huh?"

"Sure, sure, *Mâi pehn rai*. I get you beer. You enjoy."

"Thank you, we will."

He hurried back to the manager and a frantic conversation ensued, during which the manager also started beaming happily and waving across to me. I nodded and smiled politely back, and then watched as the two of them hurried away to collect our beers and spread the good news among the remaining staff. One by one, they all started smiling across at us.

By the time the others had arrived we were honoured guests. I was on my third glass of beer and feeling relaxed. Dave took full advantage of the Villa Club's hospitality by sinking excessive quantities of beer, with each generous measure of beer served in a large trumpet-shaped glass. As well as the steadily-increasing number of beers, he followed each oversized and scandalously overpriced glass with a complimentary and similarly oversized Bacardi and coke chaser.

He had drunk so much that when the stage lighting came up and the cabaret began, I was getting worried. I mentioned it to Joules, who didn't share my concern.

"Keep an eye on Dave, will you? I'm getting a bit worried. He's getting seriously pissed."

"If I'd chucked as much down my gullet as he has, I'd be seriously friggin pissed too."

"No, you don't understand. He doesn't normally drink."

His response was both worn and predictable.

"Well, that's all right then, 'cos there's nothing friggin normal about the amount he's drunk."

It was suddenly too late for further talk. The star of the show sashayed her way to centre stage to a cacophony of wolf whistles and cheers. The lights dimmed, and she began a medley of Hoagy Carmichael and Cole Porter. Joules suddenly had more important fish to fry; not that he had any love for Hoagy Carmichael or Cole Porter, but the star of the show was a good-looking woman, wearing stockings and high heels, and a glittering evening dress split to the waist. She formed extravagant Os with her mouth and held the microphone Tina Turner style, and there was no mistaking the message in that. Then she caught sight of Joules and locked eyes with him as she sang. It signalled the end of any conversation at the table.

Everyone began lecherously assessing the figure beneath the evening dress, checking out the slit in the skirt to see if she was wearing any other items of similarly risqué underwear. Everyone, that is, except Joules, Dave and me. Me because I was watching Dave and not happy with what I saw. Joules because he knew if he held eye contact with the sexy singer for long enough, whatever else she might or might not be wearing underneath that evening dress would be his for a souvenir before the night was out. And Dave because Dave was just about to throw up.

Seconds later, he did. Five litres of beer, half-a-dozen triple Bacardi and cokes and three large platefuls of partially-digested spaghetti Bolognese, all violently deposited on to the table between us and the voluptuous cabaret singer. What made it worse was that after he had finally finished throwing up, he collapsed into his chair, leaving lank strands of regurgitated spaghetti just about everywhere: dangling from his mouth, dripped down his shirt, wriggling around on the table and swimming in his glass. It looked like the poor man had been suffering from an acute case of alien worms, and those that had found their way into his glass looked to be still alive.

The sexy-looking singer halted the cabaret in mid-verse with a glare of disgust, a cry of revulsion and a sudden exodus from the stage. The management ejected us some moments after that. A disappointed looking waiter took our money and told us we couldn't possibly be British, because British people didn't behave like that. Oh, how times have changed.

Once outside, we propped Dave against a wall and tried to flag down a passing trishaw, which wasn't easy, because the usually aggressively marketed trishaws were avoiding us like the plague.

"I'll be all right. Leave me alone. I'm sorry, I'm so sorry."

That was Dave, apologising to the world. We'd all laughed insanely at the memory of the sexy-looking cabaret singer's face as she broke free of Julian Carter's gaze of lustful promise and saw the worms of spaghetti wriggling around in that oversized glass. I say we'd all laughed, but that wasn't the whole story. For some reason the enviably good-looking Joules hadn't seen the joke.

"I was in there. I was bloody-well in there. I haven't friggin well bounced around on a pair of tits like that for months. And did you see the way she was holding that microphone? You know what she was saying, don't you? You know what she was saying to me? She was offering to do the same to my dick. You bastard. You total friggin bastard. If I've missed giving her one, just because of you, you pissed-up prat. They shouldn't friggin-well allow arseholes like you out."

We laughed louder at that, while a pathetic-looking Dave continued apologising as he disentangled previously unnoticed strands of spaghetti that had somehow wormed themselves around his belt buckle.

"I'm sorry, mate, I'm so sorry. It's all my fault. Look, let me go and talk to her. Let me explain."

"Oh, shut up."

We finally found a trishaw rider who agreed to take Dave back to the hotel for an extortionate amount of money, but as we tried to shovel him into the seat he staunchly resisted and said, "I'll be all right, just give me a few minutes. I'm sorry."

Joules was having none of it.

"You must be dreaming, pal. Look at the friggin state of you. You're covered in gunge and you stink of puke. Now get into the friggin trishaw and shut it."

Dave looked vacantly down at the front of his ruined shirt and saw the truth of that. He nodded a drunken agreement, but instead of getting into the trishaw, fished through his pockets. He produced a wad of baht and U.S. dollar bills and shoved them into my hand.

"You're gonna go and get a woman, you always do. So, I want you to bring one back for me; one who looks just like that little dhobi girl at Korat: little '*Mâi pehn rai*'. I've gotta know, I've just got to. It's my whole fucking life at stake here . . . you understand?"

Despite the drunken melodrama, I could have said no. I could have lied. It would have been simple, and he wouldn't have remembered the next morning. I could have said the hotel would throw us out if they caught us smuggling in women, which was true. I could have spoken of my regard for Jenny and feigned concern for their happiness. I could have thought up a thousand excuses. If push came to shove, I could even have told the truth; if I'd only had time to think.

I could feel everyone's eyes on me as I tried to think up a sensible answer, but the brain wouldn't function, or not in time. I mutely nodded, stuffed the money into my Levi's and bundled him into the waiting trishaw. I smiled a confidence I was far from convinced of, and told him to clean himself up and sober up, then said that I would see him back at the hotel in a few hours.

It didn't occur to me that I would be doing precisely that just over two hours later, because I had fully intended conveniently forgetting Dave's bizarre appeal and enjoying what remained of that night. Unfortunately, everyone else in the group had other ideas, well everyone except Joules, who had sneaked back into the Villa Club via the stage door.

Two hours, three bars, and rather too many beers later I still hadn't managed to talk my way out of it. Instead, I found myself with the rest of them in an extravagantly decorated house of ill repute, while a genial *mama-san* paraded an enticing procession of beautiful young women before our collective gaze, and everybody argued about the relative merits of each according to their own disparate recollections of Dave's beautiful young dhobi girl from Korat.

Twenty minutes after that, I crept back into the hotel, feeling thoroughly self-conscious, having purchased the tender mercies of two of the most beautiful and sensually exciting young women in Bangkok. The girls had chattered happily and constantly to each other all the way back to the hotel, but now they clung to me in stifled silence, one on each arm. With collective breath held, we tiptoed past the snoring night porter and then shot along the corridor to the nearest elevator.

However, unlike previous assignations with morally dubious young women, I wasn't nervous or embarrassed in the least. On the contrary, as the elevator headed to our floor and my latest moment of truth drew ever closer, I was smiling and supremely confident. Even as we headed along the corridor and the room loomed toward me, there was none of the usual weakness of the knees, pounding of the heart, and trembling hands. Not because I had suddenly discovered a supply of much-needed courage, but because I secretly knew that I still had a way out of this.

You see, I had devised a cunning master plan, cleverly reasoning that I could pass the girls to my love-sick room-mate as a magnanimous gesture and slip out to a local bar for a few hours, leaving an eternally grateful Dave to assess the depth of his love for Jenny, and the extent of his passion for that beautiful young dhobi girl up at Korat. I would be the friend in need, while Dave would discover the outrageous lengths to which two incredibly sensuous and stunning young beauties with mischievous smiles, pouting lips, and dark eyes full of promise would go.

It was with a nod of supreme confidence and a grin of bravado that I left the rest to find their own rooms, and shepherded the two wiggling and giggling young beauties out of that dangerously public corridor and into the relative safety and privacy of our allotted room. Manfully guiding them through the open doorway, I stepped confidently after them and into the darkened room, then closed the door behind me, turned on the main lights, and said, "Did somebody here order a takeaway, 'cos this is your lucky. . ."

That was when the grin of bravado dissolved, and a cunningly woven master plan suddenly unravelled. Dave was there, not waiting in patient expectation as promised, but lying half underneath his bed with his legs sticking out. He stank of cheap parmesan cheese, and goodness knows what else, and was snoring loudly through blood-caked nostrils, a result of aiming for the safety of the mattress, but somehow missing and crashing to the floor.

I spent nearly ten minutes after that desperately trying to rouse him from his self-induced coma, but finally conceded defeat and left him where he lay. I began making excuses to the two now puzzled and defensive looking young women, painstakingly explaining that Dave wasn't sober enough to benefit from their undoubted talents, and wouldn't need them after all.

Having already paid most of the fee, and not anticipating a refund, I decided to cut my losses and call it a night. As an Englishman and gentleman, I offered the girls their taxi fare home and modest compensation in lieu of the anticipated balance and tip, fully expecting that to be an end to the matter. However, it seemed they either didn't understand my non-existent Thai, or, more likely, wanted the full amount. And while I persevered, with a string of apologies on behalf of the comatose Dave, they glanced knowingly at each other and then began to fondle, guide, and cajole me away from the safety of the doorway to the carnal killing ground of my own unmade bed.

I did try to dissuade as I backed nervously away and babbled an embarrassed refusal, but less than thirty petrified seconds later grudgingly abandoned what had always been a pathetically inadequate defence, and allowed the pair of them to go to work on my eternally grateful naiveté.

I can't say I fought too hard to preserve my unwanted honour. I can't say I complained too loudly as they claimed their individual shares of the spoils. I am unable to boast anything other than a pitifully rapid release, following their expert guidance through the shakes and the shame and the gropings of ineptitude. I can, however, happily report that I then shelled out the full amount demanded, before settling down to the only worthwhile education I had ever known.

Between them, they worked me in shifts throughout that wonderful night at the Grand Hotel in Bangkok. Today, with breath shortening, hair greying at the temples and a sadly expandable belly, I am in awe of the stamina and libido of that frantic eighteen-year-old, desperate-to-be stud, cramming five years of frustrated ignorance into a few hours of educational bliss.

Not that I thought there was anything boastworthy of my wretchedly artless and unquestionably robust performance, or not at the time. Perhaps the brilliance of an image needs to fade before the mind can focus on detail, or perhaps I had nothing against which to compare the feat.

I do, however, remember naively assuming, that such non-stop effort would be any healthy young women's natural expectation of a healthy young warrior. I also believed that spending a night in a hotel bedroom, with two stunningly beautiful and shamefully expert young women demanded sleep only as a euphemism.

I didn't have the faintest idea which of them had been the first to defile my naiveté that night, and I didn't bother to enquire the next morning; not because the thought hadn't mildly intrigued me, but because I had decided there was no point asking. Whoever had claimed both virgin trophy and dubious distinction was more than welcome to both.

The following morning Dave didn't remembered anything of the previous night. After he had jealously watched my knowledgeable grin, and seen those two beautiful creatures wiggle and giggle their way into the noise and bustle of early-morning Bangkok, I gave him his money back. I told him not to worry about Jenny, or that beautiful young dhobi girl, and proudly assured him that one man could indeed love two women at the same time, conceitedly adding that I could thoroughly recommend it.

I was just grateful that he hadn't been conscious five hours earlier, when the only knowledge on display had been an acutely embarrassed awareness of my own shaking limbs, fumbling ineptitude, and thrusting naiveté . . . but then, I guess that's how so many reputations are made.

Ever-decreasing circles in the sand

We flew over El Adem, and I suffered a dark despondency, because I'd been posted there for the next two years.

We had only just got back from three weeks of boredom at Wildenrath in West Germany. When I heard the news, I walked straight into the Flight Lieutenant's office.

"Permission to apply to undergo regiment selection and training, sir?"

"Do what?"

"The SAS, sir. I'd like to put in an application. I believe they need mobile comm's skills, and I'd like to apply . . . with your permission, sir?"

My subservience was uncharacteristic, and he knew why. He beamed at me.

"Not a chance. You're posted, but come and see me when you get back. I'll be happy to put your name forward. Right now you're dismissed."

His sadistic glee was not solely a wish to get back at me for a thousand past sins, but a genuine amusement at my posting. Most of the unaccompanied postings, mainly those around the Middle East, were only for nine months. They included places like Sharjah and Masirah and Salalah and Bahrain, and even farther east to dear old Gan. However, the worst of the lot, El Adem, was a full two years. For a single man, a posting to El Adem was like all of your nightmares coming at once.

Thanks to the system, and a gleeful-sadistic Flight Louie, I was in a bumping, droning Viscount, about to land on the most miserable lump of concrete on the face of the earth.

I saw the radio masts and the water tower, a lone runway and a few scruffy looking shacks, but these aside all I could see was the desert. Not, I might add, the popular picture-postcard image of exotically sculpted seas of shifting sand, with conveniently scattered oases of swaying palms and limpid pools to inveigle the nomad and welcome weary travellers. There were no romantic tales of Arabian Nights told of this place; no proud Bedouin tribesmen sprawled across satin cushions, with bellies distended by succulent lamb and harems of scantily-dressed femininity eager to please. This was a Sahara of grim reality: three-and-a-half-million square miles of rock-strewn desert and searing heat; a vast expanse of aridity and desolation, stretching to almost the size of the entire United States, and seemingly occupied only by flies and ants and spiders and scorpions.

I made my way down the aircraft steps, and across the concrete, feeling the midday sun burning through my shirt, and believing this to be the most depressing place I had ever seen. However, as the coach took me along the main camp roadway toward the southern edge of camp and my new billet, I saw there was more to El Adem than I'd first believed; not much, but a little.

The camp boasted a control tower, a communications centre, and a small air terminal, all built in sandstone or rendered blocks, all painted beige or white, and all modern. There was a large mechanical transport section with maintenance bays, a large MT compound, a tiny camp cinema, an armoury, and a medium-sized police station, stacked to the gills with 'snowdrops' and baying Alsatians. There were other buildings, too, of which a well-equipped sick quarters was the most worthy of mention. There was also a camp commandant's office and general administration buildings, as well as many other nondescript buildings of equally limited value and interest.

The shacks, I'd seen from the air, were the single men's accommodation, positioned as far to the south as possible without encroaching on any WWII minefields. The married quarters were placed as far north as possible, for obvious reasons. Alongside the single men's accommodation and airmen's mess was a NAAFI compound. It boasted a shop, modestly stocked with toiletries and other basic commodities, and generously stocked with row after row of bottles of booze and cartons of cigarettes, and a supply of mildly-titillating magazines.

Packed every night was a larger than average bar. Next to that was an under-utilised restaurant. Most importantly, NAAFI had shipped over three genuine females to serve behind the counters.

I went to the trouble of checking on them before I flew out, by asking the worldly-wise Doggett. He boasted a previous El Adem posting, but didn't personally know any of the 'current batch'. He assured me that if every other NAAFI girl he had known was anything to go by, all three would be around forty years old and with more divorces behind them than cellulite. Between tongue-loosening pints of Eastgate bitter, he went on to confirm that they would equally probably be disappointingly plain, lamentably overweight, and deplorably promiscuous.

He obviously noticed my disappointment, because with two fingers held high and firmly crossed, he nodded encouragingly, grinned salaciously, and added, "And, hopefully, bisexual."

I wasn't at all sure Doggett held the experience with non-profit-making NAAFI girls that he claimed. However, I did know that the three ladies in question would be the only accessible females of consenting age for a thousand miles. I resolved to look them up at the first opportunity.

When I arrived at the accommodation blocks I found the billets spartan, but comfortable. The windows boasted curtains, and the doors boasted locks, with each newly-built four-man room tastefully equipped with an electric ceiling fan, four bedside lights, four wooden beds and four plain bedside mats. In the centre of each room four large wooden lockers acted as a form of privacy partition, while four small wooden lockers stood alongside each bed. In addition, a large square table stood surrounded by four wooden chairs. A small tannoy-style speaker sat on the far wall for those sad enough and desperate enough to listen to the local forces radio station.

In the communal area was a shower and ablutions area, with a washing and ironing room, and a water dispenser. The dispenser should have dispensed cool fresh water, but in reality dispensed lukewarm saline water. Truth was, there was no fresh water of any description available in North Africa, or not for us. It was officially claimed that after a month or so of drinking saline water you couldn't tell the difference, but I never enjoyed the taste of it, and neither did anybody else.

My assigned room was on the southernmost edge of camp. Only a deserted Twynham, an extended tin hut that had once housed eight tragic souls, stood between me and the bulk of the Sahara. I was the only person allotted to my room, which was strange, because every other block was packed with Air Force and Army personnel. I naively thought nothing of it.

In this block the six rooms housed only two airmen in the room next to mine, and two more in the room next to them. The two airmen billeted in the next room worked in the mechanical transport section. One was off-shift when I arrived. He greeted me with some words of welcome and a firm handshake, and told me I could move into his room if the solitude and isolation became too depressing. I declined, not because I was being unfriendly, but because I reasoned the Air Force had assigned me to this room, and I'd better find my feet before flouting authority.

He introduced himself by telling me that he came from Bristol and his name was William something or other, but everyone called him Billy. He told me his job was to drive the passenger coach, which shuttled anybody who wanted to make the trip between Tobruk, with its garrison, and the El Adem camp. I had no interest in visiting Tobruk, and so I nodded politely and asked him why this block was deserted. He smiled enigmatically, and then nodded to the desert.

"I don't know. I love it here. There's such a feeling of solitude looking out over the desert, but when it starts blowing out there it's not much fun. This is the camp's first line of defence."

I peered nervously out and across the wilderness.

"Is that a serious problem; sandstorms and that?"

"No, not much. You'll see them coming from miles away; bloody great walls of orange dust, hundreds of feet high and hundreds of yards wide. When you see one coming, just lock everything up, close all the windows, and make sure you stay inside until it's blown itself out. You'll be OK."

Relieved to hear it, I said as much, but then he smiled and offered some further advice.

"Scorpions and camel spiders are the problem. This is the worst place on camp for them."

Scorpions I was aware of, but I'd not heard of camel spiders.

"What are camel spiders?"

"Big bastards, they are. Some are the size of a fucking dinner plate. Nasty bastards, too."

"I've never heard of them before. Are they dangerous?"

He shrugged his shoulders and I expected him to tell me he'd been joking, but he delivered his next comment with such a deadpan expression, the words only served to further unnerve me.

"Can be, if you get pissed and crash outside. You don't wanna do that, I promise you."

I stammered a flurry of questions.

"What do you mean, they can be dangerous? How dangerous, and why can't you sleep outside? What do they do to you? I mean, what are they? What the hell do they look like?"

"Hold on, I'll show you."

He disappeared into his room, and then returned clutching a set of photographs. They were pictures of sandy-coloured and seriously ugly-looking spiders, big ones.

"Hobby of mine, photography. That's them; ugly looking buggers, aren't they, but as long as you don't crash out in the desert and keep your door closed at night, you'll be all right."

"And if I do crash outside?"

"To tell the truth, you'll most likely get away with it, but we had this guy once who got paralytic and crashed outside. Camel spiders got to him during the night; ate half his face away."

I didn't believe a word of that, and said as much.

"Piss off."

I studied him carefully, hoping to see some sign of humour. There was none.

"Straight up, that's how they feed. Well that and insects and scorpions and that. They have fluid they inject into their victims; sort of local anaesthetic. They inject it into the victim's flesh, then they go away for a while and leave it to go numb. They come back later, when the anaesthetic's done its work, and literally eat away the anaesthetised area. It's not nice, but don't let it worry you. Just watch where you crash out. You'll be fine."

I still couldn't see any sign of humour, and decided to test his honesty with something I did know a little about. I wanted to see if he was serious, or merely trying to unnerve me.

"What about scorpions? People say that some of them can kill you in thirty seconds."

I half hoped he would lie to me, but he didn't.

"No, not in thirty seconds; not the North African varieties, not unless you've got a weak heart or something. That's a load of old bollocks. The darker ones can be nasty, mind, if you don't treat the sting immediately, but just get yourself straight up to sick quarters and they'll deal with it. The lighter, sandy-coloured ones aren't nearly so bad, but get up to sick quarters as soon as possible anyway. People talk crap about scorpions. They're nasty and they can be a bloody nuisance, but I doubt they'd kill you, not unless you're very old or very young, or don't get treatment. It's the same with everything you come across out here: just use your common sense, and you'll be fine."

"Thanks, I'll try to do that. See you around."

"Yeah, I'm only next door. Bang on the wall if you need anything."

Billy disappeared back to his room, and left me to make up my bed and put my belongings away. With that done, I wandered over to the NAAFI for a beer and a sandwich.

The place was empty, except for a mixed group of around twenty RAF and REME guys, sitting around half-a-dozen tables they'd pulled together to make one large table in the corner of the bar. Understanding the despair our current posting invoked, the fact they were all as drunk as skunks, at ten-to-two on a weekday afternoon, came as no great surprise. What caught my attention was the stack of empty beer cans, maybe three or four hundred in total, painstakingly built into an ever-increasing mountain in the centre of the table.

I wandered over to the bar and to one of the three celebrated NAAFI girls sitting on a stool behind the counter. She looked bored, chewing pink gum and constantly checking her watch. My first impression of her was not good. She looked exactly as Doggett had predicted, and reminded me of the disgraceful tale he had related that night in the Eastgate Inn, of his youth in Tiger Bay, and an ample lady, and a stack of pallets on the dockside. I recalled that conversation with a mixture of fondness and sadness, but when she spoke to me, in a voice that had clearly once boomed out from the valleys, I studied the name on her lapel badge and smiled quietly to myself.

"What do you want then?"

"Beer, please." I decided to ingratiate myself. Not that I had any intent of furthering the liaison, I didn't believe I could ever become so desperate, but because I thought I might need an edge in getting served quickly when the place was busy. "Mary, is it?"

I had anticipated that any woman with such limited physical appeal would consider my winning smile and boyish charm mildly flattering, but she didn't even bother to answer. Instead of smiling and exchanging pleasantries, she raised her eyes to the heavens, and then asked in a monotone voice, with that same evocation of Tiger Bay and a well-worn stack of pallets, "You want DD, Heineken or Amstel? Get a move on, 'cos I'm closing up in a few minutes."

"Amstel, please."

"Large or small?"

"Large, uh, thanks."

She unceremoniously dumped a pint glass and two cans of Amstel on the counter, then reached out and snatched the pound note from me. I decided to try again.

"Uh, would you like one?" She stared blankly back. I repeated the offer. "Can I get you a drink or something?"

"Fuck off."

There wasn't a great deal I could say to that; one down and two to go. I consciously closed an involuntarily-opened mouth, and quietly prayed the remaining two NAAFI girls would be better looking, or at the least better bred and more obliging. Something told me it was a forlorn hope.

I stared moodily into the glass as I poured the beer, and decided to head back to the room as soon as possible, thinking the evening couldn't possibly get worse. However, as things turned out, I didn't return to the room until late, because the group in the corner invited me to join them.

An enormous REME guy, wearing the largest pair of khaki shorts you can imagine, wandered over when he heard the sweet old-fashioned thing respond so daintily to my offer of a drink. Then again, maybe it was because he'd heard that she was about to close the bar.

"Don't worry about Mary, she's on the rag next week; it's never her best time."

"You can fuck off an all, you fat cunt."

I couldn't believe my ears. I had never even heard that term used in front of a woman, let alone by a woman. I gawped at sweet old-fashioned Mary, who was somehow managing to glare her anger and look bored at the same time. She responded to my open-mouthed disbelief with a nicotine-stained digit extended vertically. The fat man laughed, ordered three twenty-four packs of Heineken, and invited me to join them. I ordered a pack of my own, because that was the joining fee demanded. As we carried them to the table, my jaw was still hanging.

"Is she always like that?"

We dropped the four packs of Heineken on to a pile of six more. He grinned broadly.

"Should last us until they open again at five thirty," he said. "What, you mean LAs answer to Mary Hopkins over there?"

"LA?"

"Yeah, El Adem . . . LA"

"Oh, right, I see. I think I'd rather be at the other one."

"Who wouldn't?"

"So is she always like that; Mary, I mean?"

"To tell you the truth, she's not normally that pleasant to strangers. I think she must fancy you or something." And then, in response to my look of horror, "She's all right. Good as gold is our Mary. She doesn't mean anything by it; it's just her way. So what's your name?"

He told me his name was Charlie, but everybody called him Corpus, and then introduced me to the others. Each one nodded in bleary-eyed apathy, but when they heard I had just been posted in for a two-year stretch, a few of them appeared genuinely sympathetic. One of them slit open a new pack of Heineken with a wicked looking eight-inch Bowie knife, which seemed to be the standard weapon of choice, and then began passing cans around the table.

"You poor bastard. Two whole bloody years of this shit!" He turned to the others. "Ten to one, Mary's fucked him senseless before six months is out."

Someone laughed.

"You've gotta be dreaming. It won't take that long. See the way she's looking over here . . . I'm offering twenty-to-one and six weeks."

I didn't dare look to see if the sweet old-fashioned thing was watching me, but nobody seemed eager to take the bet, and so I naively asked, "Hasn't she got a boyfriend or anything?"

They all found that highly amusing, then someone else said, "What, right now? She might have. Can't see from here, because she's on that stool behind the bar. I suppose there could be somebody on his knees down there."

I didn't laugh, partly because I didn't find it funny, and partly because I was still relatively sober, but mostly because I was feeling utterly depressed. Instead, I said, "I hate this place, and I've only been here two hours. How the hell am I going to survive for two years?"

Corpus Charlie grinned.

"You'll manage, everyone does. Stop being so bloody miserable, and look on the bright side."

"What bright side?"

"Well, if you wanna go to bed pissed every night, the booze is cheap and the fags are cheaper. You can do pretty much what you like, wear pretty much what you like, and say pretty much what you like. Nobody around here is gonna give you any hassle, because everybody knows how fucking depressing this place is, and they don't want to send us over the edge."

"And that's the bright side?"

"Yeah, but best of all. . ."

"What?"

"Sloppy seconds, with our Mary over there, won't cost you a bean."

He nodded towards the sweet old-fashioned thing behind the bar. She must have mouthed something, or extended the obligatory digit, because they all laughed again and someone said, "She's got the hots for you, mate. She'll be gripping you by the ears before you've even got your legs brown."

I was suitably indignant.

"She won't bloody well get the chance. I promise you that. Anyway, you're just winding me up, she doesn't even like me . . . I can tell."

I must have sounded less than convinced of that, because they were now laughing even louder. I quietly drank my beer and silently suffered my dual role as the butt of their drunken humour and the object of Mary's reputedly fickle affections. It appeared I had made some friends, but after studying them and assessing what was undoubtedly the motliest collection of reprobates this side of Cairo, I wasn't at all sure that I wouldn't live to regret it.

As the session progressed, I got to know some of them better. I asked about the mountain of cans. They explained they were always ready for a fight, and building cans was a challenge to anyone similarly looking for trouble. Your group built a stack of cans, as did other similarly motivated and similarly retarded groups. If any group decided they wanted to fight a group on another table, as often happened, they simply knocked over the stack of cans on that table.

Moronic and immature are the two adjectives that come most readily to mind, but they were a tough bunch, my motley reprobates; a seriously tough bunch.

Frederick Joyce, another Army engineer, was the uncrowned head of the group, or Fractured Freddie as I called him. I estimated Freddie to be in his mid-thirties, with a shaved head set on the thickest bull-neck imaginable, and crudely-worded tattoos scrawled across his arms and chest. That combination, and the fact he must have weighed in at around sixteen stone of solid muscle, gave him a look that I can only describe as intimidating.

But despite his aggressive manner, Freddie wasn't all bad and boasted three admirable qualities. He had a sense of humour. He always stood his corner at the bar, and he always stood by his friends. No man has a right to ask for more from any drinking buddy.

Few people messed with Freddie, though, because Freddie was undoubtedly mentally unbalanced, and if that weren't enough to ward off the foolhardy, there was always his party piece. He demonstrated it for my benefit that same night.

The act was as simple as it was imbecilic. First he placed a chair on top of the table. Then he climbed on to the chair. Then he dived, head first, on to the floor.

There were no hands held out to save his skull or cushion the blow. There was no soft landing area carefully selected before take-off. Just a sickening thud as his skull met the floor, followed by a combined wince from the motley reprobates as they listened to the crunch and watched that great bull-neck act as a sort of flesh-coloured buffer.

With lunatic party piece performed, and granite skull seemingly intact, he climbed back on to the table and challenged anyone, and me in particular, to do the same. Not fancying a broken neck or cracked skull, and still holding some modicum of sanity, I declined, as did everyone else. Freddie sneered, downed his pint in one, wiped the residue from his chin with the back of his hand, and then loudly announced that we were all 'chicken-shits'.

How he was able to perform such a mindless act without killing or seriously injuring himself, I never discovered. Whatever possessed him to try it in the first place remained similarly shrouded in mystery, but do it he did, not once, but a dozen times during the next few months.

I sometimes find myself wondering whatever happened to Fractured Freddie; what toll such a foolishly dangerous activity might have exacted on both mind and body, and how that toll might have become obvious in his later years. . . assuming he had any later years.

Sitting alongside Freddie were the 'ticket twins', who weren't real twins, of course, but two chronically depressed Scotsmen from the same Glasgow tenement. Rumour had it they were on the payroll at the armoury, but as nobody ever saw them at any recognised place of industry, nobody could say for certain what they did, or where they worked. I never did discover their real names, but everyone called them 'The Jocks'.

They only ever seemed interested in talking to each other, did 'The Jocks'; unintelligibly, I might add, and in accents that dripped tins of shortbread and Scott's Porridge Oats from every impenetrable Glaswegian syllable. I called them 'the ticket twins', because, apart from constantly trying to out-drink each other, they spent every spare moment thinking up ever more ridiculous ruses in the hope of being classified as mentally unfit and sent home.

As with their drinking, these efforts to 'work their tickets' become a competition, with the prize being a ticket or 'casevac' home to Sauchiehall Street. Well. that was what Corpus Charlie always said, because he claimed to be able to interpret the guttural grunts that passed between them, and would astound us by translating them into intelligible conversation, but I never could.

As time passed, the competition became ever more ridiculous. When one claimed that his imaginary pet highland terrier had died, and marched around the camp perimeter every evening, naked but for a tam-o'-shanter and black armband, while playing an appalling rendition of 'Over the Sea to Skye' on a set of broken bagpipes, the other went further. Every morning he dressed in women's underwear and walked his imaginary reincarnation of Greyfriars Bobby all the way to the camp gates and back, using a piece of frayed rope as a lead, and religiously pausing at every upright structure along the way, presumably to allow canine nature to take its course.

They were always up at sick quarters, claiming incurable bouts of depression, or insomnia, or blinding headaches, or dipsomania, or something or other, but how they ever explained the symptoms I have no idea. Freddie said they wrote them down, but I doubted they could write. Either way, they always seemed to be in varies stages of sedation, compliments of the Heineken brewery, and anything pharmaceutical they had managed to wheedle out of the medics, but their presence did bolster the numbers at the table, and their antics always kept us mildly entertained.

There were many more similarly disturbed and equally bizarre characters gathered around the mountain of cans that day, but I won't go into any further description, partly because of space, but mostly because you wouldn't believe me if I did. Suffice to say, the motley reprobates were the most curious assortment of punch-drunk morons and alcoholic misfits I ever set eyes on.

That first drinking bout, which had reputedly started at five-thirty in the evening on the day before my arrival, was still going when I left that night. When I finally did get back to the block it was gone eleven. I threw my clothes on to the chair, climbed into bed and was instantly asleep, but around three hours later someone or something woke me, and that was when I first heard the noise.

It was a clicking sound, and it was coming from the floor at the foot of the bed. At first I took no notice, but it continued to invade my sleep . . . click, click, click, click, click, click. The sound was moving back and forth across the floor at the foot of the bed and I was suddenly wide awake and nervous. The chair with my clothes on was around five feet away and therefore out of my immediate reach, but the light switch was only just to the left and above my head. I leaned up and switched it on and then waited a few seconds after that for my eyes to become accustomed to the glare. It was then I saw the cause of the noise, and felt my heart start thumping against my ribs.

It was the biggest spider I had ever seen, like a sand-coloured version of one of those bird-eating spiders, and it was scuttling back and forth across the floor at the foot of my bed. The noise was the sound of its feet clicking against the floor tiles, but it stopped and reared up when it saw me watching. It was then I realised, to my horror, that it had positioned itself between my unhealthily white and embarrassingly naked backside and the chair with my shoes and clothes on.

There seemed little I could do. There was no way I could reach my clothes and boots without also having to negotiate this monster. I could probably have reached the door before it got to me, but had no intent of running around the Sahara in the middle of the night, dressed only in a sheet. Such was the garb of the Bedouin. There was nothing else for it. Embarrassment or not, I needed help, and so I banged on the adjoining wall and called for Billy.

It seemed I waited there for an eternity, with me watching the spider and the spider watching me, although Billy arrived within moments. Now, though, I had another problem, because I was naked and all but defenceless, and my midnight saviour was dressed only in a pair of flip-flops and a black leather posing pouch held in place by thin leather straps and a good deal of will-power.

"No problem, sweetie." He pouted at me, and I noticed something equally disturbing. As well as that sole item of immodesty, Billy was wearing bright pink lipstick and pale-blue eye shadow. "You just stay there and I'll deal with it for you." He pouted again. "It's only a baby."

He began chasing the spider around the floor, poking and prodding at it with the business end of a broom, and stretching and manoeuvring his all but naked body into unnecessary positions. Finally, he killed the poor creature with a succession of extravagant slashing motions and ostentatiously swept it from the room, then closed the door and checked for more spiders before returning to sit on the end of my bed. I remember dragging the sheet around me and thinking that I would have preferred the camel spider to have ejected Billy.

"You all right, lovely? Didn't bite you or anything, did it? Do you want me to check?"

I was wondering what the hell happened to the macho guy with the firm handshake I had met only a few hours before, and just where the hell this leather-clad, fully made-up, pink-and-blue powder-puff had come from. I shook my head and shrank back against the bed-head with the sheet pulled up against my chin, looking for all the world like a virgin bride on the first night of her honeymoon. He must have noticed my reticence, because he smiled coyly across at me and added in a whispered voice that screamed effeminacy, "You look frozen, poor thing. Now, if there's anything else you need? You know you only have to say. Anything at all. You just have to ask."

He began to idly stroke at my leg through the sheet. I shrank further back, pulled the sheet closer around my suddenly acutely vulnerable nakedness, and stammered back at him, "No thanks, I'm fine, honestly I'm fine. Thanks anyway; thanks for your help."

I moulded myself against the bed-head, while he shifted closer.

"You're sure now? You poor thing, you're shivering. Are you sure you're not cold?"

"Yes, I'm absolutely bloody well certain."

Colour and courage were slowly returning and I was becoming aggressive. Although it was unclear to me, given my current state of undress, what I would have done to defend myself without further enticement for him and further embarrassment for me. Fortunately, he read the warning signs, withdrew his hand and stood up. I held the glare and pretended not to notice that the leather pouch had some difficulty in containing its charge.

"Well, I'm only next door. You only have to tap on the wall, and I'll come in a jiffy."

I was under no illusion about that, and suddenly understood just how this particular camel spider had got into my room. I was also beginning to understand just why this section of the accommodation block was so thinly populated. As I shuffled across the room with the sheet wrapped around and locked the door behind him, I decided that from tomorrow it would be even less populated. First thing in the morning, I was out of here.

It wasn't until four months later that I finally gave up and took the bus into Tobruk. I had spent those four months alone in that isolated tin Twynham hut on the southern edge of camp, because, as angry as I had been that night, the following morning I hadn't the heart to complain about Billy's visit. Nor did I mention his avant-garde appearance or unwelcome overtures, because both he and his three similarly oriented companions would have been swiftly and unceremoniously booted out of the service. So I gave no particular reason for my question, and they told me that unless I had a valid reason for changing, there was no other accommodation available. It was either my assigned room or the Twynham. I moved that morning.

On the upside, and much to everyone's amazement, I liked the Twynham. It was roomy and isolated, and I could spread myself out without worrying. On top of that, and presumably because I lived there alone, it was never scheduled for commandant's inspection, and so they allowed me to fester in my own squalor with a feral dog I'd befriended and uncreatively named Rex.

When not at the Twynham, Rex ran with a pack that terrorised everyone on camp and came and went at will. When he ran with the pack Rex was unapproachable and dangerous, but when he was with me in the Twynham he was as gentle as a lamb. Rex was my only company in the Twynham during those months, but somehow the isolation and lack of human contact didn't bother me. I was so depressed, I didn't believe that human company could have done anything to lift the misery or lighten the gloom. . . and gloomy it certainly was.

Because of my depression, I was even more heavily into blues music. I bought an Akai M9 reel-to-reel tape-recorder from an airman who had served his two year tour of duty and was due to fly home. The unit had a powerful amplifier and was one of the best that money could buy, or at least in those days. I also bought a Dual deck through the NAAFI catalogue and two stacks of twelve-inch Goodman's base units, and inexpertly cobbled them together. Maybe it wasn't high-fidelity to satisfy the purist, but for pounding out John Mayall's Bluesbreakers it was awesome.

Apart from creating a sound that rattled the Twynham roof and carried all the way across camp, I organised the furniture to suit, covered the internal walls with LP record sleeves and tin foil, and changed the original clear light bulbs for red. All in all, the place looked and sounded like a cross between London's Marquee, and a backstreet Cairo knocking-shop. Few people had sufficient nerve to come near the place, and that suited me fine.

You see, isolation wasn't my problem; my problem was the seriously unhealthy quantity of booze and cigarettes I was consuming. My shift pattern at the communications centre was three days on and two days off, and then two days on and five days off. The upshot of that was a significant amount of free time, and I wasted it to the full.

As well as my regular off-shift pilgrimages to the bar in the company of the motley reprobates, I was going through a bottle of Chivas Regal and sixty Benson & Hedges a day. All this before I had reached my nineteenth birthday. Something clearly had to change, but I was so depressed there was no chance of my doing it, or not without help, but when help finally did arrive, it came from the most unexpected quarter.

I'd not spoken to the effeminate Billy since that eventful night four months earlier, and had no qualms about perpetuating the stony silence, but then, one afternoon, he parked his coach outside the Twynham and knocked on the door. I answered, with a half-empty bottle of Chivas in one hand and a cigarette in the other, neither feeling nor looking especially wholesome as I squinted out from the darkness and growled a question.

"What the fuck do you want?"

He had obviously anticipated such a reception, because he smiled and then nodded and said, "I wanted to thank you."

"What for?"

"For not saying anything about that night, when you first arrived, and to say, well, I'm sorry for all that shit I put you through. I just thought that, well, that you were . . ."

By this time I was feeling acutely embarrassed by his mere mentioning of the incident, and so I snapped an answer before he had completed his explanation.

"Some kind of fucking queer, you mean?"

The moment that I had spoken the words I regretted them. Not that I was in any way liberally minded, or even sympathetic to the plight of gays in the forces. It was because they had been cruel and unnecessary words, designed to wound and to hurt. By speaking them I had shown myself to be ignorant and aggressive. Billy didn't seem offended. He just smiled back at me.

"Yeah, something like that," he said.

He started to walk away. I called after him.

"Look, I'm sorry, I didn't mean . . ."

He turned back to me and smiled again.

"Yes, you did."

An awkward silence ensued, but then he said, "I wanted to show you something."

With that, he wandered over to the side of the hut and started kicking at some largish stones, turning them over and then moving them aside with his boot. He continued until he had found what he was looking for, which turned out to be a medium-sized scorpion. The scorpion ran out from under one of the stones and then tried to regain the safety of another rock. Billy cornered it, and then shoved it farther out and into the sunlight with his boot.

"Come over here a minute."

I had no interest in the scorpion and said as much.

"I've seen scorpions before; not as bad as camel spiders, but nasty bastards, all the same."

He changed the subject.

"Talking of camel spiders, how is the mighty Hercules?"

Hercules was the communications centre's pet, a huge camel spider kept in an old fish tank. The commcen guys would drop two or more live scorpions into Hercules' tank, and then bet on which of them he would eat first.

"He's all right, I suppose; getting bigger and uglier every day, they do say. For some reason I can't bring myself to like camel spiders. I wonder why?"

With unsubtle point made, I started to walk away, and called out to him over my shoulder.

"Anyway, I've got better things to do than to piss around here pulling the legs off insects."

"Oh, stop being so fucking precious and come over here."

I wandered over and watched as he took a tin of petrol lighter fuel out of his pocket. He squirted a ring of fuel around the insect, and lit it with his Zippo. Why he carried the fuel, I had no idea; maybe he chain-smoked, or liked torturing scorpions. Either way he knew a lot about them.

"They reckon scorpions can go without food or water for over a year. Bit like you, except I never saw one with a fag and a bottle of scotch. Anyway, watch this; watch what it does."

He continued spraying the lighter fuel in a circle of fire around the scorpion, and then started to bring the circle in, closer and closer to the beleaguered insect. After a few moments of this increased heat the scorpion became seriously agitated. It began stabbing left and right with its tail, before finally, and to my mind prematurely, stabbing itself to death.

We stood and watched the scorpion in its death throes and Billy said, "It looked like he just stung himself to death, didn't it, but all that crap about scorpions stinging themselves to death is just that; it's all crap. He was just reacting to the heat, going into spasm and that. The truth is, it's only fucked-up humans like us who sting themselves to death. Animals, birds, even insects have more sense."

He looked at me, and I began to understand there might be a moral to the demonstration, but didn't understand what. I grinned at him, hoping to cover my own stupidity.

I said, "If you think I'm gonna start touching my toes just to relieve the boredom, you can forget it."

Billy grinned, briefly and facetiously, before saying, "You see, we both do what we have to do in this world; you in your macho, heterosexual, piss-head world of blues music, whisky, scrubby barmaids, punch-drunk arseholes and clinical depression, and me in mine. Now I can't change mine, and I'm not sure I'd want to, but you can."

I still couldn't see the point and quipped back with the only answer that came to mind.

"Yeah, well, what the fuck. Anyway, why the hell should it bother you?"

"Because we each have to survive the best we can. Well, at least until that big silver bird swoops down from the sky and carries us back to where we wanna be."

"Big silver bird? What are you . . . some kind of queer fucking hippie?"

He grinned good-naturedly at my lack of grace.

"Have you ever been down to the MSC?" he asked.

The Marine Sports Centre was an Air Force club on Tobruk harbour. It was split into three sections: sailing, sub-aqua and water-skiing. I'd heard the members were cliquey and pretentious.

"Naw, I don't wanna go down there. They're all up each other's backsides; just a bunch of . . ."

I suddenly realised, and stopped in mid-sentence as I felt the colour rise. Billy shook his head.

"Why not give it a go? Treat yourself to a wash and shave, maybe even clean your teeth and wash your Levi's. Then get down there and check the place out. What have you got to lose?"

I thought about it for all of three seconds.

"Naw, it's not my kind of thing. Thanks, anyway."

I shook my head, lit a fresh cigarette with the stub of the last, and offered him the packet.

"No thanks, I've got to get going. I should have left ten minutes ago. See you around."

I grunted and watched him walk back to the coach, climb into the driver's seat, and start the engine. He turned the bus in a wide arc, heading for the road back to the north of camp. As he passed the Twynham he slowed the coach and called out, through the driver's window.

"It's a tin hut in the desert, not a circle of fire. You don't have to keep stinging yourself to fucking death."

As he drove away I lifted the bottle high, and then took a swig in an extravagantly cynical toast, but ignored the golden opportunity for riposte. Not because I had suddenly developed a long-overdue maturity, or conscience, but because I was thinking about that demonstration with the scorpion and the fire, and the meaning behind the message.

I wandered back into the Twynham's gloom, and then took a long look at myself through the tobacco film on the mirror. I took a similarly long look around the Twynham. It was a mess, and so was I. Maybe I should do something. Maybe it just might be worth taking that trip into Tobruk.

Tangled webs, and the temptation of too many clichés

The road from El Adem to the main Benghazi highway was single track and roughly ten miles long. Unmarked W.W. II minefields lay on either side, with dwellings set at intervals.

The dwellings were mostly packing cases, tied together to form some rudimentary protection from the heat and dust. One, I particularly remember, had camels and donkeys tethered outside, with a few chickens, while some grubby-looking children could often be seen playing in the dirt. However, the discovery of oil and all that brought was never more graphically illustrated than outside that particular hut, because sitting in pride of place was the owner's brand-new Mercedes.

How anyone could live in a cardboard box under the glare of the Sahara sun, sweltering in temperatures of 130 degrees, and then drive to and from work cosseted in one of the world's most expensive cars, sitting on soft leather upholstery and basking in air-conditioned luxury, was utterly bizarre, but they always seemed content enough with the absurdity of it.

At the end of the track the drive into Tobruk, along the main Benghazi highway, was similarly bizarre, because it was a modern dual carriageway, the equal of any major transport artery in North Africa. However, just as drivers rounded the bend and began the descent into the harbour-side town, the dual carriageway abruptly ended and rock-strewn track resumed.

No markings or warning signs were in place to warn drivers, and so, for travellers unaware of the foot-high drop from modern transport artery to cratered track, a sudden bout of terror preceded a jarring shock to the coccyx, and an equally-destructive jolt to the tyres and suspension.

From that point, assuming both spine and shock absorber had survived, sixty miles an hour became fifteen, sometimes less, and twentieth-century impatience slipped into a microcosm of old Arabia, called Tobruk.

Apart from an apartment block erected by the British to house married families, Tobruk in the sixties was much the same as the days when Rommel and Montgomery had flexed their Second World War muscles. Around the outskirts every wall had bullet and shrapnel damage, and every road was cratered from artillery fire. For drivers, a secondary need was to avoid the donkey carts weaving around the craters, with no thought or consideration for drivers or pedestrians.

Billy drove the coach on that first trip to the MSC. He collected me from the Twynham and shot off like a rocket. We turned along the dual carriageway and then charged into Tobruk, before skidding to a halt outside the garrison, a British Army base staffed by the Royal Irish Rangers.

"We've got twenty minutes to kill. Get yourself a cup of tea. I've got to meet someone."

He pointed out the NAAFI cafeteria just inside the gates on the right-hand side.

"I thought it was only a ten minute wait? Well, it is according to the timetable."

"Yeah, that's right, but I'm early and I need to kill some time."

"But you drove down here like a lunatic, nearly killed us twice."

Billy grinned, and headed on into the cafeteria, bought a cup of tea, and then sat down at a table in the corner alongside a young squaddie who had obviously been waiting for him.

"I'm beginning to see why we broke the sound barrier on the way down here."

I grinned at Billy, who glared back at me, his face like thunder. He came over and sat down.

"Look, I know you don't mean any harm, but, for Christ sake, shut it."

"What's wrong? Nobody cares. Look, they're not even taking any notice of you."

Billy glanced around, casually studying the half-dozen or so squaddies who were sitting talking at the various tables, then returned his attention to me.

"Maybe not, but you don't understand," he said.

"Understand what?"

He spoke in a whisper, but there was no doubting the urgency in his voice.

"If I'm found out, they'll just kick me out of the Air Force with a dishonourable discharge."

"Well, to some people that might seem apt."

I had expected at least a flicker of a smile in response to my crude and oafish humour, but he ignored the comment and continued whispering.

"With me it'd be lack of moral fibre, but if he's found out they'll more than likely kill him."

"Bollocks."

"It's not bollocks. I'm serious. So shut up. Please."

I saw he was in earnest, then looked across and saw that the young squaddie had gone.

"Come off it. You can't be serious. They might beat him up, but they wouldn't kill him."

"No, of course they wouldn't. They'd just find him hanging from a shower fitting one morning. Didn't anybody tell you? Suicides from depression are a fact of life in a place like this. Anyway, forget it. I think we were lucky and nobody noticed. Now, let's get out of here."

Viewing the seeming unfairness of today's society, there are times when I rue the fact that the social pendulum has become detached from its original axis of conformity. I sometimes think, as a white Christian heterosexual male, I'm in the least popular category for just about everything, or it seems that way from a judicial and discriminatory view. But, then I think back to Billy that day, to his earnest plea, and to the look of panic and fear on the face of his young squaddie boyfriend.

It's then that I remember the vilification and physical abuse so many individuals suffered in progressing society to a point where people don't have to live in fear because of race or colour or religion or sexuality. It's also around then I realise that perhaps I'm not so hard done by after all.

I didn't say any more as we headed on into the town, and Billy seemed happy enough with the silence. I was thinking back to my comment outside the Twynham that day, realising just how few and dangerous are the steps between unthinking scorn and violent persecution.

As we travelled, Billy pointed out places of interest, including Tobruk's only hotel and the local dry-cleaners. Then he headed to the town square and stopped to allow a young married family to get on. He switched off the engine, and we sat waiting for a few minutes. He showed me the souk, which was the local market place and centre of commerce, and then pointed across the square to the town's only coffee shop. He talked about what you could buy and the various places you could buy it, which wasn't much and weren't many, then restarted the engine and drove down to the harbour.

When we arrived at the top of the hill leading to the harbour, he showed me the entrance to the MSC, and said the road was too narrow to go all the way down. I nodded, thanked him, and then headed down the track to the entrance, not realising I was entering a world that would become my sole source of comfort, company and relaxation.

"Don't worry about him. He only bites Arabs."

I had been nervously negotiating a snapping and snarling feral dog tied up outside the sub-aqua club with a disquietingly frayed and inadequate rope. I had no idea who had called out, but took the opportunity offered by the dog's momentary distraction to dash into the centre.

There wasn't all that much to the centre. The larger of two oversized garages had the snarling dog tied up outside and housed the sub-aqua club's inflatable dinghy and other equipment. The smaller housed the ski-club's two brightly-coloured speedboats. A well-stocked bar farther along housed a kitchen area, a good-sized lounge and small dance floor, while a set of iron railings ran along the harbour. A fair-sized concrete area lay marked out for storage and cleaning of sailing dinghies. Behind the sub-aqua club, a concrete ramp allowed the launch and retrieval of boats.

Thirty yards out, and permanently anchored, a solid-looking raft belonged to the water-ski club. In the centre of the harbour a couple of dozen sailing dinghies tacked back and forth. Each was of the same obviously popular but unmemorable type, with a retractable centreboard, a jib, a mainsail and two crew. One crew member sat proudly at the stern, managed the mainsail, handled the tiller and had all the fun. The other squatted uncomfortably toward the stem, ducked whenever the boat altered course, and then dragged the jib across and secured it when the boat's lord and master had completed the manoeuvre and the vessel had come about.

As you can probably imagine by reading this and assessing my ignorance of sailing, I'm no aficionado. Neither did I, nor do I, have any interest in becoming one. Something to do with that first-ever passage from Weymouth to Jersey, I guess. But, if I didn't intend having anything to do with the sailing club, the sub-aqua and water-skiing sections were a different matter.

A severe looking man called Harold Cartwright told me about the various sections. I found him working behind the bar when I arrived. He introduced himself, told me he was a sergeant from El Adem, and that he worked in the main administration centre. He then introduced me to his wife, who I had already noticed candidly studying me from the other side of the bar. Her name was Paula and she worked part-time during the week in the NAAFI shop up at the garrison.

Harold was middle-aged, tall and skinny and thinning on top, with a hooked nose and austere expression to go with a puritanical outlook. Paula was a good fifteen years younger, perhaps in her early thirties, slightly plump and short, with wavy brown hair, dark-brown eyes, a beautiful smile she rarely used, and the largest pair of breasts I'd ever seen on any woman with a waistline.

The sergeant and his wife tut-tutted their displeasure as they minded the bar and watched all the comings and goings. He was a member of the sub-aqua club, and lived only for the next expedition. Paula didn't share his enthusiasm, and preferred the sailing club. The unlikely couple did have something in common, though. Neither of them had any time for members of the water-ski club in general, and three or four of its more colourful characters in particular.

According to the submersible sergeant, and his buoyant young wife, the water-ski club boasted a nucleus of 'strutting young peacocks', who sped across the harbour in coloured speedboats powered by Mercury outboard motors. They slalomed their bronzed and pretentious athleticism in and out of the boats' wake at unnecessary speeds, and regularly drenched the local fishermen with fan-shaped walls of water, presumably to confirm the metaphor's aptness.

I bought the unhappy couple a drink and asked them to tell me more about the respective clubs. They seemed happy to oblige.

"Well, they're nothing more than a bunch of degenerates in that ski club, as far as I'm concerned. They have no morality, no decency, no standards, and no respect or consideration for anybody but themselves. If I had my way, I'd close the place down, kick the lot of them back up to El Adem; get somebody to teach them some values and give them some discipline."

The thin-faced sergeant had begun the conversation, while his buxom young wife look bored. She poured herself another large vodka and tonic before coming out from behind the bar and sitting down next to me. She settled herself onto the stool, gulped down a good third of the tumbler's contents, and then confirmed a severe husband's severe opinion.

"Harold's right; that's just how they are. They have barbecues at one of the coves up the coast. Goodness knows what they get up to. Well, to be truthful, I happen to know that . . ."

Clearly fearing an indiscretion as he listened to his wife wrestling with the laws of slander and groping for the right words, the sergeant butted in.

"Yes, they take steaks, and champagne, as much as a couple of dozen bottles or more . . ."

"And that's not all."

Despite the sergeant's effort at censorship, his wife had obviously discovered the right words. Disturbing a middle-aged husband's conversational flow, and a young man's fickle concentration, she leaned closer and breathed the words.

"They take women, too, when they can get them . . . Married women, I might add."

I wasn't at all sure if she was talking about the ski-club's impromptu barbecues, or a raiding party of pillaging Moorish pirates plaguing this section of the coast. I said nothing, and tried my best not to look too obviously at the mesmerizing rise and fall that was now dominating my every consideration. Instead of a lecherous survey, I tried to appear as genteel and polite, a young man whose only interest was the lady's conversation. For her part, the voluptuous Paula continued to tell outrageous tales of infidelity, sinfulness and debauchery.

"I'm not prepared to say who these women are, well not their names. Anyway, most people around here already know who they are." She glanced furtively around, as if checking for eavesdroppers or hidden microphones. "But there are certain husbands, up at that El Adem camp, and over at that garrison bar, who should be paying a little less attention to getting drunk every night, and a little more attention to their wives' physical needs."

"So it's the husband's fault, huh?"

"Women do have needs, you know, Harold, physical needs I mean. You can't buy every woman off with presents from the NAAFI catalogue, or increases in the housekeeping allowance. They're not all married to monks, and they're not all expected to be nuns."

He had made the observation, and she had responded angrily and glared at him, while I looked out of the window and pretended not to notice. It seemed she had triumphed in this particular skirmish of wills, because the unsmiling sergeant chose to ignore both pointed remark and pointed glare. Instead, he resumed his defamation of the ski club membership.

"They're all degenerates in that ski club. They take drugs, too . . . Hashish mostly, shipped from the Lebanon. It's so cheap, they buy it by the kilo from that tatty-looking dry cleaners in town; quarter of a kilo for a couple of cartons of cigarettes, I'm told. That amount on the black market, or on the streets of London, would cost a small fortune. Around here they almost give it away."

I nodded politely, and tried to appear interested as he went on.

"I've warned them about smoking the stuff around the club, warned them on so many occasions, I can't tell you. I reported them for it once. They just laughed at me; think they're so clever. Not that the authorities could give a damn about what they smoke, or where they get it from. They'll get their come-uppance one day, you mark my words."

The sergeant's wife suddenly leaned even closer. With her eyes staring deeply into mine, and her voice little more than a seductive whisper, she added, "Not only that, but they think they're God's gift. They think every woman in the place only has one thing on her mind and is fair game. I watch them sometimes, strutting around the bar as if they owned the place, expecting every woman they meet to just lie back and let them do whatever they want." She grinned slyly and fluttered her eyelashes. "I'm sure you wouldn't expect a woman you hardly knew to do something like that for you, would you? Michael, is it?"

I cleared my throat and babbled, thinking I should either change the subject or leave.

"Uh, yes, I prefer Mike, but no, no, of course not."

I watched her mischievously toying with both my discomfiture and the band of gold on her third finger, then looked into her eyes and blushed violently as I heard her say, "Are you sure now? Are you sure you're not the sort of man who sees a woman he wants and just takes her, whether she's spoken for or not . . . whether she's married or not?"

I spluttered a denial and glanced anxiously at the grim-faced sergeant. He seemed not to notice the sudden shock of sexual electricity which had flashed between his young wife and my rising embarrassment. Neither did he hear the disgraceful suggestion so implicit in her tone, or see the blatant eye contact that she wilfully preserved, despite my obvious unease.

To my amazement, he showed neither concern nor alarm. Instead of a quiet warning or glare of censure, he merely shook his head and resumed his denigration of the ski-club.

"They don't even bother to dress properly; wander around the place unshaven and half dressed. When they're not smoking hash, they're smoking those filthy-smelling French cigarettes, and they never use a glass, just swig whatever they're drinking straight from the bottle, and that can't be hygienic. I don't know who they think they're impressing. If I had my way I'd . . ."

She tut-tutted him into silence, and I felt myself blushing again as I heard her say, "They wear those tight jeans, and sometimes less than that, sometimes only tiny little bathing trunks. Sometimes they come in here when they're still dripping wet; don't care that sometimes you can see. . . Well, there are times when I have difficulty holding my tongue, and then there are other times when I simply don't know where to put myself. I'm sure you can imagine."

I was trying my level best not to. I was also trying to ignore the all too obvious double-entendres, so inadequately hidden among the hollow protest.

There was clearly one deprived young hen in this menagerie who was more impressed with strutting young peacocks than she cared to admit. An apparently unaware and recklessly inattentive husband seemed lost in his own private conversational time warp, because he continued to advise me as though oblivious to his wife's flirtation.

"You seem like a decent fellow. You take my advice and stay well clear of them."

I gave a start, knowing that I must have looked guilty, and only too aware that I had been openly ogling his wife's breasts. Not that I had any wish to demean the lady, or offend the prudish Harold. I had been gawping at her breasts because I was incapable of doing anything else. No matter where else I tried to look, and no matter how hard I tried to think of her in purely platonic terms, my eyes kept returning to that same area.

It took a moment before I realised that his warning hadn't been an effort to dissuade me from molesting his wife. He had been talking about the perils of ski club membership. It seemed Harold had issues with certain members of the ski club. It also seemed his wife had issues with him.

"Oh, for goodness sake leave him alone, Harold. He's young. He's allowed to be reckless. Can't you remember when you were like that? I can, but it seems like a million years ago now."

Harold Cartwright looked solemnly across at his wife.

"We have to grow up and settle down as we grow older, Paula. We have to adjust to the different stages we go through in life. It never used to worry you."

There was an underlying sadness in the comment. I'd noticed it, and so had the playful Paula. She looked across at him and smiled gently.

"It still doesn't, Harold. I'm only teasing."

"No, you get yourself over to the sub-aqua club." He had resumed his briefly interrupted monologue without answering or returning the smile. I watched her scowl as she considered his indifference and listened to his preoccupation. He didn't seem to notice. "You don't want to involve yourself in all that juvenile ski-club nonsense," he went on. "There's going to be some major trouble with that lot. What with all those so-called barbecues and drunken parties and what have you. You're better off joining the sub-aqua club. We even have our own bar; in the club, I mean. There's always good company there during the evening, if you ever want to pop over."

"Oh, so you don't run this place full-time then?"

"Oh, no. There's far too much work involved in running a place like this. Anyway, present company excepted, I can't abide most of the people you get in here. I'm only watching the place while John, that's the regular bar manager, nips up to the souk."

"Oh, I see."

"I'm a senior member of the sub-aqua club. That's where I spend my time; couldn't stand this place for more than an hour at a time. I don't understand why Paula spends so much time in here, not when she could join the sub-aqua club and do something worthwhile."

"Because I prefer to belong to the sailing club, that's why."

She had answered indignantly and he sniffed his disdain.

"We go on expeditions, up the coast and that. I always go, wouldn't miss it. I tell Paula, you do what you like, but I'm not wasting my life sitting around here, listening to pop music and drinking myself into a stupor. I spend my spare time doing something worthwhile, exploring the sea, studying all the different formations and fascinating marine life beneath the waves. There's a whole world waiting out there, a whole living world that most people know nothing about."

I nodded, and asked politely, "Is it especially interesting, this area of the Mediterranean, I mean?"

"Oh yes, enthralling. There's so much history to this area. There's an old Spanish wreck a few miles up, which we still haven't begun to fully explore. Some of the sights I've seen around that wreck and on some of the other dives are so beautiful they're almost indescribable. It's not just that, though. It's the sense of comradeship and learning about the world, marvelling at the wonders of creation and sharing experiences with true friends. That's what life's about. Well, it is to me."

He was clearly in his own private world, a world that he was passionate about. I watched him come alive as he talked. Despite his austerity, I was warming to him.

"We're going again next weekend. You might be able to come. Not to dive, of course, you need to get through the training programme first, but we'll get you through that as soon as possible. Meantime, you could come along, maybe snorkel and meet the others. You should get your name down on the membership list. You'll need to do that as soon as possible. It's difficult getting into any of the clubs, and sub-aqua is especially popular. I only dive with teams I like and trust, so there might just be a place open for the right man."

I felt a twinge of guilt as I saw him smile and listened to his offer of support, knowing I'd been mentally undressing his wife for the last ten minutes. I had to admit, though, it all sounded interesting. I agreed to place my name on the list, but not because of guilt or any contemplation of the wonderful sights beneath the ocean. My immediate interest was purely self-preservation.

You see, I may have been on the juvenile side of twenty years old, but I was old enough and smart enough to know the severe sergeant had been right. His warning about those dangers inherent in the ski club's wickedness were well-intentioned and well considered.

Not only that, but common sense told me the armed forces frowned on single men having affairs with married woman. Despite the obvious charms of the plentiful Paula, an affair with a lonely and neglected young wife could prove more trouble than it was worth.

I decided to be sensible, for once in my life. There was no point in looking for trouble. I should steer clear of both the ski club and dangerously lonely married women, and apply for membership of the sub-aqua club at the earliest possible opportunity.

I saw his earnestness and knew immediately that my decision was right. Whether she had been playing games or not, I was too young to risk becoming enmeshed in such a potentially dangerous liaison. Apart from anything else, there was the sanctity of marriage to consider.

But then I studied Paula's soft-brown eyes as they stared into mine.

"You shouldn't rush him, Harold. Let him make up his own mind. Let him look around for a bit; see what takes his fancy. He doesn't realise all the possibilities that could open up around here, all the opportunities that are there for the taking. If he takes his time and looks carefully, I'm sure he'll figure out what he wants and come to the right decision."

I tried to divert my eyes, but failed miserably as she collected my gaze with hers, and then dragged it down to where she lifted her foot from the stool's lower rung and placed it on the upper. Then she gradually slid the hemline higher, allowing me an unobstructed view of milk-white thighs surrounding a black satin triangle of gently swollen femininity.

It was an unbelievably vulgar display of shamelessness and coarseness that in many ways repulsed me. But, after four months of imposed celibacy in that spartan tin hut, I also believed it was the most incredibly erotic and sexually provocative vision I had ever seen. It sent shocks of sexual adrenaline straight through me, jolted every nerve in my body, and left me feeling both drained and elated. At that moment I was so captivated by the raw sensuality, I had to stop myself from reaching out and claiming that magnificent vision for my own.

Five of the briefest electric seconds after that she brought her knees together, returned her foot to the lower rung, and tugged the hemline down. The show, if that is what it had been, was over.

I tried to compose myself, not sure if she had intended me to see, or had merely been careless. Not knowing, either, if she had done it to punish an insensitive husband or seduce a potential lover. I looked to Harold and saw him preoccupied with refilling his pipe. Then I saw her smile, and knew the truth. She had fully intended me to see, and fully intended me to want what I saw.

From deep among the panic and confusion and electric excitement, I heard a warning voice calling out, but as I helplessly followed the rise and fall of her breasts and hazily tried to focus my mind, she leaned closer and breathed some further and unnecessary provocation.

"There's so much to explore, and so much to enjoy around here, Michael. Don't just rush in without thinking. Relax, take your time, it's all here ready and waiting for you. All you have to do is make it happen. Where there's a will, there's always a way. Isn't that what you boys say?"

I couldn't believe what she was saying, or the way in which each seductive syllable seemed to drip from her lips. I frantically glanced to where the oblivious Harold continued filling his pipe. Then I saw her smile at my stunned expression. "That's always assuming you're interested?"

The soft brown eyes widened to again stare an obvious invitation, while a criminally imperceptive husband put down his pipe, refilled our glasses, and began describing the precise detail of last weekend's underwater expedition.

Until then, you could reasonably excuse the incident as risqué fun and harmless flirtation, the meaningless contact between male and female that happens at a million dinner parties on every weekend of the year. But this wasn't harmless flirtation. This was an attractive married woman, sitting right in front of a foolishly uncaring husband and publicly offering herself to me. This was serious. This was immoral. This was reckless. This was downright dangerous.

I looked at Harold and suddenly felt sorry for him. He was a boring man, unsmiling and stern, and, from his wife's earlier remarks, a frustratingly celibate one. However, from the little I'd seen, he was also decent. He didn't deserve such cruel deception. I looked at the provocative Paula and suddenly felt disgusted by her. Yes, she was unbelievably sexy, still relatively young and attractive, but also shameless and callous, and driven only by an appetite for lust and pleasure.

I quietly studied her as I mentally phrased my rejection, ignoring the smoothness of her thighs as they slid beyond the hemline, not considering the firmness and roundness of her buttocks as she shuffled and fidgeted on the stool, dismissing the seductive pouting of her lips as she moistened their aridity with a flickering tongue, not seeing the fullness of her breasts as they rose and fell in breathless anticipation, not caring to recall that fleeting and violently erotic vision.

Slowly and deliberately, I nodded a confirmation of my own shallowness and wickedness and weakness. . . It seemed I was joining the ski club, after all.

The following weekend I stood and watched the sub-aqua club's heavily loaded inflatable dinghy head out of the harbour for a weekend expedition up the coast. An uncharacteristically happy and smiling Harold Cartwright had charge of both the Evinrude outboard motor and the expedition. I waited until lunchtime and sank a couple of whisky chasers for courage before leaving the centre, then walked up the hill to their apartment off the main square.

Arriving at the block, I made my way up the stairs and then knocked on the door. She took a minute to answer. She wore a simple printed smock that did nothing for her figure, the minimum of make-up on an unsmiling face and a pair of worn and tattered slippers. I didn't know what I had expected, but I did know this wasn't it. She invited me in and sat me down in an armchair.

"Would you like a drink?"

"Beer. . . thanks."

She collected a beer from the kitchen and poured herself a large vodka and tonic from the drinks trolley. Then she handed me the bottle and sat down on the settee opposite.

"I think that's how the ski-club takes it; the same way Harold wants to take them, by the neck."

It was then I noticed that her hands were shaking and suddenly realised that she was even more nervous and uncertain about all of this than me. I was also beginning to realise the wanton harlot performance, so convincingly given during that first adrenaline-laced meeting at the club, had been an elaborate façade, no doubt due to drink. Now, though, she was clearly sober, openly trembling, obviously embarrassed and, to my mind, acutely vulnerable.

I suddenly felt terrible. No, I felt more than that. I felt like the bastard I undoubtedly was.

"Look, if you want me to leave and forget all about it, you don't have to worry. It's not a problem. We can still be friends."

She didn't answer, but looked across at me and in a dull monotone voice said, "How old are you?" It was my turn not to answer, and so she said, "I'm thirty-five years old."

"So?"

"So you're so much younger than I am. You couldn't possibly understand, but I've never done anything like this before." She looked intently at me. "You have to believe that; never. We've never been all that happy, but I've never done anything like this."

"I'll let you into a secret; neither have I."

I'd tried to lighten the moment, but she looked even more miserable than when I'd first arrived. I shuffled my feet as I studied her misery, thinking this wasn't getting any better. In fact, it was becoming uncomfortable. I gallantly, if not especially convincingly, offered to leave.

"Perhaps I'd better go?"

"I don't want that."

"I'm sorry, I don't understand. What do you want?"

"I just want someone to want me, someone to care about me and want me."

"And Harold doesn't?"

They had been simple enough clichés. This entire affair was undoubtedly something of a cliché, but at the risk of flogging clichés to death, they opened a floodgate. As she considered the question the tears began and all the loneliness and misery and unhappiness came gushing out.

She had only taken the part-time job up at the garrison because she had been so lonely, but a puritanical Harold had disapproved and told her to quit. When she refused, he threatened her. He even mentioned divorce. When she still refused, he became taciturn and refused to speak to her unless they were in public. She said he spent most evenings, and every weekend, away from the apartment, leaving her alone in the centre of a desperately depressing Tobruk.

I didn't know how much of the story had been true, but this wasn't the provocative Paula I'd expected. I'd expected a perfumed and painted seductress, flouncing around a candlelit bedroom in her negligee; a wanton harlot, ruining my appetite for other women.

Whatever she might or might not have pretended at the bar that day, I could see this was a lonely woman, trapped in a desperately unhappy marriage, living in the centre of a wilderness, away from friends and family and loved ones, and as far from civilization as one could imagine.

I suddenly felt so sorry for her, and so helpless to do anything about it. I was just a nineteen going-on twenty-year-old idiot, who'd spent four of the previous eight months screwing his brains out with any female who so much as looked sideways at him. What the hell did I know about marriage or serious human relationships?

"We haven't made love for over twelve years."

"What?" She had suddenly confessed, and I remembered how she had behaved, and how seductive she had looked in the bar that day. I couldn't see how any man in his right mind could refuse her. "With a body and a face like yours, he'd have to be crazy. You've got to be joking."

She clearly wasn't, and smiled briefly and painfully at the crude compliment before the tears began again. I crossed the floor, put my arm around her and listened as she talked.

"Harold tried, I know he did, but he was only doing it because he felt he ought to. I didn't want that. No woman wants a man to sleep with her because he feels he has to."

"No, of course not, I understand how you must feel."

I didn't understand, at all, but I could feel the warmth of her body beneath that thin printed cloth, and I could smell the headiness of her perfume. I just said whatever I felt she needed to hear. It worked, because she began to relax, then snuggled closer and went on talking.

"All I wanted was to feel special and desirable; for him to want me, to want to make love to me. Why am I saying all of this to you? You're just a boy. I'm probably old enough to be . . ."

I placed my fingertips on her lips.

"Shush. I'm listening, because I think you're beautiful and sexy and I want to help you. And you're talking to me because you have to talk to someone."

I'd surprised myself. This was all so simple. I was finding it so easy to say the right words and make the right moves. It had seemed only five minutes before when I'd been laid out on that Bangkok hotel bed in petrified submission and had my virginity forcibly removed. Yet here I was all too expertly seducing a reluctant conquest, a beautiful woman, a married woman, a sexually naïve and repressed woman, a woman old enough . . . Well, let's not go there, but, as she rested her head on my shoulder and poured out her misery, I could see that everything was going well.

"Even when we tried to make it work, it was never all that successful. After a while we just stopped trying. We never said anything about it. It just happened that way. For the last six years we've even had separate bedrooms. I think secretly he knows he's . . . "

"Not another one."

I had made the insensitive remark without thinking, and immediately felt ashamed of myself. Worse than that, my outburst had ruined the moment. Perhaps I wasn't the sophisticated seducer I'd imagined myself to be. She just smiled that same painful smile and quietly explained.

"Oh, no, nothing like that. Harold's too straight-laced for anything like that. He'd go mad if he heard you suggest that. No, he's just not interested in all that physical stuff; never has been. But he loves me, and he needs me . . . and I need him too, God help me."

"What about all those guys in the ski club? Why didn't you just go to bed with one of them? Maybe go on one of those barbecues that Harold hates so much."

She looked guilty and seemed ashamed.

"I did consider it once. They were always coming on to me, trying to get me to go up the coast with them in the boat, but I didn't want to. Anyway, if I had gone they'd probably have told everyone and made hurtful remarks to Harold. They can't stand him."

"Yeah, I think someone mentioned it."

"I couldn't have that. I couldn't have them hurting him because of me, and I couldn't see myself becoming a tramp. That's not what I want. I want someone to want me and love me. I don't just want men to use me, not like a whore, not like some of those women they take up there."

"So why did you act like . . .?"

"So why did I act like one with you? I don't know. It's not like me. I think Harold's comments must have hurt me, and you seemed lovely. I thought you might be different. I thought you might not want to just have me, then walk away. I'm sorry. I also think I must have been a bit drunk."

It was time to relax the reprimand and turn up the seduction, or so I thought, because for some foolish reason I still naïvely believed that men seduce women.

"Don't be sorry. I thought it was incredibly sexy, and you're beautiful. But, if that's so, why did you invite me here?"

"I don't know. I think I wanted you. I don't know what. . ."

That was my cue to move in for the kill. The cue for a nineteen-year-old boy, with four months of frantic sexual experience, to teach a stunning, thirty-five-year-old married woman about the wonders of love. If it hadn't all been so intense, it would have been laughable.

I pulled her close, and began the same sadly perfunctory routine I always used. She drew back.

"What's wrong, don't you . . . ?"

The shaking started again, and then the tears started again. I watched her fumbling for words and couldn't believe she was the same woman who had so blatantly offered herself to me that day. She took the glass in both hands and downed the contents, and looked embarrassed. "I'm sorry, but I'm so frightened. I don't think I'm ready for this. I'm so sorry."

"It doesn't matter . . . Don't get upset."

"Look at me. I'm thirty-five. I'm not even sure I ever had ever had an orgasm before. Perhaps I've waited too long. Maybe I'll never . . ."

She smiled a pathetic smile and I was lost. I reached out to her, sealing her lips and silencing the words of self-doubt with my fingertips, then told her what she wanted to hear. I kissed her gently on the forehead as I spoke, and reassured her anxiety with a well-worn line.

"Don't worry about all that. Just close your eyes. Let me show you how beautiful and sexy you are, and how much I want you."

As I held her and calmed her and watched her confusion, it occurred to me that I had learned so little about love during my life; so much about using, and so little about caring; so much about taking, and so little about giving, and nothing whatsoever about true love. But there was one thing I had learned. I'd received the best education money could buy, taught by some of the world's most gifted tutors, and all without so much as a mortarboard between them.

I don't intend to describe all that happened during the rest of that afternoon and night, or over the rest of our brief and frantic affair. Mostly because it was private and precious and full of poignant memories that, despite the circumstances of our parting, I still cherish to this day. I can remember, though, that as I touched and caressed and soothed and calmed, and then slowly unveiled that incredible body, I felt so privileged to be the one she had chosen. And as I looked down on her nakedness, and saw the apprehension and shame and embarrassment and guilt written across those beautiful features, I fell completely in love for the first time in my life.

I will always remember studying that beautiful face as I slipped into love with her and began to pass on the sum total of my education. Watching the brow furrow as the shame receded and the excitement increased. Seeing her rise again and again to greet each caress, and hearing the groans of indulgence gather. Marvelling as that magnificent body filled with lust, and experiencing such a delicious sense of power as I watched her thighs slowly and helplessly separate. Listening to the cries of shock and disgrace as I violated her mind and gorged on her flesh, before finally allowing another frantic release to wash away all of that guilt and shame and repression.

And as I saw the beauty in her smile and the lust in her eyes, I realised I had been wrong about her, and wrong about myself, wrong about my reasons, and wrong about my desires. I'd expected to spend a few hours of selfish enjoyment, fucking a faithless slut, but instead had found myself in love with a lonely and beautiful lady. And when we made love, all the despair and all the misery I'd seen in her eyes seemed somehow replaced with tenderness and happiness and love.

If that's all corny and clichéd, I don't care, because in all my life until then, and in all my life until now, I have never known another moment when I felt so intensely proud of being such a complete and utter bastard.

On the dangers of life and love

Sadly, the ski-club didn't prove quite the den of vice and iniquity anticipated. We had fun and did some crazy things, but any fickle young married women who might have yearned for clandestine assignations in deserted coves were often scarce, and more often only notable by their absence.

For the next five months, I spent every off-shift weekend with Paula, and most free weekday time around the club. I even moved some of my belongings out of El Adem and into a house in Tobruk, living with a generous young Air Force family who had taken pity on me.

I still kept most of my belongings in the Twynham, though, and I still saw Rex. But, as time passed he become ever more feral, ever more attached to the pack and detached from humankind. And so our reunions became less and less frequent, until one day they stopped altogether.

I suppose, in a way it was a natural progression. For a while, our isolation and loneliness had forged a marriage of convenience. Now, though, he had a permanent place in the pack, with all the companionship and security that went with it, while, in joining the ski club and beginning an intensely physical and thoroughly reprehensible affair with Paula, I had discovered mine.

Everything about my life during the ensuing months was incident packed or dangerous. I made two new friends in Tony and Steve, and took part in so many dangerous activities that I'm amazed I survived. We had some good times, though, and I miss their companionship to this day.

Steve was a Londoner, wide and fast-talking, with all sorts of barrow-boy mannerisms that sometimes amused and other times annoyed. Tony was yet another Welshman from Cardiff, but as different to dear old John Doggett as chalk is to cheese.

Tony was one of those pretentious ski-club peacocks Harold had warned me against. He was aged somewhere in his late twenties or early thirties, although precisely where he wouldn't say and I couldn't guess. He was a former RAF boxing champion, something of a poseur with long blond hair, which he parted down the centre, and handsome weathered features. Like me, Tony was in a clandestine affair. She was a French beauty from the Côte d'Azur and in the throes of divorce. Unlike me, he made no effort to hide the truth.

Today I value my life and would never consider taking the risks I took then, but at that time and in that place, life wasn't precious. We would spear barracuda and moray eels, or pull octopus from the sea bed with our bare hands. Not because we especially wanted to catch these creatures, but because of the danger that each species posed. A shoal of barracuda would go berserk the moment you hit one, a fair-sized moray would literally come up the spear at you, and any octopus had to be just the right size; not so small they wouldn't make a decent meal, not so big they could keep a hold on both the seabed and you.

It was the strangest phenomenon that life meant so little to us. We were young and foolish, but it was more than simply the impetuosity of youth. Our contempt for life was a product of the despair and hopelessness of that place, at that time, and this was never more in evidence than a fishing trip we took with two of Tony's Libyan friends. One was Faraj, a well-known Tobruk resident. The other, whose name I never discovered, was a dark-skinned man, who never spoke and stood at five-foot-nothing in his flip-flops.

Faraj was a wealthy man, a friend to everyone and a fixer extraordinaire, who drove around town in a Fiat 124 saloon and did deals with anybody who would offer him a percentage. He was a friend to Tony, but I always steered clear for a reason that I don't now care to recall.

We headed up the Benghazi highway for a few miles, and then turned left on to a track that wound its way through the dunes to the sea, with the little Fiat lurching and crunching and occasioning serious damage to both bodywork and suspension, not to mention my spine.

Battered and bruised, we arrived at a deserted cove, climbed out of the Fiat, stretched our aching bodies, and then checked for damage. I smiled as I surveyed the cove and began scanning the dunes for discarded underwear. Tony, who knew the place well, said that a boat was the only sensible way to get there. Others had clearly been here before us, because there were champagne bottles and the charred remains of campfires liberally dotted along the beach.

So this was it. The infamous Buffalo Beach, where bored and fickle housewives drank champagne and lost their inhibitions, and steaks and reputations were irreparably blackened. We weren't here for a barbecue, though, or to drink champagne and violate loose and lonely women. We were here to fish.

"Wake up. We need stones."

That had been Tony, shaking me from my reverie.

"What stones? What for?"

"Small ones." He indicated the rough size with thumb and forefinger. "About so big."

"What for?

"You'll see."

It occurred to me as I began collecting the stones that I hadn't seen any fishing rods, or even a spear gun. It wasn't until I wandered over to the opened car boot that I realised why.

A large pile of what looked like coarse cement lay unwrapped in the centre of the boot. I estimated about twenty pounds of it or so, but it wasn't cement. It wasn't anything to do with building, in fact, quite the reverse. I stepped back and turned to Tony.

"That's gelignite. Are you telling me that we bumped and scraped our way all along that bloody track with a boot full of fucking gelignite? There's enough here to blow up Tobruk."

"Relax, it's not dynamite. It's stable, and it's safe. Well, it is without a fuse."

"Why the fuck didn't you tell me?"

"Because you wouldn't have come."

"Bloody right I wouldn't have come. What are you, crazy?"

"Oh stop being such a big tart. It's fun. We do it all the time."

Faraj arrived back at the car, carrying a handful of small stones that he'd gathered. He put them with ours, alongside the gelignite, and then took an empty coke can from a plastic bag in the corner of the boot. He had obviously prepared the cans earlier, because each was dry and clean and had the top sliced cleanly off. He filled the bottom half with a handful of gelignite, packed the top half with the small stones, and then gingerly inserted a waterproof fuse from a box that he kept in the glove compartment. Then he painstakingly folded over the top of the tin to prevent the contents spilling, and handed the completed article to his undersized friend, who had readied himself by climbing into a wetsuit, complete with face mask, snorkel and flippers.

"He may have been short of stature that little friend of Faraj, but what he lacked in feet and inches he more than made up for in courage. We stood and watched as he padded out into the water, and then began slowly swimming farther out, with the coke tin held above his head. As he

233

swam his eyes peered through the goggles, scanning the depths for shoals of fish.

"You don't mind if I stand back a bit, do you?"

That had been chicken me, of course. Faraj just smiled and said, "It's O.K., Mike. It's quite safe."

"I notice you didn't volunteer to take it out there."

He grinned at me again.

"Do I look that crazy?"

It seemed the undersized friend had spotted something, because he suddenly flicked the waterproof fuse and dropped the can, then turned on to his back and lay floating on the surface. Ten seconds later, a muffled explosion preceded a sudden flurry of agitated water, which boiled up from the depths and bobbed the little fellow up and down like a cork on the tide.

The idea was laudable enough. The stone- and gelignite-filled can would act as an underwater grenade, leaving stunned and splattered fish to float to the surface, compliments of inflated swim-bladders. All we had to do was charge into the water and collect the haul.

But you know what Burns said about the best laid schemes.

Three times more that crazy little man snorkelled his way out. Three times more he dropped the can into the water and turned on to his back. Three times more we heard the explosion and saw him bobbing up and down like a cork, and three times more we had nothing to show for it.

"Not so much as a damp squid."

I thought my little play on words amusing, but nobody else did. With a mixture of emotions, we headed back to Tobruk, with me flinching every time the Fiat went over a bump, the little dark-skinned man looking thoroughly dejected, Faraj scowling his embarrassment, and Tony and Steve looking disappointed. Despite their obvious disappointment I hadn't minded, though, because spearing fish with a compressed air or spring-loaded gun was acceptable. Outwitting them with rod and line demanded skill. Even pulling them away from the seabed with our bare hands was fine. But this seemed a little too far away from anything that I could even loosely describe as sport.

The Libyan coup, in September nineteen sixty-nine, wasn't quite the blood-curdling event you might imagine. There was no crackling of gunfire in the distance, no rampaging rebel army, no beleaguered loyalists holed up in the King's Palace, no tanks on the streets, well, nothing worth calling a tank, and no raping and pillaging. All in all, it was uneventful, as regime changes and military coups on that continent tend to go.

The only way you might have guessed was the flyover of five F5 freedom-fighters from the Libyan Air Force, and then, two days later, a couple of round-shouldered and sorry-looking Libyan foot soldiers arrived. They had been too frightened to look directly at us as they shuffled along, keeping their eyes to the ground and dragging their feet as they threaded their way through the town and on to the deposed king's palace.

Gaddafi was a different matter. He arrived in Tobruk a couple of weeks after the coup, and immediately did some serious rabble-rousing down in the square. A week or so later he came up to El Adem to negotiate with the British government, via a direct communications link we'd set up.

From my admittedly peripheral viewpoint, I saw two separate Muammar al-Gaddafis in the new Libyan Republic. The first was the rabble-rouser and sponsor of lunacy, who screamed his hatred of everything western to an illiterate mob gathered down in the square. The second was an intelligent and articulate man, who negotiated our withdrawal with firmness and reason.

Not that he had all that much choice in the matter, because, according to unconfirmed intelligence reports, only two of the original five F5s remained airworthy. Not only that, but the armoured personnel carrier that ferried supplies and reinforcements between Benghazi and Tobruk had broken down on the Benghazi highway. Its occupants walked all the way up to the camp and asked us to help them repair it.

The Americans had a massive airbase up at Wheelus Field near Tripoli, which was typical, when you come to think of it. They base themselves near Libya's answer to St. Tropez, while we base ourselves smack bang in the middle of a scene from *A Fistful of Dollars*. With all that firepower and might at their immediate disposal, Gaddafi knew there was no chance of bullying the Americans into submission, and when he arrived at the camp that first time, we similarly left him in no doubt about the folly of trying to bully us.

As he drove up the single track road and then sat at the camp gates waiting for approval to enter, he could see two tanks, ready and waiting at the gates. Either side of the tanks, a battery of old Bofors field guns pointed menacingly out, and a contingent of fully-armed Cherry-Berry Paras just happened to be passing. On the pan, a squadron of Lightnings from Akrotiri had landed, and, as the minutes ticked by and he continued to wait, a Vulcan glided innocuously over his head and then went to full-boost.

Today the Vulcan bomber is obsolete, and that's a shame, because if you ever saw one tilt skyward and go to full boost, you would know exactly what happened to Gaddafi's party. The ground for about a mile in diameter started shaking, as did everybody and everything on it, and the noise was deafening. So much so that Gaddafi's driver and bodyguards put their hands over their ears and looked to the sky in terror, and even the man himself stole a nervous glance skyward.

With show over, he was allowed to continue to where the Commandant waited to greet him, and the strictly non-interventionist policy of the British Government survived one of its sternest tests. We were only thankful that he hadn't arrived a day earlier, because he would have seen the death-or-glory Seventeen-Twenty-First Lancers, of old Balaclava fame, pushing one of the tanks into position, because it had flatly refused to start without an engine.

Not that Gaddafi or his rag-tag army and fast-depleting air force concerned us. A platoon of Irish Rangers from the Tobruk garrison and a lone Harrier jump jet could have despatched the lot without raising a sweat. Nor did we care about rampaging mobs from Tobruk, fuelled by Gaddafi's rhetoric, or avenging armies of blistered foot soldiers charging along the Benghazi highway, because we were nervously peering in the opposite direction, out to the bulk of the Sahara, where rumour had it the Senussi were massing.

You see, we weren't sure how the Senussi would take Gaddafi's ousting of their beloved King Idris I. He had been a good friend to Britain over the years, but when it came to repaying that friendship, our diplomats and politicians did what diplomats and politicians around the world are wont to do when faced with a need for decisive action: they perched on the fence and did nothing. The Bedouin Senussi could legitimately argue that Britain and the West had failed to stand by their good friend Idris, despite him standing loyally by them in fifty-six and sixty-seven.

The upshot of all that negative diplomacy was that we weren't sure if the Senussi now saw Britain as friend or enemy. So our nervous camp guards spent their days and nights peering south.

Not that we'd have been any great shakes if the Senussi had come, because the RAF, in its infinite wisdom, didn't bother to enquire about small arms competence when they drew up the guard-duty rosters. They just started at surnames beginning with A, and went through the camp roster until they reached Z. After that they went back to A again. This meant we now had RAF personnel on guard duty and in charge of loaded rifles who weren't sure of either the location or purpose of the weapon's safety catch.

I would estimate that on El Adem camp there were only a couple of dozen RAF personnel who knew anything about small arms. Those who held enough knowledge to break down and reassemble a pistol, rifle, or submachine gun, and then load, aim, and hit what they aimed at were in even shorter supply. The majority were clerks and cooks and drivers and medics and technicians. They were people who had no need for such knowledge, and hadn't touched a weapon since the bolt action three-o-threes they had fired just that one time in basic training. However, that didn't stop the RAF from calling them up for guard duty, and then happily handing over the latest seven-six-two self-loading rifles.

The only time I was foolish enough to allow them to press-gang me into guard duty was one night in late September. They assigned me to the water tower, handed me a loaded SLR, and told me the day watch came on at seven. When I got to the top of the tower, I found three nervous-looking airmen with loaded rifles, and with not the first clue of how to use them, other than a hazy awareness of what the trigger did, and a rough idea of where the bullets came out.

It was around two a.m. when a shot rang out. It echoed around the tower and made me jump out of my skin. I rushed over to the guy who'd obviously fired the shot and nervously asked, "What was that? What's going on?"

"I thought I saw something."

He was lying. I could see that, because he was looking everywhere but at me. I remember thinking that if he was going to lie he should learn to lie properly, and if he was going to invent a story he could have been a little more creative than that.

"O.K., so what did you see, and where was it?"

I made it clear that I didn't believe a word.

"Honest, it was out there. I saw something."

He had pointed to the blackness of the desert, all three-and-a-quarter-million square miles of it.

"Bound to be something moving somewhere out there, I suppose."

"No, honestly, I saw it."

"Don't be stupid. You can't see a hand in front of your face out there."

"Well I saw something . . . I did."

237

"Look, the snowdrops will be here soon. If you can't think up something more believable than that, we're all in the shit. Have you any idea of how much paperwork you've just caused?"

The snowdrops were the RAF police, so called because the top of their hats were white, as opposed to the Army police, named redcaps because theirs were red; simple, huh? The snowdrops' guardhouse was three hundred yards from the tower, and I expected them to come charging up at any minute. Thankfully, the nervous-looking airman who'd fired the shot decided to own up.

"Look, I was trying out this double pressure thing on the trigger. It just went off."

"Oh, for fuck's sake. Which direction?"

"What?"

"Which way were you pointing the fucking gun, when it just went off?"

"I don't understand."

I was getting angry.

"Look, we need to know if you fired it out into the desert, or if you've just killed somebody sleeping in their bed. Which fucking way were you aiming?" He suddenly understood and pointed to the desert, and so I said,. "You're sure about that; you're certain?"

"Oh yeah, that's what I was looking at. You see, I thought I saw . . ."

"Don't start that crap again."

We finally agreed on a concocted story about him seeing a shadow move, challenging whoever or whatever it was, and then firing a warning shot into the air, which had roused the rest of us. It was the best we could do, and there was no way I was going to lie. Not when there was still an outside possibility the idiot might have hit someone. We needn't have bothered, because it wasn't until daylight, five hours later, when the snowdrops finally put in an appearance.

They arrived by Landrover, having driven the three hundred yards from the guardroom at breakneck speed, and then slammed to a halt with a squeal of tyres and a cloud of sand. They jumped out, and immediately began strutting and posing, John Wayne style, staring belligerently around and threateningly fingering their nine millimetre sidearms. One of them shouted up to us.

"Are you lot OK up there?"

"Yeah, we're fine, why?"

If they had only jumped back into the Landrover and driven away, they might have escaped with strutting reputations and dignities intact, but in a reflex response one of them shouted back.

"We heard a shot."

The most unexpected news of that autumn wasn't the coup, or that I would be on my way home before my two-year tour of duty was up. The most unexpected news broke in the MSC bar in late October. I walked into the club and found the place packed.

"You'll have to join the local bowls club or something, Harold."

One of the sub-aqua crowd had shouted across the bar. Harold Cartwright answered, "Why's that?"

"Well, you'll soon be too bloody old to walk, let alone go diving."

Everybody laughed, and so I asked the first person I met, "What's all this in aid of?"

"It's Harold; he's done thirty bloody years. Can you imagine that? Thirty years of this crap. Anyway, we're helping the poor old sod celebrate."

Somebody else added, "Poor old sod, my arse. It'll be Mister Cartwright this time next week, and he'll be supping pints of bitter down at his local. I'll still be in this God-forsaken place . . . What'll you be doing?"

I suddenly felt a knife go through me.

"Where's Paula?"

I don't remember who it was, but he lowered his voice and then turned to me.

"I don't know, but I bet wherever it is she's flat on her back with her legs open. Lousy bitch didn't even bother to turn up and help the poor old bugger celebrate his retirement."

I suddenly felt numb, but then I looked across at Harold Cartwright and saw him looking straight at me. He was smiling, but even from ten yards away I could see the smile didn't reach his eyes. He relaxed the smile and pushed his way through the crowd to where I stood.

"She didn't tell you, did she?"

There had been no hint of triumph, either in voice or attitude. I looked blankly back at him and said nothing. He suggested we get some air.

We pushed our way out, and then walked to where it was quiet. I finally found my voice.

"How long have you known?"

"About you and Paula, you mean?" I nodded. He smiled ruefully. "Since the beginning; since she picked you up in the bar that day." Then, when I'd obviously looked surprised, he added, "Well, let's face it, neither of you were especially subtle about it, were you? At one point I thought you were going to spread her across the bar and fuck her in front of me."

The remark was out of character, and he was obviously bitter. I couldn't say I blamed him.

"I'm sorry."

It was a pathetic thing to say, after all the humiliation I'd heaped on him, but at that moment it was all I could think of."

"Don't be. With a wife like mine you learn to ignore it after a while." He studied my surprise. "You didn't think you were the only one, did you?"

I suddenly began to understand just what he was saying, and why he was saying it. Not wanting to believe, but knowing it to be the truth, and suddenly realising just how stupid and gullible I'd been. We stood and looked out across the water for a while, not speaking, but then I had to ask.

"The ski club? Did she . . . ? Is that why . . . ?"

He stared out across the water and didn't answer, but then took a deep breath and told me the whole sad and sordid story.

"That's what started it all; about fifteen months ago."

"Started what?"

"I hadn't suspected anything. Oh, I knew the rumours about what went on up there, and knew that some of them were about Paula, but I didn't believe it, or not at first."

"I'm sorry, but I don't think I want . . ."

He wasn't taking any notice of me. I tried to interrupt, but he ignored me and continued with his story. It was almost as though he needed me to listen, but that my opinion didn't matter.

"The longer the rumours went on, the more I started to worry. So, one day I left work early and came down here. There was nobody here, apart from the usual weekday crowd; none of the ski club people, and no Paula. I took the inflatable out and went to see for myself. I drew into the cove next to Buffalo, and then walked across the dunes."

He suddenly stopped and looked vacantly out across the harbour as he relived what was obviously an acutely painful memory.

"There were five of them. They were drunk, laughing and shouting and spraying champagne around. She was with them. They were groping her and kissing her, and making crude remarks, and then someone pulled her top off. At first she pretended to be shocked, but she let them maul, and I could see she was laughing, too. But then she stopped laughing. She reached out and kissed one of them, and then pushed her hand inside his trunks and started grabbing at him.

I stood there and watched while he pushed her down on to the sand, pulled her pants away, took his cock out and just shoved it into her. It was like she was nothing, like she meant nothing; no tenderness, no gentleness, no affection. He just shoved it into her, and she just let him do it, with everybody watching and cheering. After that they all had her, every one of them, some more than once. . . They were worse than animals."

"Didn't you try to stop it?"

He drew back from his trance and considered the question.

"What could I do? They were all over her, and she was encouraging them and enjoying every minute. There was nothing I could do, nothing I could say. It went on for ever. I just sat down in the dunes and cried. I didn't know what else to do. There was nothing I could do.

"When she got home I told her I'd seen it all. I said I wanted a divorce. She started crying. She's good at that; turns it on and off like a tap. She swore they'd tricked her and got her drunk. She said she was so ashamed. She said she loved me and didn't want to hurt me. She promised it would never happen again. . . And I believed her, because I wanted to believe her, so very, very, badly."

"Why are you telling me all this?"

"Because there are always consequences. You're young and stupid and cruel and selfish, and you don't care who you damage, but I want you to understand. There are always consequences."

"I know. I'm sorry."

He ignored the soulless apology and continued talking.

"But then there were others . . . so many others."

He looked accusingly at me, and I found myself apologising again.

"I'm so sorry."

"It doesn't matter now. After a while you have to accept the inevitable and let go. If you don't, it'll destroy you. We're divorcing as soon as we get home. The funniest part is, she's leaving me. Can you believe that? She's leaving me."

"I'm sorry."

It was all I could think of to say. He just kept shrugging his shoulders.

"Don't be; she's not worth it, and I don't care any more. I suppose she told you I didn't like her working up at the garrison?"

He looked questioningly across at me. When I nodded, in stunned silence, he went on.

"Not that we needed the money, but I thought it would give her some interest, something to occupy her time. After a few weeks she started getting home later and later. It was obvious she was seeing someone from work. I don't know who, and I don't care, but then, neither does she. She doesn't try to hide it any more. Some nights she doesn't even bother coming home."

"You mean it's still going on?"

"Of course. It's been going on for over a year. I told you that you weren't the only one. Did you seriously believe you were?"

He looked at me with contempt in his eyes, but I didn't answer, allowing him a minor moment of long-overdue revenge and expecting him to start tearing into me at any moment. He didn't. Instead of showing the anger and bitterness he must surely have felt, he turned and walked away without saying another word. I could only watch in silent shame as he headed back to the bar, and his special thirty-year celebration, with the weight of the world on his shoulders and a poorly-manufactured smile on his face.

I stood and looked out across the harbour with tears in my eyes. I felt so foolish and cheated and bitter and hurt and used, and so angry about everything. I didn't care or even consider that I was the guilty party in all this misery and sordidness . . . or one of them.

I had seriously thought myself the consummate lover that day: the great seducer of a reluctant beauty, an instructor in passion, the maestro of the female orgasm and the liberator of repression. I couldn't have been more wrong. All I'd actually done was allow a stupid male ego, that couldn't tell the difference between love and infatuation to flatter and deceive. Then I thought about Harold Cartwright and realised how dignified he had been during all those months of knowing and hurting. I couldn't have begun to understand how he must have been feeling.

Fifteen minutes after that I was knocking on the apartment door. She looked surprised, but invited me in. I looked at the deep-sea boxes, and then said rather unnecessarily, "You're packing?"

"What? Oh, yes, sorry, darling, haven't had the chance to tell you. It was all so last-minute. I was going to tell you this weekend." She linked her arms around me and put her head on my chest. "It won't be for long.

You'll be home soon, and we can start seeing each other again. I'm going to miss you so much. I don't know how I'm going to survive without you."

The tears started to flow as she snuggled against me. God, she was good, or maybe I was just gullible. I changed the subject and said matter-of-factly, "Went bomb fishing up the coast the other day, saw the infamous ski club beach. You know the one; the one you've never been to. There were empty champagne bottles everywhere."

"Oh, did you?"

She was a little too casual, but then she probably guessed why I had suddenly turned up on her doorstep, midweek and midday, and could equally probably see what was coming.

"Strangely enough there were plenty of empty vodka bottles there, too."

I pushed her away. She feigned surprise, but then abandoned the pretence and looked sullen.

"Who told you?" I stared blankly back, and she knew. "That bastard. That bloody bastard."

"That's not all he said." She looked puzzled. I went on. "The garrison, your so-called part-time job. The one that regularly goes on all night; the one that's still regularly going on all night."

"Do you want a drink?"

"No, I want an answer."

She poured herself the usual large vodka and tonic. She obviously needed time to think.

"An answer to what?"

"Why you played that game, when I first came up here? All that crap about never having had an orgasm, and never having any real experience of love? I want to know why you lied, and why you did that to me; all those tears, all that bullshit; you even dressed down to play the part. Why?"

"I didn't dress down. I didn't expect you so early. I was still in my housecoat, and I'd only just finished drying my hair. I was going to dress up for you, give you a treat. The black satin chemise and those little satin panties, and the silk stockings and suspenders . . . everything you like."

I may have been gullible, but I wasn't buying that.

"Come off it; you'd only just met me. How could you know what I liked?"

"Because all men like that, and because I'm an expert at giving men what they want . . . didn't your new friend Harold tell you? Anyway, I'd seen the way you couldn't tear your eyes away that day, the way your mouth fell open when I showed you those little satin panties."

"And all the rest of the bullshit. What was all that about?"

"I liked you, I liked you a lot. I didn't want you to just have me and leave me. I wanted you to want me, to want to be with me."

I wanted to let her know how much she'd hurt me, to tell her what she'd spoiled.

"I fell in love with you."

"I know. It made me feel wonderful."

"Not wonderful enough to be honest with me. Not wonderful enough to love me in return."

"That's not true." And then, when I stared angrily back, she added, "Shall I tell you something? That first day, the first time we made love, it was the most wonderful experience I ever had."

"What, you mean it was even better than taking them on five at a time, or however many it is you're screwing up at the garrison these days."

She ignored the comment, and I found myself wanting to believe her.

"It was so beautiful, I swear to god. I couldn't believe that anything could feel so good. That first climax was the most incredible thing I'd ever known. I couldn't stop coming, and when you started again and it happened again, I thought I was going to pass out. It's the truth. I swear it. If you don't believe anything else about me, please believe that."

I was just thankful that I didn't have an ego left to believe her with.

"I wasn't talking about how many times you came off. I was talking about love; about being in love . . . about me being in love with you."

"So was I."

"I don't think so."

I wanted to tell her that I had needed her to be faithful to me, but suddenly realised the hypocrisy. I decided to say nothing. When I started to turn away, she said, "I didn't mean to hurt you, I'd never hurt you, I love you. Look, I'll write when I'm settled, send you my new address. We can try again, properly, without all this sneaking around."

"Don't bother."

I went back to living in the Twynham after that, because it all seemed so much more civilised than the life I'd been leading and the things I'd been doing. I went back to downing a bottle of Chivas a day, and to chain-smoking myself to death. I went back to sitting and staring morosely out across the desert, and to building cans and fighting alongside the rest of the motley reprobates in the NAAFI bar. I went back to crying myself to sleep in nightly fits of drunken regret, and playing all those slow-blues tracks that made me feel even sadder; telling myself how much I'd loved her then, and how much I hated her now; squandering so much precious youth and indulging in so much self-pity while I waited for the pain to go away; yearning only for that blessed moment when a big silver bird would swoop down from the sky and carry me away from that dreadful place.

The end of an era

It was early evening, on a desperately-cold February day in nineteen-seventy, when I flew back into the same R.A.F. Lyneham I'd left sixteen months earlier. I was dressed in a pair of faded and frayed Levi's hanging over a pair of scuffed bondai boots, had the obligatory eight-inch Bowie knife dangling from my belt, and only the benefit of a thin khaki shirt to keep out the February inclemency. I was freezing.

I carried an old canvas bag with a pair of binoculars hung around my neck and a mono ski resting on my shoulder, my share of the disbanded ski-club spoils. I wore a floppy desert camouflage hat, with my hair long and bleached almost blond by the sun. I looked unkempt, my face unshaven for the best part of a week, and my complexion tanned and weathered by sixteen months of the Sahara. All in all, I looked like the sort of deranged knife-wielding lunatic that most sane individuals would cross the street to avoid.

In my pocket burned a large roll of cash, the product of all the paid leave I hadn't taken, a month's disembarkation, and a chunk of previously unpaid Local Overseas Allowance. All that, and the fact I'd had nothing to spend my money on for the last sixteen months, apart from booze and cigarettes, added up to wealth beyond the dreams of . . . well, perhaps not that, but I wasn't hard-up for readies.

I arrived home in the company of a little Scottish corporal, I knew from El Adem, and with whom I'd shared a scotch or two on the journey into Lyneham. He dressed in similarly unnerving fashion, but instead of a water-ski , he carried an acoustic guitar without any strings. I don't know which of us looked the more desperate.

Lyneham said we could spend the night in the transit block, and they would ferry us to the railway station next morning. However, neither of us intended spending our first night back in the U.K. on a lumpy mattress and a metal bedstead. Instead, we ordered up a taxi, and told the driver to take us over to the Bear Hotel in Hungerford. Although around twenty-five miles away, it was the only decent hotel I could remember being in that area.

I will never forget the look on the face of the young duty manager at the Bear Hotel when he first saw us walk up to the reception hatch. It was priceless, but to give him credit, he didn't turn us away. He just stood there with his eyes wide and his mouth open, and nodded blankly when we asked for a room apiece. Then, presumably fearing for his employment more than his life, he plucked up his courage, apologised profusely and asked for the money in advance.

When we each produced a huge roll of cash his eyes nearly fell out of their sockets, and when we printed Tobruk, Libya firmly and boldly in the book, you could see the wheels going round. He stood there, nervously eyeing us and obviously considering all the military ramifications of being in that place at that time, and factoring in our gaunt and intimidating appearances.

I don't know who or what he thought we were, but he suddenly didn't want to meet our eyes. I have to admit, though, from that moment on the service at The Bear Hotel was exemplary and I would recommend it to anyone.

I phoned my parents from the hotel, but they didn't seem especially pleased to hear from me, and so I followed my first night with two weeks of juvenile excess in London's West End. I spent the days around Carnaby Street, and nights sleeping at the Britannia Club in Waterloo. Unsurprisingly the roll of money rapidly disappeared, and I headed to Tangmere a week early.

At first sight nothing had changed. Many of the old faces were still there. A few had never left, and others had gone and then returned, having completed the more usual, sensible and acceptable nine-month tour of duty. The same basic ramshackle organisation and lack of management seemed in evidence: the same scruffy prefabs for work, the same spartan barrack blocks for rest, and the same old NAAFI bar and television room for relaxing. But, despite all that, something was missing.

Doggett was there. He had been to Gan and back on a nine-month tour, but, horror of horrors, he'd got engaged. I congratulated him, and then bought him a beer and asked about his fiancée.

"So, what's she like? Where did you meet her?" I glanced knowingly across the table, and then mischievously added, "What's it like to be in love, John?" He didn't rise to the bait, but shrugged his shoulders and answered matter-of-factly.

"She's OK, I suppose. Names Trudy . . . great fuck, and she goes down like the Titanic."

"I'm sorry, what . . .?"

"You know; straight down . . . one minute she's . . ."

"John, I know what the term means, but you're talking about your future wife here. You're not talking about some old scrubber you just paid a tenner for."

"I know."

"So why are you marrying her? She's not . . . ?"

"No, nothing like that. To tell you the truth, I'm marrying her because she's the only woman I ever met who could drink me under the table. She's unbelievable. Can I borrow your best blue?"

"Sure, where's yours?"

"I haven't seen it for years, and I want to look my best . . . on the day and that."

"Yeah, sure, John, it's no problem; as long as you promise to wear a clean pair of shreddies."

"You have my word."

So dear old John Doggett married brown-eyed Trudy in my best-blue uniform and SD hat, someone else's shoes and someone else's shirt, collar and tie. They obviously weren't short of something borrowed and blue, and with John they had something old, but the lady wasn't new, and neither was anything else I could see. This was especially true of John's attitude to the fair sex, because he continued to win every sweepstake, whenever and wherever we travelled.

The last I heard of John, he was renting her out in Cyprus to those more needy and less thrifty than himself. Although, I never got that from the horse's mouth and so it may not have been true. But knowing John as I did, and knowing the dark-eyed Trudy and her obliging nature, I would have to imagine it could well have been.

John wasn't the only one who married around that time. I also heard they sent the enviably good-looking Joules on a two-year tour to Changi in Singapore. . . lucky SOB.

I received a letter from Singapore a few weeks after I got back to Tangmere, and knew immediately who it was from. There was no note inside the envelope, but there was a photograph of a happy couple at an impressive-looking formal wedding.

The groom was classically good-looking, with an Adonis-like bone-structure, and a smile that could charm the birds from the trees and the knickers from a nun. The bride was a consummate beauty, with porcelain features and expensively streaked blonde hair, who looked like she'd just stepped off the cover of a glossy magazine. Stapled to the picture was a Singapore dollar bill.

Despite further visits to the Far East, I never saw or heard anything of the enviably good-looking Joules after that. Someone told me he bought himself out of the service, and I suppose that would fit, given the boast his new wife made about the impressive connections of her social circle, but I never knew the truth with any certainty. I do know, though, that I will always remember him with fondness, and often find myself wondering whatever happened to that impish-looking friend with the auburn hair: the one we had seen in the company of his petulant, but perfectly formed future wife that day, and offered to me by the lucky lothario himself as a consolation prize.

After a few weeks back at Tangmere, I moved out of the accommodation block and into a caravan, living in the middle of a farmyard in Pagham with a friend of mine who worked as a clerk in the TCW headquarters. He was a part-time disk jockey, who managed the camp radio station, and we had some good times. We strung a counterpane across the caravan's main sleeping area to offer some privacy, and placed the television in the far corner, at an angle, so we could both watch the programmes from our individual beds. The problem was, when we switched off the television, the blank screen acted as a mirror. Little did our sexually-liberated female guests realise that while giving their all to one, they also provided X-rated entertainment to the other.

The idiot Aps was still at Tangmere. They had posted him to the Gulf: nine-months in Masirah. He arrived back at Tangmere a few weeks after I moved into the caravan, and seemed just as cretinous as ever. I tried to steer clear of him. In fact, the more I saw of him, the more he annoyed me, and I had long since passed the point where I was willing to suffer fools. I knew if I saw him leer his pock-marked face at one more of my girlfriends, or heard him say 'any port in a storm' or some other childish or derogatory remark, there was a good chance I'd punch him.

For a while I found it easy to avoid him, living away from the camp and in that farmyard caravan, but then they sent us on the same exercise, a three-week stint to Malta and Cyprus.

I thought about how I would deal with my hostility toward him, and decided there was no point in unpleasantness. I would bite my tongue and keep away, and for the most part my new avoidance strategy worked. But then we moved from Luqa to Akrotiri and it failed spectacularly.

The exercise was uneventful, but the nightlife was good and the girls were dusky and beautiful. I loved Malta, because Malta, pre Dom Mintoff, boasted an area in Valletta known as 'The Gut', a long narrow street running down a steep hill from the heights of Valletta to the shore. It boasted nothing but bars and brothels and restaurants, and was thoroughly entertaining.

I held a similar affection for Cyprus, because Cyprus had Limassol, and Limassol had 'The Square', and that was always similarly entertaining for similar reasons. I haven't returned to either island for over thirty years, and those areas may well be flourishing to this day, but in those days the nightlife, for a young and foolish serviceman, was something to behold.

But back to the moronic Aps and my non-confrontation strategy, because the most memorable event wasn't the nightlife, or the bars, or the girls, or even the exercise. The most memorable event happened on our arrival at the bedding store in Akrotiri. The Corporal, handing out the clean bedding, was someone most of us knew well.

"You do yourself a favour and shut it, laddie. Now take your bedding, and piss off."

I had been standing at the back of the queue and hadn't seen those involved in the kerfuffle, but I knew that voice better than my own. It was a voice I would never forget.

Aps had caused all the commotion. He walked back down the line, carrying his bedding, sneering and scoffing in a voice loud enough to hear at the front of the queue.

"Have you seen who's up there, handing out the sheets and taking in the dirty washing? It's only the Wee Beastie . . . What a tosser. I mean, is that a fucking career move or what?"

Most of the others sneered and smiled. Some made similarly derogatory remarks. They remembered Corporal Campbell as a psychotic drill instructor with delusions of grandeur, and a streak of viciousness and cruelty a mile wide. They recalled a man who took his inferiority complex out on a group of terrified boys. I didn't agree.

They each arrived at the counter and each made nasty remarks; not directly to him, but just loud enough for him to hear. They obviously had scores to settle and I could understand their anger, but I hadn't seen him in that way. There was no doubt I had, during my early days at Cosford, because during those first few weeks I had only seen the façade. I had only seen the small man talking big, the pint-sized Scottish psychopath with a slashed peak and a belligerent pose. I had only seen a man who bullied and frightened the weak and intimidated the strong. But that had been in the beginning.

When I reached the counter, he made no comment. I smiled across at him.

"It's good to see you. How are you keeping?"

He nodded, and I could see that he had been upset by some of the comments.

"Fine, laddie, fine . . . you?"

"Yeah, great, thanks. I wanted to . . ."

"There you go; name, rank, and serial number."

He had interrupted me. It seemed my lack of belligerence was more embarrassing to him than others' wealth of the same, but I needed to say something. I jotted down the necessary information on the form, then signed my name at the end and spoke to him as I scrawled a signature.

"I wanted to say thanks, for everything. I never got the chance before."

He nodded a cursory acknowledgement, and then shoved the pile of bedding into my arms.

"You're welcome, laddie . . . Come on, who's next?"

My appreciation obviously made him feel uncomfortable. I nodded back at him and moved away, and then headed out and across to the transit block. When I got there, I found Aps standing in the centre of the room. He'd obviously heard what had happened, and what I'd said.

"You fucking little wanker. That bastard made our lives a living hell for a year, and you just thanked him for it. You'll be offering to bend over for him next, you brown-nosing bastard."

I dumped the bedding onto an empty mattress, walked over to where Aps stood sneering, and then hit him, hard and in the face; in fact, too hard, because I hurt my hand. However, he went straight down and so I figured it was worth some bruising and a swollen hand. Punching him was something I had wanted to do for so long. When he started to get up, I stood over him and said, "You get up now, and I'll finish this, I swear." He thought about that and stayed put. "Oh, and if I wake up in the night with a fractured skull, you'd better make sure you finish the job, because if I ever come out of hospital I won't just beat your face in . . . I'll kill you. You understand me?"

That had been a reference to the last time that Aps had fought with a comrade. I hadn't been there, but they told me it happened a week or so before they posted him to Masirah. Some said it was the reason they posted him. The fight had been vicious, and he'd lost that one, too, but a few days later the other guy was taken to hospital with a fractured skull. Somebody hit him over the head with a house brick while he was asleep.

Although they never proved it, everybody knew who had done the cowardly deed.

I decided to finish my little speech for the benefit of those watching as much as for his, but also because it was the truth.

"That guy taught me a hell of a lot. He taught me to see my faults and to deal with then. He taught me to be honest with myself, and he taught me to grow up. And do you know what else he taught me? He taught me to deal with nasty little pieces of shit like you."

I turned my back on Aps and walked back to my bed at the other end of the room. Nobody else said a word. Back at Tangmere they transferred him into a different unit, and never sent us away on the same exercise again. Nobody ever explained why they transferred him and so obviously kept us apart, but I guess they had all heard about the set-to in Akrotiri. I do know that Frankie Aps and I never spoke another word to each other from that moment on.

I fully intended forgetting the incident, but a few days after we got back I was sitting in the Lamb in Pagham village with an affable Irish friend of mine called Connor Moran. Connor was a great guy, who hailed from Belfast. He held a placid, common-sense attitude to just about everything, and was without so much as a bigoted bone in his body. Given Ireland's problems of the time, it was nothing short of remarkable

We were drinking, as we were wont to do, and the conversation revolved around women, as our conversations were wont to do, and the beers were going down well, as they . . . Well, I'm sure you can see where this is going. But then he changed the subject, looked closely at me.

"Heard anything of Frankie Aps?" he asked. "I mean, since you gave him that smack."

The comment took me by surprise. I knew Connor had been in the room when it happened, but he hadn't shown any interest. I assumed the question had merely been a gap-filler.

"No, I haven't seen him since, but I've wanted to do that for as long as I can remember."

"Obviously. You cracked his jaw, I hear."

I gave a start and looked at him, hoping he was joking. I could see immediately that he wasn't.

"Really?"

"Yeah, hairline break. They only just found out."

I could see that he was less than impressed with my fighting prowess.

"Oh, shit. I didn't mean to do that."

"Then why hit him in the first place?"

I immediately began justifying the action. I should have known that by doing so, I was merely confirming there was no justification to be had.

"Because he's a back-stabbing, greasy, crude and nasty little shit, and he had it coming."

"So?"

"What do you mean . . . so?"

"So, you've always known that. Why hit him now?"

I wanted to tell him that it was because Frankie Aps had called me names in the transit block that day, and had taken his spite and disenchantment out on someone I respected. Sticks and stones came instantly to mind, and so I didn't give a reason. Conversations with Connor were like games of verbal chess. One unthinking comment could result in an unwinnable position. Although, in truth, I already knew that my position on this had been unwinnable from the outset.

"You know why."

"Let me hazard a guess. Because he called you some stupid names?"

"Yeah, something like that."

"And nobody ever called you names before?"

I shrugged, because we both knew the truth of that. He pressed home the attack.

"Let me ask you something . . . Do you think Frankie Aps gets up in the morning and says to himself, 'I'm going to be a shit today; a nasty, greasy, back-stabbing little shit, so everyone will hate me?' Or do you think he gets up and tries to think up ways to make people change their minds and start liking him?"

"I don't believe he thinks of anything at all. He doesn't have that much of a brain."

"Isn't that even more reason to show some compassion?" I stared blankly back. He went on. "You see, Frankie Aps has to go through life like that, with the whole world hating him, the whole world belittling him and sneering at him. That's why he does what he does, to try to compensate, and to somehow make people like him. But the truth is, in doing what he does, he only makes people despise him all the more. It's his own vicious circle and he can't escape from it."

It was a familiar scenario. At that moment Connor didn't realise just how familiar.

"Perhaps he should stop trying and take up fishing instead."

He looked quizzically across at me, then suddenly remembered and smiled knowledgeably.

"Like you did, you mean; when you were a kid? I'd forgotten . . . So you should know better."

"Yeah, but I was just a kid. I didn't go through my childhood insulting people and telling tales, being nasty and calling people names."

"Maybe not, but you still pissed everybody off. Isn't that just the same? The real difference between then and now is that nowadays nobody's gonna fuck with you. You see, you came out the other side. You learnt, and gained a reputation for being able to take care of yourself. So why not let him learn? Maybe, one day, he'll come out the other side, too. What's it gonna cost you?"

"If I allow him to call me names like that? Whatever that reputation means, I guess."

"Come on; you made that little speech after you'd hit him, and everybody understood why you'd said all that to that little Scottish corporal. They understood, because you're good at that. You have the ability to convince people, and make them understand. You know as well as I do, you didn't need to hit him. You could have won the point without that. You're big enough and ugly enough to take a few abusive comments, aren't you?"

"Yeah, but I don't have to, so why should I?"

"Because you can." He shook his head. "The world needs a lot more people with brains and voices, people who can make other people understand, and it needs a lot less people who use reflex violence to make a point. Don't you realise that, because if you don't, you should take a quick trip over to the Falls Road, and you'd soon see."

I half-heartedly nodded.

"Do you remember that traffic light grand prix, in Regent Street that night?" he asked. "When we were in that little Mini Cooper S?"

I laughed at the memory, because it had been a wonderful exercise in the foolishness of juvenile machismo. There had been five of us, crammed into a little green Mini Cooper S with a white stripe down the middle, and we'd been in the West End of London, on our way home from a party around two a.m. We'd pulled up at a set of lights in Regent Street and were sitting waiting for them to change, when a sporty-looking car pulled up alongside. Nobody looked directly at the car, because you never admitted the presence of another. We used our peripheral vision though, and decided it was a Lotus Elan plus 2. The plus 2 was a fast enough car, but if we got away quickly we might just beat it to the next set of lights. We decided to race it.

The upshot of it all was that we screamed off with wheels spinning and engine racing and easily won the race, because the other driver pulled quietly away from the lights and dawdled along Regent Street. He was already fifty yards behind before we hit third gear. It was only then, when we looked back and saw what car it was, that we realised why he hadn't bothered. It was a Monteverdi 450; one of the fastest cars in the world. The number 450 reflected the car's brake-horsepower, and the car could easily have left us standing, had the other driver been so inclined. We slowed down as soon as we realised, looked sheepishly at one another, and felt utterly foolish.

"Yeah, I remember."

"Do you think that Monteverdi driver worried about his reputation? Do you think everybody started pointing at that 450 and claiming it got burnt-off by a Mini? You see, that's the beauty of having a car like that; you don't constantly have to prove yourself."

"OK, I understand, point taken."

"I hope you do understand, because you're a decent bloke, you don't need that reputation. I know it was different in El Adem, because over there a mass bundle was just a way of letting off steam. But if you go around punching people just because you don't like them, just because you can, you're no better than a thug. You understand?"

I nodded back at him and thought about it while he went to get the refills. It had been a salutary piece of advice. The fact it had come from one of my best friends had made it more so.

After that, I went back to Tangmere with a more magnanimous attitude to people in general, and comrades in particular, and I tried to keep my distance from those who riled me. I still found the Frankie Aps of this world to be infuriating, but I walked away more times than I confronted, or I tried to. When I did confront, I tried to lead with my tongue and not my left. In fact, now I come to think about it, after that chat, I don't believe I ever got into another fight with a comrade, whether I liked and respected them or not, and I never forget those words of advice.

I still travelled widely, still had many good times, and a few bad ones, one of which was a trip to Peru, in May of the same year. The trip wasn't bad because of the country or its inhabitants, who were charming and gentle people. It was bad, because we had only got back from Lima a week or so before that terrible earthquake hit and thirty thousand people lost their lives. I still sometimes wonder about the people I met there, remembering their lowly homes and simple lives and uncomplicated sincerity. I hope they're safe and well, and I wish there had been something we could have done to somehow help and to maybe even save some lives, rather than merely use their lands and hospitality for our own purposes.

Slowly the personnel in TCW changed, moving on to other lives or posted, and the Cosford graduates seemed younger and more naïve with each successive influx. Although they abandoned the farcical morning parades for a haphazard roll-call in the canteen, the new Cosford graduates appeared as little more than schoolchildren. I thought back to my spotless presence on that first-ever morning parade. I hoped to goodness that I hadn't looked as young and naïve and scared as they looked, although it was odds-on that I probably had.

I guess I somehow felt that the old camaraderie and passion had gone. I don't know why, and I'm not sure if my assessment was real or imagined. Perhaps it was because many of the old personnel were no longer around. Perhaps it was because I'd grown up. Perhaps it was because things are never the same when you go back to them. I don't know, but it didn't feel the same.

There was another phenomenon that undoubtedly contributed to my dissatisfaction with the RAF in general and the Tactical Communications Wing in particular. It was a new style of warfare that had only just begun in earnest, and I could see immediately that Thirty-Eight Group couldn't deal with it. It wasn't the conventional conflict we'd trained for, with perimeter guards and patrols surrounding a mobile communications centre. It was a new and inglorious war, brought right into ordinary everyday lives, by a new breed of lunatic . . . the international terrorist.

We had only just returned from Jordan after having to sit and twiddle our thumbs while they blew up three commercial airliners. Suddenly the old caricatured terrorist smoking Havana cigars and telling the pilot to take him to Cuba had become a far more menacing and deadly foe. That escalation, combined with people like Gaddafi sponsoring terrorism around the world to fuel their own bigotry and hatred, was threatening our lives in a new and disturbing way.

In TCW we knew about survival and conventional warfare on different levels, but the Air Force hadn't trained or chartered us for anything like this. When it all came down to the wire, we were impotent. Anybody who knew anything about counter terrorism conceded the SAS and the Cherries and Marines and many units of the regular Army could provide the necessary skills, but not us. After all, there was unlikely to be any need to guide air-strikes against half-a-dozen terrorists holding civilian hostages.

Then the rumours began about us transferring from Tangmere to Benson. I have no idea which high-ranking clown suggested such an idiotic and bureaucratic idea, but placing the great TCW unwashed alongside the Queen's Flight was an exercise in ignorance.

The Queen's Flight held responsibility for ferrying royalty. They lived for everything pristine and pretentious in middle-class Oxfordshire, where every surface was dusted and polished until it glinted and gleamed in the sunlight, and the air was acrid with the stench of freshly-applied paint.

The Tactical Communications Wing of number Thirty-Eight Group didn't fit the same mould. Every surface belonging to them was matt green and camouflaged, and while the air may have been acrid, it was only with the stench of diesel fumes and subhuman sweat.

Not only that, but technology was moving on. Aircraft were becoming smarter, and the need for human eyes and ears at the front line was becoming less critical, to the point of obsolescence. I began to wonder if we had any future in a technically-advanced and politically-correct RAF. Maybe it was time for me to do something else, although I wasn't certain what that might be.

I had three choices. I could go back to civilian life; take my telecommunications skills, and work for a commercial company. I could stay with TCW, and see how everything went for a while, or I could move on to another branch of the armed forces, maybe apply to the Paras or even the SAS, as I had tried to do before they marooned me in Libya.

I had no wish to go back into civilian life, and no idea whether the regiment would consider me. Maybe they'd laugh in my face. Nevertheless, it had to be worth the effort to find out, because I fancied joining them, or something like them, and badly wanted to learn all those skills that had kept me in such awe for so many years. I didn't want to stay with an organisation that considered TCW as a group of ageing dinosaurs, people not even worthy of their own base.

I thought about that for some time, but couldn't make up my mind, and, for reasons I didn't recognise at the time, began to consider the possibility of taking a trip home. I thought I would discuss the decision with my adoptive father, ask him what he thought I should do. In the past he had never shown an iota of interest in me, or my decision making, but he had once been in the forces, and so I decided that he would be a relatively knowledgeable third-party to consult.

An island called Perspective

And so that was how I came to be standing in Sunninghill High Street on an unseasonably chilly evening in late September of 1970, staring through the railings and into my old junior school playground beyond, five years after having walked away from my adopted home.

I thought a lot about my life and times as I clung to those railings, and came to some surprising conclusions about a mother and father I had never known, and an orphanage that I couldn't really remember; about my subsequent adoption and all those resulting years of childhood solitude; about my constant failure to succeed and my constant failure to please; about what truly constitutes success and failure, and where we draw the wafer-thin line that divides the two.

In the beginning, my new parents had tried their best to accept me and care for me, I'm sure of that. They had looked on with pride as the vicar re-christened me, and then they graciously and charitably took me into their home, fully expecting that we would all move on as a happy family unit; fully expecting the future to be tinted pink; fully expecting the difference not to matter.

But blood is thicker than the most blessed of holy water, and that umbilical cord just wouldn't stop tugging at their consciences.

And so, in true Cancerian fashion, I retreated ever further into my shell, hiding myself away, with fishing rod in hand, along the tree-lined margins of Johnson's Pond, or celebrating my anonymity on the anonymous streets of London's West End, financing the loneliness with the fruits of my caddying, and making no further effort to achieve any further success, however slight.

"How the mighty have fallen," I will always recall my sister gleefully saying when they had unceremoniously kicked me out of the grammar school and sent me down to the local secondary modern, while my only response had been to shrug my shoulders and head for the sanctuary of the lake, continuing to fail in the eyes of the world and in the futile hope of currying favour with the only family I had ever known.

I still respected my adoptive father, and was as desperate to please and impress him as ever, and I would always be grateful to my adoptive mother for the sacrifices she had made along the way. But, ungrateful little bastard or no, it was respect and gratitude which had fuelled a young boy's untutored emotion, and that could no longer be confused with love.

"What are you thinking about?"

The voice interrupted the melancholy. It shook me from my memories and made me start. I let go of the railings, and all those unhappy memories, then turned to find him standing behind me.

"I thought you had a dinner party to go to?"

"It can wait."

I looked down the High Street and saw that he had parked the car across the road and further down, in front of the village cinema. My mother was still perched on the front seat, glaring back at us, with crown slightly askew and feathers severely ruffled.

"She's not going to be happy, if you get there late. She'll never let you forget it."

He smiled and pulled a face of indifference. It seemed he wasn't all that bothered.

"You asked me a question . . . I didn't finish answering it."

"I thought you did: born killers and murdering cut-throats, wasn't it, just about anything would be better than that. Wasn't that the gist of it?"

He smiled and nodded.

"You kind of took me by surprise. We've never really talked before. I wasn't ready."

"And you're ready now?"

"I was thinking about it on the way back here, thinking that if joining these people is right for you, Michael, then that is what you must do. Other people's opinions are important, my opinion is important, but we none of us hand out tablets of stone. You have to make up your own mind in this life, and, when it all comes down to it, you must do what makes you happy."

"Is that what you do?"

I looked pointedly down the road, to where my mother sat fuming, and then looked back to see a smile pass quietly across his face as he listened to the words and took the unspoken point.

"Sometimes it's best not to hurt people's feelings; sometimes the easy way is the best way."

"You think I don't know that? I spent half my life trying not to hurt your feelings, trying not to answer back, or say anything that might hurt or disappoint you."

I was suddenly angry, and for some peculiar reason started recalling some of the isolated incidents that had combined with his indifference to make my childhood so unhappy.

"Do you remember what I used to do every time I needed a birth certificate, for school or for anything? Do you remember? You'd always hold out both, and ask me which I wanted: the large one with my birth mother's name on it, or the small one with only my new name and date of birth?

"In all those years I never even looked at the larger one; not once, not ever. I always took the smaller, because I figured that it would hurt you if I asked for the other one. But when did you ever do the same for me? When did you ever think about not hurting me?"

"All the time."

I shook my head in contradiction. I could feel the tears welling up. I hadn't shed so much as a tear for the unhappiness of my adoption and childhood for well over five years, not since listening to my sister's conversation with the gorgeous Diana that day, but I was close to tears now.

"That's not true. Maybe at first you did, but you haven't given a damn about my feelings for years." I blinked, and wiped away a tear; there was no way that I was going to stand in the middle of the High Street, crying like a baby. "You remember the tennis racket?"

"What?"

"The tennis racket. Angela's tennis racket. She lent it to me that day, but then she changed her mind, or maybe she just planned it that way, I don't know. I do know that she sent you to get it back. You drove down to the school and walked all the way across the tennis courts. Then you took it out of my hand, right in the middle of a game, right in front of all the other kids. You didn't say a word to me. You just walked back to the car, and then drove away and left me standing there."

"Yes, I do remember doing that. I was told that you'd taken it without asking."

"That wasn't true. I wouldn't have dared do something like that, and you know it. I'd asked her, and she'd said yes, but even if I hadn't asked, and even if she hadn't said yes . . . don't you think that was just a little too cruel?"

260

He thought about that, and then gave the answer he knew I wanted to hear, but for all of that he still couldn't admit to being completely wrong, and even the apology was qualified.

"Right at this moment, with the benefit of hindsight, I think that it may well have been harsh, and I'm sorry if it hurt you, but we all do things that upset people at times and none of us can turn back the clock."

"It probably meant nothing to you at the time, it probably doesn't now, but I never forgot what you did that day, and I never will. That's why I worked so hard to win that tennis medal at Cosford, to somehow show you that I was worthy of my own tennis racket." He favoured me with an old-fashioned look and I shrugged, because it didn't make any obvious sense to him, and I couldn't explain further. "It wasn't just that. That was just an example. It was the same with everything you did, and everything Mum did, and everything Angela did. There was never any kindness or love or consideration for me. It was the same with everything. Gran told me about it once; she said that it was all to do with the umbilical cord."

"She would."

He stood for a second, looking closely at me.

"You know why we're going over to Angela's tonight?" he asked. I shook my head. "We're going because Angela wants to convince us to sell up and help her start her own nursing home. She tells me that a lot of people are making a great deal of money out of it. Your mother told her that the bungalow's fully paid for, and so she wants me to sell up and invest everything in this nursing home scheme; go into partnership with her, throw in our savings and possibly even take out a new mortgage."

"She's aiming high, but then she always did. Now, why didn't anybody see that coming? A nursing home of her own, huh, which presumably she sees you becoming an ageing resident one day and sees herself owning outright at about the same time?"

He smiled ruefully, knowing the truth of that. It seemed Angela wasn't quite the apple of his eye she had once been, or not this week.

"That's a distinct probability. But how would you feel about me doing that? How would you feel about me putting all my money, and the bungalow, into Angela's nursing home?"

"I honestly don't care."

"Are you sure about that? You do realise that you'd more than likely lose any chance of inheriting when we go? Doesn't that bother you?"

He was doing his best, but he hadn't understood a word I'd said.

"No, it doesn't. In fact, I couldn't care less about it. You see, I never wanted your money. . . don't you understand that? I don't care what you do with it, and I don't want the bungalow either. I don't want so much as a stick of furniture from it. I never did, and I never will. What I always wanted from you and Mum wouldn't have cost either of you a bean. What I always wanted was just a little bit of kindness, a little bit of understanding, a little bit of warmth, a little bit of love . . . it wasn't much, but I guess it was still more than either of you could afford."

He thought about that for a while, then shrugged his shoulders.

"We did our best, you know, to make you feel wanted; to make you feel this was your home."

I shook my head.

"No, you didn't."

"Well, if it's of any interest, I'm not going to do it . . . the nursing home, I mean. I haven't told them yet, and I expect that there'll be hell to pay when I do, but I'm not going to do it."

"It doesn't matter if you do or you don't. Angela will get whatever you leave, I know that. She'll get it all in the end: the money and the bungalow and that. I know she will, because she wants it so badly. What's more to the point, she wants to stop me getting it, and whatever Angela wants, Angela gets. She always has and she always will. And you know something else? I really don't care enough to fight her for it. I hope to God I never do."

"I do believe you mean that."

"I do mean it, I swear to God."

"And so . . . are you going to join these people? Start killing your fellow man for a living?"

He smiled as he said it, but I didn't rise to the bait.

"I don't know; maybe, but then again, maybe not. There's probably something in what you said; not that bit about the born killers, but some of the rest of it. I'll see how I feel in a few weeks."

"What about the eyesight?"

"What about it?"

"Surely you'd fail the medical?"

"No, I don't think so. My eyesight's good enough. Oh, sure, the left's a bit on the weak side, but not sufficiently to prevent me doing what I want to do. It shouldn't be a problem. You see, it's just like so many of those things that I was always criticised for, or always made to feel ashamed of, or always made to feel worthless for. When it all came down to it, there was nothing all that much wrong with me; not with the eyes, not with the feet, not with the intellect, not with anything, really. It took me a hell of a long time to figure that out."

It wasn't an overly subtle point, and there was little or nothing he could say by way of response, and so he nodded sagely and changed the subject.

"So why did you want my advice?"

"I didn't really. I think I just wanted to show off a little bit, wanted you to know that I've got a choice, and that I've finally achieved something on my own. Can you believe that? For the first time in my life, I've actually got a choice, and if I do transfer to them it'll be because I choose to, not because I have to."

He shuffled from one foot to the other and looked uncomfortable. There was nothing much left for either of us to say, and I could see he wanted to get away.

"You'd better get going. Don't want to miss out on the horse's doubres."

He seemed thankful for the opportunity to retreat, and joked back weakly in an effort to hide his discomfort and mask an awkward silence.

"I never was all that keen on Ritz Crackers, but I suppose I'd better get going before somebody explodes all over my upholstery."

"Yeah, right, that wouldn't do at all. Well thanks, Dad, thanks for coming back and that. I do appreciate it; although something tells me you're probably going to suffer for it."

Not for the first time that evening, he seemed surprised. I'd never called him dad before, it had always been Father, but then he smiled and shrugged again.

"Sometimes moody silences can be really quite relaxing. I just wish we'd taken the time to talk like this a few years ago."

It was my turn to smile and shrug.

"Yeah, so do I, but we didn't, did we? Spilt milk, huh? Well look after yourself, Dad."

"Yes. You too, Michael."

I nodded sagely and shook the outstretched hand, and then walked away from him without looking back, knowing he had made a great many sacrifices for me over the years; knowing, too, that, for all of those material things he'd provided, something had been missing. It was something vital, something fundamental, something that love required in order to be. It was something that we had never managed to discover during all of those unhappy years together, and it was something that, sadly, we never would.

I wandered farther up the high street and around by the side of the school, before turning the corner and walking on and up along the back road leading to the fish and chip shop.

It was as I approached the illuminated façade that I saw him, and so many more unhappy memories came flooding back. I hadn't seen those belligerent features, or suffered their owner's aggression, for over five years, and that had been something of a welcome interval, but now, here they were again, the same as ever – the great and terrible 'Punchy George'.

He was leaning against the handrail on the steps outside the fish and chip shop, laughing and joking with a couple of apprentice morons, all of them talking too loudly and too crudely, all of them posing too belligerently. I remembered how easily I had been intimidated, those few short years ago, and smiled inwardly as I recalled the foolishness of my own fear and naiveté.

'Punchy George' clearly remembered me, as easily and as immediately as I had remembered him. He came away from the railing and drew himself up as he watched me approach, and then he began to smile, the same mockingly sadistic smile that he had always smiled while he and his friends had punched and kicked me around the schoolyard.

I carried on walking and then in true 'regiment style' looked both straight at him and straight through him, with a determination in my stride and a cold smile on my lips. I was over half-a-foot taller than I had been five years previously, and more than four stone heavier, but then George had grown by a similar amount during that same time. No, it wasn't the weight or the size, but, just as a gleaming, psychotic old Scottish corporal had once explained, the great and terrible are never so great or so terrible when ordinary people refuse to be victims.

'Punchy George' faltered for a second, and then moved back by half a pace, momentarily unnerved by my show of confidence, momentarily shaken by the purpose in my step. I stopped less than two feet away from him and intensified the look, concentrating on that imaginary spot at the back of his head and mocking the uncertain features with a contemptuous smile. He looked again, trying to understand what had changed, trying to recall the memories of slaughters past.

He regrouped and then tried again, attempting to stare me down, attempting to dominate my gaze with one of his own, as he had always so easily done. But my own stare didn't waver and the belligerence in his began to visibly dissolve. This wasn't the terrified schoolboy he had once so easily bullied, so often punched and kicked for the amusement of the rabble. This wasn't the easy mark that he had remembered beating on so many occasions in the dim and distant past, with a flurry of unanswered punches and the schoolyard bully's sadistic glee. He took another involuntary half-pace backwards, a retreat unnoticed by his acne-studded entourage, but he knew only too well that I had seen it and recognised it for what it was.

All those haunting recollections of pain and fear, all of the loneliness and isolation that had lived with me for so many years, and all of those recriminations which had gnawed away at my intestines for a similar length of time were still there, but in the two disjointed seconds that it had taken for those two separate half-yards of concrete turf to be abandoned, they had finally been exiled to an island called perspective.

Scornfully dismissing his insignificance, I sauntered into the shop, ordered a fish supper and then stood at the counter and nonchalantly watched him while I waited for the fish to fry.

It seemed to me that 'Punchy George' was just the same as he had always been. He was that much older, of course, and now he stank of stale beer as well as stale sweat, but in truth he was just the same. I recalled those words of wisdom spoken by my gran that day, and for the umpteenth time I mentally thanked her for them. 'Punchy George' hadn't been living his life during the last five years, he had been wasting his life, and at first glance the only thing that seemed to have changed for him was his legal entitlement to purchase a nightly drunken stupor.

But that wasn't the whole story, because something else had changed. Now it was 'Punchy George' who ruled the village roost, and 'Bad Bobby Day' was nowhere to be seen. Maybe somewhere, somehow, and sometime during those intervening years, 'Punchy George' had outgrown his psychotic mentor, or maybe the psychotic mentor had outgrown 'Punchy George'. Either way, at some point on that mindless journey between the school gates, the Carpenters Arms, and the fish and chip shop, George had assumed the mantle of leadership, and had himself become the psychotic Peter Pan, with the same local reputation for belligerence and a similarly aggressive version of the same mutant teenage gang.

They were accompanied by a similarly mindless brace of trainee Tinkerbells, dressed in short leather skirts and black fishnet tights, with lank, unwashed hair, under-sized tank tops and cheap-smelling perfume that struggled to overpower the more wholesome aroma of fish and chips. They chewed pink bubble gum with open mouths and stared out with sullen eyes from behind emaciated masks, mistakenly believing a disenchanted frown to be more seductive than a ready smile, as they sneered their ignorance at the world through thick, coarse layers of cosmetic paint.

They had looked me up and down in sluttish admiration as I climbed the steps, and now they started giggling and shrieking in unconvincing 'slapper' mode, offering up coarse remarks and senseless *double entendres* in a pubertal effort to impress.

I continued to watch 'Punchy George' as he slouched against the iron railing which ran down and alongside the steps, setting himself in that familiarly belligerent pose. I smiled quietly as I watched. Yes, I could walk out of here now and knock him and his trainee thugs all around the village, and it was a high probability that I wouldn't be required to break sweat, but why on earth would I want to do such an ignorant thing, and who would I be doing it for? I doubted it would teach George anything more than my stare had already told him, and I already knew the answer.

Whilst he had been leaning against that metal hand rail, waiting for another bag of grease-laden chips, with his juvenile thugs and jailbait entourage hanging on to his every drunken syllable, I had travelled Europe and Asia, Africa, Australasia, and the Americas from North to South. I had learnt to battle and survive in the aridity of the desert and the jungle's suffocating stickiness, I had slid my way across frozen tundra, and negotiated the vastness of the outback. I had met and marvelled at the world's best, across different terrains and in different scenarios, and I had come to know the stark and numbing terror which always accompanies that thing they call real.

I had learnt of love and life and sex and sin, in affairs of unrequited love and lustful convenience, and financed my education in the fleshpots of the world. I had walked among the native tribes of Central and South America, the traders of the Hudson Bay, the Senussi of the Northern Sahara, and those many victims of South-East Asia's plight. I had shared a beer or three with pilots weary of the perils of Hanoi and the horror that was Vietnam, and had chatted and laughed in the company of so many different peoples along the way; people of all races and all creeds, of all political persuasions and all social castes.

I collected my fish supper, and then walked out of the shop and past the drunken sneer that still somehow imagined its invincibility, only too aware that I had always dreamed of one day settling my score with 'Punchy George'; of one day doing to him what he had always so cheerfully done to me. But now, when the time was right, the skills at hand and the opportunity there for the taking, I kept on walking. I had decided to allow him his illusion, because that was all he had, and I above all people understood the pain and isolation of living in such an empty shell.

The young and frightened little boy who had lived the sadness of that similarly empty life just those few short years ago had learnt so many things since then. That same frightened little boy who had so often picked himself up from the pavement, rubbed the pain from the bruises and wiped away the blood during those dreadful days at school had seen so much more and become so much more since then.

He had learnt to defend and to attack, to survive and to overcome, but he had also learnt to look a little harder and wait a little longer before damaging or hurting, criticising or admonishing, jumping to the conclusions of hatred, or resorting to the violence of impotence. He had learnt not to despise people for their hostility and aggression, but to understand their frustration and pity their weakness; to accommodate their stupidity, and to know his own for what it was. Somewhere along the way that same frightened little boy had become a man during those five short years.

And George?

Well, somehow, George really didn't matter any more.

Footnote

On the 11th November 2007, at Exeter airport, Michael and his birth mother, Doreen, met and held each other for the first time in fifty-seven years.

Doreen now lives in Halifax, in West Yorkshire. Michael and his wife, Pamela, now live in Spain. Doreen regularly visits them. She and Michael talk on the telephone at least three times a week, trying to catch up on all those wasted years.

Michael's adopted parents died some years ago, and yes, Angela got everything. True to his prediction, and true to his word, Michael received nothing, and made no attempt to contest the will.

Printed in Great Britain
by Amazon.co.uk, Ltd.,
Marston Gate.